KEY
ISSUES
in the
Afro-American
Experience

Under the General Editorship of

JOHN MORTON BLUM   *Yale University*

VOLUME  TO 1877

KEY
ISSUES
in the
Afro-American
Experience

Edited by

NATHAN I. HUGGINS   *Columbia University*

MARTIN KILSON   *Harvard University*

DANIEL M. FOX   *Harvard University*

Harcourt Brace Jovanovich, Inc.

New York / Chicago / San Francisco / Atlanta

COVER:

Detail from the painting *Ambulance Call* by the Afro-American artist Jacob Lawrence. Courtesy of Dr. Bernard Ronis, Philadelphia. Photo by Robert F. Crandall.

SECTION OPENING PHOTOGRAPHS:

Pages 2–3   Slaving coast, Elmina, West Africa. Photo by Joel Baldwin, © Look Magazine.

36–37   Hausa tribe mud homes and streets of Kano, North Nigeria. Photo by Marc and Evelyne Bernheim, Rapho Guillumette Pictures.

37   Seacoast, Accra, Ghana. Photo by John Bryson, Rapho Guillumette Pictures.

96–97   Slaves in front of their quarters on a South Carolina plantation. Courtesy of The New-York Historical Society, New York City.

97   Details from an 1862 photo of slaves on the James Hopkinson plantation, Edisto Island, South Carolina. Courtesy of The New-York Historical Society, New York City.

158   Nat Turner and fellow conspirators, detail from a line engraving, 1863, after Felix O. C. Darley. Courtesy of the Granger Collection.

158–59   Detail from *Slaves Escaping Through the Swamp*, painting by Thomas Moran. Courtesy of the Southwestern Art Association, Philbrook Art Center.

210   Black recruits in training for the Union army, as shown on the cover of *Harper's Weekly*, 14 March 1863. Courtesy of the Schomburg Collection, New York Public Library.

211   Robert Gould Shaw with the first black regiment from a free state to serve in the Union army. Robert Gould Shaw memorial, Boston, by Augustus Saint-Gaudens. Photo by Carl Chiarenza.

Maps on pages 42–43 by Vaughn Gray.

ISBN: 0-15-548371-4

Library of Congress Catalog Card Number: 76-141607

Printed in the United States of America

Dedicated to four scholars of the American Negro:

Carter G. Woodson

Horace Mann Bond

Ralph J. Bunche

John Hope Franklin

Preface

New World Africans, from their first awareness of themselves as Americans, have wanted to assert the uniqueness and importance of their experience. They have called on the poetic muse: Phillis Wheatley, Jupiter Hammon, and Alberry Allson Whitman were among the early classic voices that sang the black consciousness in lyric and epic form. Polemicists and activists like Frederick Douglass, Martin R. Delany, and David Walker hammered out prose designed to awaken black men and women to their moral obligation. And from at least 1841, with J. W. C. Pennington's efforts, black Americans have had a keen sense that their story needed to be told as part of the history of America. For most blacks, there has never been any doubt that their identity is embedded in the general American history, and that they will never know themselves until they mine and refine that history themselves.

So it is only a trick of ego—a sleight of mind—that permits some observers to imply that the discovery of the Negro's place in American history and American studies is a recent event. It is arrogance to ignore or deprecate men who began their work near the beginning of this century, men like Carter G. Woodson and W. E. B. Du Bois. Many important black scholars followed, some of whom—J. Saunders Redding, John Hope Franklin, Benjamin Quarles—continue their work into this day. These men labored in a discouraging scholarly environment; indifference to their work kept the highest honors and acclaim just beyond their grasp. That they persisted despite the many obstacles was nothing short of heroic, and we are much the richer for their dedication. Consider, for instance, Carter Woodson's commitment and sense of purpose in starting, in 1915, and sustaining the Association for the Study of Negro Life and History. Because of his effort, we have had ever since the *Journal of Negro History* and the *Negro History Bulletin,* which have welcomed the essays of black and white scholars often thought too ethnic and too narrow in scope for the standard journals.

Thus formal and informal study of the Afro-American experience has existed for a long time. Nevertheless, there is something new about contemporary efforts to study Negro life and history. For the first time, Negro history has become a central concern of the general academic world. Indeed, concern has often been forced on colleges by student pressure. Growing numbers of black students found that the standard studies of "our" past—Western civilization no less than American history—failed to sound true to their lives and experience. Many white students, perplexed and annoyed by the disparity between officially stated ideals and sensed reality, suspected with good reason that a better perception of the irony and paradox that defined their present might well be achieved through an understanding of the Afro-American experience. That experience challenges conventional rhetoric on uninterrupted national progress and the success of the American Dream and is itself the essence of irony and paradox. But the new concern goes even beyond students' demands for relevance. White and black scholars have begun to see study of the Afro-American experience as a way to illuminate and reconsider perplexing problems in the American past.

The two volumes of *Key Issues in the Afro-American Experience* are designed to bring the specialist's interest and knowledge to the service of students, instructors, and general readers. We wanted to direct the energy, intelligence, and training of academicians to the creation of a collection of sharply focused essays that would both capture interest and demonstrate disciplined analysis. We wanted to choose topics that were central and essential to an understanding of the Afro-American experience. And we wanted the best people available to address themselves to those topics. These could not be essays already printed in scholarly journals—they presume a different audience.

Of the twenty-seven essays in these volumes, all but three—those by Philip Curtin, Kenneth Stampp, and Stanley Elkins—were written expressly for this collection. All other essays are fresh statements of principal issues by specialists in the field. For each essay we have provided a headnote that includes a brief biographical sketch of the author. For each section of the volumes, we have supplied a list of suggestions for further reading.

Defining relevance was a major problem in choosing the topics to be treated. Some issues that seemed urgent also seemed likely to be transformed by changes in national policy or economic conditions. We tried to make distinctions between the transient and the enduring. The definition of an Afro-American history, a black culture; the influence of Africa and the impact of slavery; black efforts at organization and resistance; the economic and social realities of Jim Crow and racism—these issues are central: relevant to the past, the present, and the foreseeable future.

It is from among these enduring issues that we have drawn the topics of these essays. We have not attempted to present a unified point of view—except for the feeling that the Afro-American experience is important to us all and deserves serious treatment. Nor have we attempted to create dispute for its own sake, though we realized that these topics and these authors would provide spirited, sometimes conflicting, statements. That is as it should be. We hope that this conflict and tension will be amplified and extended as readers talk with one another in the classroom and informally. None of these essays are thought to be definitive or to close the issue. If the essays help point the way to a meaningful perception of the Afro-American experience, if they offer some suggestions of how to probe more deeply and how to ask new questions, then we will have done something of what we set out to do.

We are indebted to Frank Freidel, from whose course on the Afro-American experience, given at Harvard College in the 1968–1969 school year, the idea for these volumes emerged. We gratefully acknowledge the constructive comments made by the following specialists who reviewed and commented on our original plan for the work: Jacob U. Gordon, University of Kansas; Peter Wood, Harvard University; Arthur Tuden, University of Pittsburgh; and James M. McPherson, Princeton University. We also thank Lenworth A. Gunther for his help on the volumes.

Nathan I. Huggins
Martin Kilson
Daniel M. Fox

Contents

2

African Beginnings   37

3

Slavery · 97

4

Ante-Bellum Black Activism

5

Emancipation and Racism 211

KEY
ISSUES
in the
Afro-American
Experience

1

The Conceptual Framework for Afro-American History

Afro-American History:
Myths, Heroes, Reality

NATHAN I. HUGGINS

Nathan Irvin Huggins, professor of history at Columbia University, is the author of *Protestants Against Poverty* (Greenwood, 1970). He has recently completed a study of the Harlem Renaissance of the 1920's for publication by Oxford University Press in the fall of 1971. In the following essay, Mr. Huggins explores the methods and the meaning of Afro-American history. Sharply critical of the myth making and hero building that have threatened at times to add an element of fantasy to the study of the Negro's past, Mr. Huggins argues that Afro-American history is in the end inseparable from American history and essential to it—that a recognition and an objective appraisal of the Afro-American experience are necessary if we are to achieve a full and realistic assessment of the American past and a cohesive national identity.

Most people think that American history is the story of white people, and that is why black people, in recent years, have been demanding a history of their own. Actually, standard histories have been even more restrictive than is generally allowed. Except for the necessary discussion of Afro-Americans in slavery and some treatment of immigrants, the taught history of the United States has been that of Anglo-Saxons and Northern Europeans. Even the current consciousness of Negro history on the part of textbook publishers, though it has resulted in efforts to improve the nonwhite's image, has made no fundamental changes in the character of the history. It is now more likely that Negroes will be mentioned as participants in the development of the country; heroes, achievements, inventions, are duly recorded. But in very important ways, the history has remained untouched; the ethnic conception of American history persists. In the past, Negroes, Oriental-Americans, and American Indians were educated in their native land as though they were no real part of it. In many ways this is still true. The pronoun "we," so often used in school textbooks, has never really included the nonwhite reader. It is probably not too much to say that the authors, publishers, and teachers have never fully appreciated the implications of the ethnic diversity of the United States.

It is little wonder, then, that Afro-Americans have labeled taught history as racist. In fact, the best one can say is that it is ethnocentric. Yet the complaint that the Afro-American has been "left out" cannot be answered in any simple way. Certainly, the scattering of more nonwhite names in the texts or the adding of paragraphs judiciously salutary to the Negro is not enough. But one must ask whether the idea of a separate and distinctive Negro culture—fashionable among some proponents of a black history—can serve historical needs any better. Surely, it is useless to claim that Negroes have figured importantly in American history unless this can be demonstrated within the history itself. Further, it may be pointless to "create" a culture if, in the end, it will not sustain itself in historical terms. The problem is that the discipline of history makes demands upon us that are really independent of our wishes. Whatever we should like to do with Afro-American history, what we are able to do will be contingent on the character of that social science.

The first challenge for Afro-American history (as for any history) is that of discovering and utilizing evidence. During a considerable portion of his experience, the Afro-American kept only the slightest written record. Indeed, the vast majority of black men and women from the time of the first settlements to the middle of the nineteenth century were mute witnesses to the events of their lives. The problem of evidence brings to mind the old conundrum about the tree that falls with no one to see or hear it. Did it really fall? How does one know, and how can one report on it? Without a record, can there be a history? Of course, from one point of view, everything that happens is history. Your breakfast this morning, your reading of this book, a recent discussion you had with a friend—all are part of the past. But much of what happened in the past went unobserved—like the falling tree—or unrecorded, which, in time, amounts to the same thing. Without evidence for historians to work with, it is as if nothing ever happened.

It takes a special kind of character to keep a diary, save letters, or write memoirs: one must have a sense of his own historical importance—if not to society, at least to his heirs. Some free Negroes were literate enough and felt sufficient obligation to the future to leave an account of their lives, but the institution of slavery deprived the bulk of Afro-Americans of any historical sense. Also, as a result of the absence of blacks from official roles in government and industry (where other kinds of historical records are created), much of our knowledge about the Negro's historical experience has come from the testimony of others. Through reading the comments of whites—travelers, planters, abolitionists—we have been able to infer something of the actual experience of slavery. This has been a poor substitute, however, for the slave's own account of his experience. And it has encouraged the tendency of historians to see black men through the eyes of others, who often view them with contempt or pity. We should not be deceived, however; there has always been more of a usable black record than historians have chosen to employ. Doubtless, with more inventive use of available data and some borrowing of techniques from other social sciences, a fairer story might have been told. Had American historians thought the Negro's voice important enough, we would all have read a different history. Nonetheless, those who now wish to rewrite history are limited by the scant data left from very important periods of the Negro's past. With little evidence, unless extremely skillful use is made of what is available, it will be as if nothing ever happened.

Unlike a poem, which should not mean but be, the historical record, statement, act, must be significant. Through it, the historian should be able to gain a better understanding of a past event. Historical evidence should tell him the why, the how, or the effects of some occurrence. This is why even if you dutifully recorded your breakfasts, your study habits, and your discussions with friends, the record would be unlikely to become historical evidence. Unless your life is extraordinary, these facts are not likely to expand anyone's understanding of the past. Historians do not collect facts like rare art objects. An event from the past that has no meaning beyond itself is not historically significant and can serve only antiquarian interests.

To take a case in point, several commercial enterprises (mainly whiskey companies) have recently published, as part of their advertising, notes about little-known accomplishments by Americans of African descent. The public has been told of Esteban with the Spanish explorers, Du Sable with the French, Benjamin Banneker the mathematician, Matthew Henson in the Arctic. Similarly, one Boston radio station has broadcast a series of spot announcements called "Black Facts." This is just what they are, no more and no less. For to make such facts history, one must charge them with meaning. One's sense of history is hardly enriched by the knowledge that George F. Grant, a black man, invented the golf tee, as one whiskey company has informed the public. It is possible, perhaps, to make even Grant's achievement serve some historical purpose, but in order to do so, one needs to go beyond the fact itself, to ask larger questions, to make the connections that give the fact meaning. This process is the craft, the art, the discipline of history: the sifting of raw data and the attempt to give them meaning within their broader context.

Because the historian chooses among his data, and because his craft requires that he ask questions and convert his data into meaningful form, the written product of his labor necessarily reflects his biases. It cannot be helped. Yet the scholar is never completely free to indulge his prejudices, to choose his data by whim, or to consider merely the questions that amuse him. He depends upon professional judgments. Foolish, capricious, and egregious work will affect his reputation with his peers and cast suspicion on any future judgments he might make. Of course, there must be some in the profession who are free of any given bias before it will be detected and censured in others.

The problem that concerns us here is that, from the beginning, American historians have not considered the Negro's testimony valuable enough to search it out, nor have they raised the kinds of questions that encourage curiosity about the black man's role in America. This bias could be indulged until circumstances exposed the distortions that resulted. As long as the Negro was out of sight, he could remain out of mind. But the events of World War II (the shock of societal racism), America's subsequent world role, awareness of the failure of the "melting pot" (as witnessed by the extreme ethnocentrism of our major cities), the fact that the great majority of the black population has not moved into the middle class, the violence and disruption in our cities—all have forced upon historians a new set of questions about our past, questions that may help the present make sense. The history most of us have learned is not satisfactory precisely because it has failed to ask the right questions and to call upon all the witnesses.

Negro history has come in vogue because it has become apparent that we cannot understand present American development without knowing about it. Of course, Negro intellectuals have been interested in it for some time. Among others, J. W. C. Pennington and William C. Nell attempted to construct Negro histories in the nineteenth century, and later Carter G. Woodson and W. E. B. Du Bois were active agents in the promotion of Negro history. But, for the white American historian, historical significance has been dictated by the exigencies of his own era. The crisis of the moment has always given rise to new and pressing questions. Thus, in our time, it is not sentiment, liberalism, humanitarianism, nor sudden enlightenment that has compelled historians to take a new look at the American past, but simply the demands of the American present. And historians find themselves unable to perpetuate the bias that has made the Negro an invisible man, a problem, or a project—someone to be acted for or acted on, but never an actor in his own right.

Recognizing the inherent relativism of history, many have been satisfied to dismiss it all as distortion or lies—some out of disillusionment with the academic, some out of the understandable rage of the denied. Several advocates of a black history have gone so far as to say that since all histories are distortions, one that is devised by blacks is preferable to one created by whites. Like most cynical observations, this is the result of a deceived idealism that has failed to go beyond the obvious. Of course history (all history) is distortion. But there is a difference between the distortion of interpretation and that of conscious deception. The first is open to correction because, presumably, it honors truth, when told. The second is closed to all discovery, all discussion, and therefore all learning. Few historians would deny that their work distorts in the first sense, but then few ever expected to attain absolute fidelity to the past or absolute truth. Rather, they hope to achieve a valid and satisfactory interpretation, an explanation of the past that can be "lived with." When a historical interpretation is so grotesque that the distortion becomes obvious, it must be revised or rejected. But little is gained by the creation of countervailing grotesques. Those who want to contribute to the new interpretations of American history will have to work within the obligations of the discipline if their work is to have telling effect.

The correction of past interpretations would be simpler if the problem were merely, as some argue, that the Negro has been *systematically* excluded from American history. That would imply a conscious plan on the part of the historians, a conspiracy. If that were so, it could easily be corrected by forming a new conspiracy that includes the black man. In my opinion, however, the exclusion has been unconscious. The Negro (like the Chinese-American, the Mexican-American, the Nisei, and the American Indian) has been ignored or considered only incidentally. He has truly been an "invisible man." But to say this is to say he has not been in the minds of the historians, which means he has not been considered a man at all. The oversight is far more damning to the profession than any conspiracy could have been. For, as historians effectively omitted them from the story of the culture, they contributed to the emasculation and the dehumanization of all colored peoples in America. That the general public—including intellectuals with pretensions to some historical understanding—could "live with" such a view of American culture is of great significance to a new insight into American society.

The remarkable thing about the crisis that we now face is that the Negro (and, along with him, other colored minorities) can no longer be ignored. Some may regret it, but the Negro is now being seen and heard. And since he is so much in sight, he must now be in mind as well. Even the most conservative of academic disciplines is forced to take him into account. So, most American historians, some grudgingly, are beginning to reconsider the traditional histories. And their revisions are inspiring very lively discussions. For the new histories are raising more interesting and more fundamental questions about American society than the hoary debates about the tariff, reaction and reform, and so on which once served as the mainstay of the profession. Furthermore, allied social sciences such as sociology, anthropology, psychology, and economics, along with modern techniques of quantitative analysis, have expanded the ability of the historian to deal with the subject, especially where literary evidence is not available. All these developments are helping to invigorate the history—and to ensure that as we bring the Afro-American and other non-whites into the account, we will produce a history that measures up to the variety, richness, and infinite complexity of American life.

Black Myths, Black Heroes, Black Rage

It is myopic, some will say, to consider history, as I have been doing, primarily as a professional undertaking. After all, history and historical concepts are part of the general culture; what gets written by professionals is merely the top of the iceberg. Not only the educated man but every man lives his life with a sense of the past and his tradition. Most of the time, however, the ideas that determine his attitudes are not informed; they are mere impressions. Evidence and logic play a small part in his judgments. Most Americans, for instance, are unable to believe that the United States has ever been an aggressor nation, despite its history of territorial expansion. Most Americans assume the validity of the melting pot metaphor even though they actively work against the effective assimilation of the varieties of men who have come to this country. Such common-sense history is really myth, since it is sustained by emotion and self-concept rather than by evidence and reason. Some have argued that history is more important (and more pervasive) on this level of myth than as written, rational analysis. Thus, to them, it is not as important to revise history as to create new myth. Some have gone further and asserted that professional historians have helped to sustain these myths, and that, therefore, written history is merely rationalized mythology. Granting such arguments, one could say that Negroes should create their own myths, call them history, and thus serve their own emotional needs and self-concept.

Such an argument is much too cynical and, again, much too simple. For while it is true that national history tends to serve the generalized prejudices of the population, one cannot ignore the very important role of history in exposing the myths. The "Gone with the Wind" version of the reconstruction of the South has been more persistent than most romanticisms; it has a deep emotional hold on the American imagination. But, if that hold is to be loosened, it will be more the result of the scholarship begun by W. E. B. Du Bois in his *Black Reconstruction* and of the painstaking work he has inspired than the result of any substitute mythologies. Because scholars like Du Bois, John Hope Franklin, and Kenneth M. Stampp, who cannot be dismissed as myth makers, have compelled a reinterpretation, students are now at least required to confront the facts.

Most historical interpretation is actually myth-destroying. Almost every age has its Young Turks, who challenge the traditions and seek to make new and better sense of the old forms. Charles Beard attacked the apotheosis of the founding fathers. Richard Hofstadter exposed Abraham Lincoln as a shrewd politician who had a hand in the making of his own myth. And Hofstadter went on to challenge the accepted notion of the democratic, agrarian Populists. Kenneth Stampp showed that slavery was primarily a labor system and not a social system for the accommodation of the races. And, in the last year or so, by considering racial attitudes, historians have even been challenging the mythology of the "democratic" frontier.

To dismiss all history as mythology is not only to deny what conscientious historical scholarship has contributed to our understanding of ourselves, but it is to evade the intellectual problem altogether. For to consider the problem of historical judgment as merely one of choosing among myths is to preclude any obligation to understand what has been written (that is, to realize the nature of the distortions) and to correct it. The assumption that one myth is just as good as another—that every group should establish its own mythology —is not only anti-intellectual, but it is based on a faulty conception of mythology. Myths must be sustained by deep emotional springs, and, for this reason, some are more compelling than others. Only myths that are congenial to preexisting dispositions can take root in the imagination. And, once a myth has taken firm hold, it cannot be easily invalidated. The story of George Washington and the cherry tree, for instance, was planted in soil that was extremely receptive to its morality; in truth, it was an illustration of already accepted mores. Because it was so generally believed that truth is preferable to lies and that honesty is a manly virtue, the cherry tree story was a useful moral lesson. What would-be myth makers should recognize today is that a favorable Negro mythology that might substitute for history cannot simply be created and promoted. Myths that are unrelated to history and tradition and unsustained by deep-rooted emotional and spiritual validation will be short-lived and of questionable service. For no matter what urgency caused the mind to construct them, the heart will at last deny them. It is sobering to realize that one of the common bonds between whites and blacks in America is a tendency to accept the same myths—even those with racist implications.

It is appealing, nonetheless, as black men talk of black nationalism, to consider devising a myth that defines the black nation. Here there is precedent enough; most nationalisms have been accompanied by an epic that has glorified and defined the national character. Thus Homer's *Iliad* served ancient Greece; *La Chanson de Roland,* France; the *Morte Darthur,* the legend of King Arthur's Round Table, England. The Old Testament has been an epic to the Jews, who have used their history of slavery and persecution and the concept of being a "chosen people" to sustain a sense of "nationhood," even though they are dispersed throughout the world. Immediately following the American Revolution, Joel Barlow, among countless others, tried to write a verse epic for the new American nation. As it turned out, the work that became the American national epic was George Bancroft's *History of the United States,* which assumed that a divine hand had led the Americans into their more perfect union. All these epics involved considerable fantasy; that is what myth is. But the fact of national existence and national power sustained the myths and allowed the fantasies to be indulged. The same can be said of racist fantasies throughout the years. It was such a fantasy that allowed Englishmen, Europeans, and Americans to interpret their exploitation of colored peoples in the nineteenth and twentieth centuries as a "white man's burden." But the facts of power were such that the distortions were not, at the time, forcefully exposed; white men could live with the myth, and the colored people were made to.

Nothing, however, is more pathetic than a people clinging to a legend or myth that has outlived its basis in actuality. Homer was a powerful ideological force for the Greeks as they stood (more or less) together against the Persians in the fifth century B.C. The Athenian victory at Marathon, indeed, reminded the historian Herodotus of the united effort at Troy. But the *Iliad,* for all its glory, counted for nothing against Philip of Macedon, and for even less against Rome. Sometimes, in fact, the legends built up among a people can become very dysfunctional. Doubtless the Jews' historical view of themselves as a persecuted people has made it difficult for them to view black complaints of Jewish exploitation as anything other than the familiar anti-Semitism coming from a new direction. What is more, it probably exacerbated racial tensions in New York City's recent school decentralization dispute to the point of hysteria. In much the same way, the persistence of France's notions of empire led that nation into the ignominy and deep tragedy of Vietnam and Algeria. Historical concepts that encourage people to think of themselves in ways that are indifferent to the realities of power, economics, and human behavior tempt disaster. People must be able to separate fantasy from reality in order to know how to act and what to expect from their actions; misconceptions can be ruinous. The task of disciplined historical analysis is always to provide people with a fair chance to perceive their own reality so that they may act with a good sense of possibilities and consequences.

Demands for an Afro-American version of the past have arisen from yet another idea about the function of history—one which is closely related to the concept of national myth. It is claimed that history should serve emotional needs as well as purely rational ones—that it should contribute to one's sense of identity. Quite understandably, many want to find heroes and great men in the past with whom black people—especially children—can identify. In addition, they want to use a new history to exercise their sense of righteous rage at the oppression of their people and to collar their white contemporaries with the responsibility and the guilt for historical racism. Because taught history gives black youngsters few manly and influential ancestors to emulate, and because racial arrogance persists even among the most liberal whites, it is human enough for blacks to see an Afro-American history as a way to celebrate (and to create) great black men and to expose and condemn their white enemies. Nonetheless, this approach is problematic in historical terms. Not only would it make bad history, but in the end it would be self-defeating.

No one will deny that history can be a means of developing a positive and constructive self-concept. All too often, history as taught in the lower grades is little more than that. Although George Washington's cherry tree story has fallen by the wayside, other tales designed to uplift and to build character still fill a large portion of the curriculum. Indeed, many people believe that all education should be a promotion of moralisms. Certainly it is necessary to encourage children to associate themselves with elevating past events and with approved social behavior. And no doubt this can most easily be done by providing them with historical personalities to emulate. This easy road to building a positive self-concept has been closed to the Negro child because the national educational system does not honor his people; thus he is alienated from broad social identification. There is surely no harm in citing black heroes as often as white heroes—in honoring blacks along with whites for their real virtues. Crispus Attucks aside, Nat Turner was as much a fighter for freedom as Nathan Hale (and was surely more historically significant), and James Beckwourth was as exemplary a frontiersman as Davy Crockett.

There is a difference, however, between history and moralistic hero worship. The ends that can be served by the celebration of black heroes are extremely limited. Intelligent and critical people, as they sense the complexities of human life and motivation, find the hero unsatisfying. In the first place, like the isolated and inconsequential fact, the hero alone seldom tells us much of what we want to know about history. Second, the moral preachment involved in any invocation of heroes is ultimately condescending to mature people. And, finally, the very notion of a hero requires such a distortion of normal humanity, such exceptional character and experience, as to severely test credibility.

Heroes, black or white, become problematic whenever one goes beneath the surface characterization. They are, necessarily, bigger than life, which is precisely why mentally healthy adults are unlikely to find them satisfactory models for real life. They are of necessity two-dimensional; their motives and their acts are always simplified to make some point. More troublesome yet, the more one learns about the circumstances of a hero's life, the less of an unqualified hero he becomes. Crispus Attucks, for instance, may not have been African at all, and surely he and his white comrades were more motivated to harass the British military than to strike a blow for liberty and independence. It is possible that Denmark Vesey was wrongly accused and convicted of conspiring to revolt. Nat Turner's uprising may be seen as more desperate than revolutionary, and it did have disastrous consequences for many blacks in Southampton County, Virginia. Those who were mutilated and the one hundred or more who lost their lives in the hysterical backlash from Turner's raid could hardly have thought him a hero. However much one may appreciate Beckwourth's exploits as a mountain man and Indian scout, it is necessary to realize that he was not happy with his African ancestry, and that his value to the white men lay in his ability and his willingness to betray the Indians. This is not to diminish the achievements of these men, but merely to point out that to see them as heroes is not to see them as human beings in a real world. Real history demands no less than that.

Or, consider the "heroism" of Frederick Douglass. Surely he should be honored for his remarkable achievements. He struggled against his enslavement, taught himself to read and write, escaped to freedom in the North, became one of the most articulate and effective spokesmen in the antislavery cause, and served the federal government in many capacities, last as minister to Haiti. Few men in American history could boast a comparable record. Some of my black students, however, have been deeply disappointed in Douglass when they learned that his second wife was white. Others have been disturbed at his lack of militancy in the years following the Civil War. Heroes, however great, are extremely vulnerable in the eyes of would-be worshipers.

Historians want Douglass' life to tell something more than the obvious fact that he was a great man. They would like to understand the rather deep differences that he had with his white abolitionist friends. They would like to explore his dilemma in recruiting black men for a humiliating and racist Union army so that they might join in a war effort that was questionable from the Negro's point of view. They want to know something of the mollifying process that converted Douglass, by the end of his life, from a militant abolitionist to a self-effacing black federal functionary. Because Douglass was a great man, his life raises these and similar questions. And answers to them will reveal far more about the Afro-American experience and American culture than would simple genuflections to his greatness.

The idea that history should serve emotional needs has also given rise to its use as an outlet for anger and guilt. It is not surprising that black people, whose sense of the race's experience is overwhelmed by the crippling effects of racism and oppression, should welcome history as a convenient way to exercise their rage. Similarly, sensitive and well-meaning white people, who cannot escape the social responsibility of racism and who find their greatest efforts at expiation slight compared to the enormity of the problem, welcome Afro-American history as a means of finding substance and focus for their guilt. Such historical emotionalism finds its real satisfaction in the brutality of the African and domestic slave trades, master-slave relations, racial violence. It does not care to see much more than the abundant ugliness of the white-black racial experience. It is like biting on an aching tooth, sucking pleasure from the pain of it. While human and understandable, such masochism is self-indulgent and cannot expand anyone's sense of the past. The historical significance of the events and personalities described is generally obliterated by the strong feelings of black rage and white guilt that are aroused. Students—black and white—must press beyond the level of wounded sensibility if Afro-American history is to acquire deep, abiding, and constructive meaning.

Furthermore, the rage and the guilt that accompany the emotionalization of Afro-American history are too vulnerable when faced with all the facts. One is safe enough as long as one knows only that white men controlled the African slave trade or that white men ravished black women in slavery. But what happens when it becomes clear that African chieftains were allied with Europeans in the slave trade and, indeed, were crucial to its success; that some black women were not in fact ravished but, like other women in history, used their sex as a weapon, sometimes merely to improve their situation and sometimes as a means to actual power; that the institution of slavery often depended on slaves as drivers and informers? Surely, no amount of evidence can reduce the horrible, dehumanizing aspects of the slavery system. But black complicity in many areas certainly mitigates the racial righteousness that is assumed by the enraged and the guilt-ridden. And surely, it is vastly more instructive and interesting to try to understand the black women who willingly became consorts to white men, and even the slaves who betrayed their brothers, than it is to ignore them or to dismiss them by lumping them into simple categories.

Ironically, many advocates of a black history conceive of history in much the same way as nativist groups such as the Daughters of the American Revolution. That is, they see it as a means of preserving the past in order to feel good about themselves and their people. However, the achievements of the past cannot really reflect on the present. In our property-oriented society, one can receive wealth, power, and prestige from his ancestors, but each generation has to make its own history. However much the members of the DAR may glory in their heritage, they hardly share the spirit that made their forebears the agents of rebellion and disorder. The DAR can only lay claim to its own kind of tea party and its own notoriety. Likewise, whatever was achieved by Harriet Tubman, Nat Turner, Frederick Douglass, and others does not give living black men the right to any special glory. The past can point the way, can suggest possibilities, but it cannot substitute for one's own victories over his time.

It is doubtful, in fact, whether a positive historical sense necessarily improves one's life and self-image. Those who belong to the Native Sons and Daughters organizations and other groups like the DAR are not better people for their genealogy, though they may think they are. Such self-illusions, like myths of all sorts, are possible only as long as the circumstances of life do not belie them — as long as there is wealth and power to back them up. When the pretended glory is not accompanied by power, the results can be sad indeed. Following the decline of the European monarchies, for instance, Western capitals were filled with displaced persons with pretensions to glory and a history to prove it. They were lucky when they also had money. Many were forced to sell their jewels and other valuables and finally to seek very inglorious work. Their pretensions became ludicrous as they took jobs as doormen and washroom attendants. Or, consider Henry Adams. He was born in the line of one of America's greatest families, one that had served mightily in the shaping of the American republic. Two of his ancestors had been Presidents (one of them a founding father), others had served in various state and federal capacities, and he had been tutored in the same tradition of public service. Yet Adams was perceptive enough to see, at the close of the Civil War, that the America in which he found himself had no need for his style of service. His deeply ingrained sense of history only made him feel alien to the time in which he lived. There was little glory in that, but merely a sadness and despair.

In another way, the black psychiatrist Dr. Alvin Poussaint has made the same point on the pitfalls of the historical self-concept. Writing about the Negro psyche in the *New York Times Magazine* of August 20, 1967, Dr. Poussaint tells of his own encounter with a policeman in Jackson, Mississippi, while working there on a civil rights project. One day, leaving the project's office in the company of a woman, Poussaint was rudely stopped by a policeman, who called him insulting names and otherwise abused him. Like countless other black men, whatever their educational and social standing, Poussaint merely withstood his humiliation and, when he was permitted to leave, walked away pleased that it had been no worse. For he knew that the policeman would have been happy to do him serious injury and would have been under absolutely no obligation to answer for it. No understanding of Afro-American history and no memory of black heroes could have mitigated the humiliation of that moment.

The power—whatever the glory—was in another's hands. Dr. Poussaint's experience and good sense had given him a more usable feeling for his predicament than any glorified history could have.

One of the most important tasks of history is to give people an understanding of exactly where power lies and what their relationship to it is. A man with a good sense of history may choose to take an ultimate risk, but he does so knowingly. It is in this sense that the Blackstone Rangers demonstrated an astute grasp of their history when they refrained from joining street demonstrations in Chicago during the 1968 Democratic convention. They claimed that the police were out to get them. Their intimate knowledge of the police, of their propensity toward violence, told them they would be in danger of serious injury and even death at the slightest provocation. They knew, also, that they would be powerless to control what happened. Others, unfortunately, were less aware of what might occur. Few whites anticipated the demonstrators' encounter with a riotous and hysterical police force. And the press hardly imagined that the police would turn on them in their rage. Yet a more practical understanding of American history might have told them all that police—especially Chicago police—have acted before with uncontrolled violence against the powerless. Hopefully, Chicago–1968, Berkeley–1969, and Kent State and Jackson State–1970 have served to give many the realism of the Blackstone Rangers.

Of course, building a favorably historical image of blacks, as well as cataloging black heroes, can serve a purpose: it might help white Americans understand American history in nonethnocentric ways. But it is far better for blacks to understand their past realistically, so that they will know where they stand in relation to power and be able to judge the probable effects of their actions. This is more serviceable to blacks than dwelling on truth or fable about black heroes and a black martial spirit. The historian, to help build a realistic historical sense, must stick to his task of hard analysis. He cannot be a servant to irresponsible fantasy.

Culture and History All Our Own

Finally, there are those who argue that Afro-American culture is best understood as separate and distinct from white America, and that the historian's task is to define it and write about it. This idea, too, has its appeal. A certain black-white dualism has always been manifest in American life. And the generalizations that seem to apply to whites are sometimes inappropriate to blacks. Even the fact that the traditional histories have tended to ignore the black man's voice tempts us to believe that Negroes were doing and saying something remarkably different from whites. Certain more discernible differences have appeared as well. On the lower-class level, the Negro church and family have seemed distinctive. Surely, Afro-Americans have had a unique voice in matters of culture: their view of the gospel, a distinctive rhetorical style, and major innovations in music have been exclusively their own. Many have described the argot of the lower-class black community as a separate language. Although it started (as does most argot) as a cryptic language, ghetto and class insularity have made it, for some, an only tongue.

There are still other matters—felt concerns—that support the argument for cultural distinctiveness. Most Afro-Americans have sensed, at one time or another, that they understand other blacks without language; shared experience and emotion allow a kind of knowing without words. How common it is for black students in white schools to feel the frustration of trying to explain some of that experience to whites, while knowing that they can never understand. And what a relief it is to be back in the company of a black person (stranger or not), because the questions do not have to be asked nor the words searched for. The emotional bonds among black people can give rise to a sense of brotherhood that seems to uphold the notion of distinctive culture.

W. E. B. Du Bois, in his *Souls of Black Folk,* described Negroes as "living within a veil." He meant several things by that image—notably, that Negroes see America from within, yet apart; that they have an alienated perspective. He believed, as do many Negroes, that Afro-Americans understand the white world in a way that whites themselves do not understand it. It should also be said, and it seldom is, that a history of oppression has denied to most black people the skills and training that would permit them to understand aspects of their own world as precisely as they should. Nonetheless, all the shared problems and experiences, coupled with a unique perspective, give Negroes, one to another, a shock of recognition that runs deep.

This argument has strong claim to truth. It explains the justifiable demand for separate black student unions on white college campuses. Black students often feel the need to come together to discover their ethnic distinctiveness, to crystallize their common experiences in a sea of undiluted white culture. But it is another question whether all this explains and justifies a history which presumes so distinctive a culture that it must be studied in isolation.

I think that it does not. The very fact that this culture is such a self-conscious thing—that people have to decide what it is—suggests that it is not such an overwhelming fact of life as to demand formal study of its own. Even those who support the idea of separate culture most strongly are hard pressed to suggest its character or dimensions. It is impossible to give serious academic study to something so vague. Perhaps, after considerable scholarship on the Afro-American experience, we will discover that there is a definable black culture. But we cannot simply make this assumption. Cultures (whatever they are) either exist or they don't; they are never successfully manufactured and promoted.

What is most remarkable about much that is called black culture is its Americanness; and, conversely, much of what is considered most uniquely American is essentially Afro-American. However distinctive the Negro idiom has been in religion, for instance, it has remained Protestant Christianity;

Negroes have merely tended to rest their religion more heavily on the Old Testament than have white Christians. As the Negro church developed through slavery, from the earliest revivals and the Great Awakening, it remained more fundamentalist in tendency. It was little affected by the liberal Protestant reforms that occurred in Northern churches in the mid-nineteenth century. If anything, the Negro church has hewn more to the tradition of American Protestantism than white churches have.

The most distinctive product of black culture has been music. But Afro-American music is indebted to Europe as well as to Africa. "Jelly Roll" Morton, the self-proclaimed father of jazz, was quick to acknowledge the influence of Italian opera on his innovations. And modern American music is derived so heavily from Negro folk tradition—gospel, blues, rhythm and blues—that it is impossible to separate the two. Even the argot of Negroes has become a part of standard speech in America. "Up tight," "nitty-gritty," and "soul," for example, are expressions that have become part of common speech. Even words that were once cryptic terms for whites—"ofay" and "gray," for instance—no longer belong to Negroes exclusively. Some words—such as "fuzz" and "bread" —have come into the general language almost as soon as they were coined.

There is no doubt that on some levels one can distinguish a Negro ethos. But, again, I doubt whether such distinctions are sufficiently important in the lives of blacks or whites to warrant a separate historical study. On the contrary, I think that much of what we must understand about the Afro-American experience is best understood within the context of American history. For instance, considering Frederick Douglass in the context of nineteenth-century reform will help us to understand the limits of his vision as well as that of his white contemporaries. It is important to see black men who advocated the recolonization of Africa by Afro-Americans, men like Edward Blyden and Marcus Garvey, in terms of their basically American sense of mission. Black leaders around World War I, like W. E. B. Du Bois and James Weldon Johnson, cannot be understood outside the framework of American progressivism; only within this context can we grasp the significance of their rejection of manipulative urban politics, their self-styled upper-middle-class reform.

In art, the same can be said; black artists are best understood in terms of the major schools that have influenced them. Paul Laurence Dunbar's poetry, like that of his friend James Whitcomb Riley, served the school of local color realism. The artistic judgments of Countee Cullen and W. E. B. Du Bois were squarely within the genteel tradition. When Richard Wright wanted to tell the story of Bigger Thomas, child of oppression and racism, he chose as his method the same naturalism that had served Theodore Dreiser. Although Melvin Tolson's *Harlem Gallery* often seems to parody the academic poets of the mid-twentieth century, it is firmly within the academic school. LeRoi Jones's plays—whatever the author's feelings about "black art"—join those of Edward Albee in the theater of the absurd. If one thinks that some special ethnic genius is the sole inspiration for Jones's work, one should consider the origin of the tale of the "Flying Dutchman" that gave form to one of his plays. Even if a black art could be successfully postulated, it would become American in its very creation.

In short, there is nothing wrong with the Americanness of black culture; to the contrary, it is natural and expected. But if we really want to understand what Afro-Americans have done and are doing, it is best to consider them in terms of the traditions they continue.

Toward a National Identity

One of the most important reasons for studying Afro-American history is that through it we may come to a better understanding of American history. The true character of American culture and tradition can be fully understood only when the Negro is included in the account. This means going back to the beginning. It means asking new questions—questions that provoke full testimony from the long-muted evidence. It is necessary not merely because Afro-Americans were there from the beginning, but because men like Thomas Jefferson and George Washington and Woodrow Wilson lived in a world affected by black men. Surely, we will know these men better too when we know more about the racial realities of their world. Indeed, the whole of American history will take on a different aspect. It seems that the black man has always been beyond the limits of what appeared to be a limitless America. The American Revolution stopped short, democracy stopped short, progressivism and liberal reform stopped short, and always the Negro seems to have marked the limits. Despite the fact that the Negro has been ignored in American history, he has always been deep in the consciousness of Americans. Whatever the aspirations of whites for this country, whatever their sense of its possibilities, they have always had to make careful distinctions to exclude black men from the dream. When we know the Negro's history, we will know the failings of the dream itself.

Our times are compelling. The traditional, absolute faith in progress has been abandoned by many Americans. Many struggle now to understand themselves in terms of the impossibilities that define their present: the racial and urban crises, poverty, war, and the need for peace. The inclusion of the Afro-American in American history will help illuminate the impossibilities that have been there all along. As we Americans, black and white, struggle to understand how we can survive in peace with one another and how we can finally transform ourselves into a people with a true and inclusive national identity, it is essential that our history encourage us to abandon all fantasies for realistic conceptions of ourselves and our past.

Completely Well: One View of Black American Culture

HOUSTON A. BAKER, JR.

Houston A. Baker, Jr., is associate professor of English at the University of Virginia at Charlottesville. He has taught black literature at both the University of Virginia and Yale University and has edited *Black Writers in America,* to be published by McGraw-Hill in 1971. In the essay that follows, Mr. Baker takes a positive stand on the question of the existence of a distinctive black American culture. Holding that true culture is the product of one's whole life and experience, Mr. Baker argues that black culture is wholly separate from and in opposition to white culture. Further, he contends that the white world's definitions of culture—and the social pretensions to which they give rise—have been profoundly damaging to black Americans in the past.

The Question of "Culture"

Most of modern Western civilization uses the word "culture" to mean only "a body of intellectual and imaginative work"[1] and considers it something spiritual and transcendent. In general, those who have this reverential attitude toward culture also have the greatest vested interest in preserving its present limited connotations. Hopefully, through sound reasoning and serious effort the true meaning of the word can be re-established. Culture is not transcendental and ethereal; while some of its manifestations—some of its arts and artifacts—may often be defined in spiritual terms, culture itself is a more inclusive concept that accurately means "a whole way of life." To define or analyze a culture, therefore, one must pay as much attention to historical factors as one pays to technology and sociological patterns. The proposition here is that the history of a culture is, in effect, the culture. Culture is not a body of intellectual and imaginative work that can be set forth as a sanctuary from our technological age; it is not a series of artifacts displayed by curators of culture; it is not the curriculum of even the most advanced and highly rated

---

[1] Raymond Williams, *Culture and Society, 1780–1950* (New York: Columbia University Press, 1958), p. 325.

university; and it most certainly is not the supernatural ethos that surrounds these things. One does not worship, display, or teach culture; one acknowledges it as a whole way of life grounded in history, and one necessarily lives a culture.

The central question of the discussion that follows is whether a way of life known as black American culture is distinct and separate from a way of life known as white culture. The relevance of historical information in arriving at an answer cannot be overrated. If, as proposed here, the history of a culture is the culture, then the history of the black American is black American culture. The only way to arrive at an understanding of black American culture is to comprehend fully the history of the black American. Moreover, to survey the evolution of his way of life is to analyze why "culture" came to be defined in America as something spiritual, transcendental, and white. For some, the most vexing problem surrounding such an examination is the fear that black American culture may prove separate and unequal. However, "separate and unequal" in the question of culture is as much a myth as "separate but equal" in the question of school facilities. Any whole way of life differs from any other whole way of life in content and form; but discussions of the equality of different cultures can only lead to distortions and faulty evaluations. The attempt here, then, is not to demonstrate the equality of black American culture but to deal with its distinctiveness from another whole way of life. We must begin with history, the primary factor in such a discussion, and move on to study the distortions occasioned by race and culture theorizing, the literary reflections of a black culture, and, finally, the wholesome effects of acknowledging a distinct black American culture.

The History

Any black American might paraphrase Countee Cullen and ask: "What is America to me? / Spacious sky / And land of liberty?" The answer history supports is that America is something apart. Black Americans were plowed through the amber waves of grain, their stars and stripes the engravings of cat-o'-nine-tails on black flesh. The legends of men conquering wild and virgin lands are not the legends of black America; the stories of benevolent theocracies bringing light and salvation to pagans are not the stories of black America; and the tales of pioneers enduring the hardships of the West for the promise of immense wealth are not the tales of black America. When the black American reads Frederick Jackson Turner's *The Frontier in American History,* he feels no regret over the end of the Western frontier. To black America, "frontier" is an alien word; for, in essence, all frontiers established by the white psyche have been closed to the black man.

In a recent work, Dr. James Comer deals with America's conception of frontiers. He points out that the early wealth of America was contingent upon the produce of its great land area and upon the ships that carried that produce to foreign ports; together, agriculture and shipping ensured the survival of the country in its early days, and the wealth acquired from the partnership filled their white coffers. Each proclamation of a new frontier brought substantially increased wealth to these two enterprises.

Both agriculture and shipping, however, were closed to the black American; when the American grab bag was opening—when new territories were being annexed and handed out to humble homesteaders—the black American was toiling from day clean to first dark. The railroads received phenomenal doles; miners claimed hundreds of acres; immigrants made their way into the Northwest Territory and established thriving communities. Meanwhile, the black American was sold or bartered back and forth as chattel. Only when the frontier had closed, only when the strings of the grab bag were pulling tight, did the black American begin to make his presence felt in a society that had not included him on its list of recipients. As Comer puts it: "Much of the wealth of America was given away while blacks were still in slavery. Almost all of it was given away before 1915 when 90% of the black population lived in extreme poverty and oppression in the Deep South."[2]

Yet, there are those myth makers who insist on reassuring the black man that whites came to North America with pennies and parlayed them into fortunes. They talk of the competitive spirit, justice for all, and bootstrap philosophies of advancement. This is simply naiveté. Even now they do not realize that the dreams, tales, and manners of black America are things apart from this American *Weltanschauung;* they do not realize that with every law and grant America took calculated steps to set the black man outside the larger society. While the myth makers gaze back at what Baldwin has called a period of "European innocence," while they hear drums beating out the Spirit of Seventy-six, the black American looks back to Elmina on the Gold Coast and hears the debate on behalf of the three clauses in the Constitution that ensured the continuance of American slavery—the fugitive slave clause, the slave trade clause, and the three-fifths clause.[3] Slavery was written into the American Constitution; and, when its usefulness had begun to wane, the effects of the cotton gin revived this fading institution. The perspectives of black America and white America are as far apart as the captain's cabin and the quarters of "black ivory" during the middle passage (the eight-week voyage from Africa to the New World).

On one side the word is:

> If you see my Pompey, 30 yrs of age,
> new breeches, plain stockings, negro shoes;
> if you see my Anna, likely young mulatto
> branded E on the right cheek, R on the left,
> catch them if you can and notify subscriber.

---

[2] James Comer, *Beyond Black and White* (Chicago: Quadrangle Books, forthcoming).

[3] Benjamin Quarles, *The Negro in the Making of America* (New York: Macmillan, 1968), p. 60.

On the other side the word is: "Mean mean mean to be free." The polarity is so great that it is perhaps meaningless to debate what was left of an African heritage after a "voyage through death / to life upon these shores."[4] Melville J. Herskovits[5] argues that much was left after the middle passage—African linguistic traits, religious practices, patterns of family organization, and modes of song and dance. However, E. Franklin Frazier tells us that "the Negroes were practically stripped of their social heritage and their traditional social organization was destroyed as the result of the manner in which they were enslaved and became the labour force in the plantation economy."[6] After Herskovits, Frazier, and others have spoken, the fact remains that the black American's perspective on history, his patterns of social organization, his life style as a whole, are significantly different from those of white America. Some have attributed the differences to race, while others have attributed them to culture. Heretofore, few have been willing to look steadily at America's past and acknowledge that the differences stem from the fact that the black man was denied his part in the frontier and his share of the nation's wealth.

Race and Culture Theorizing

If one is to come to terms with the history, one must face the fact that no meaningful definition of "race" exists. All arguments to the contrary, "race" is simply a heuristic term that is often invoked in support of an existing order or in an attempt to unify a body of people for political purposes. The theories—from Gobineau to Shockley—merely serve to perpetuate superstition.[7] The practice of superstition consists in setting the generalization over the fact, and that is what all race theorizers have done; they have generalized from individual cases. According to the race theorizers, if one black man acts in a particular manner, all black men must act in the same manner. Similar skin color, features, and hair type mean that all who possess them are to be subsumed under a particular race theory. As Jacques Barzun has pointed out, such theorizing is not only insupportable but also dangerous; it can only lead to global blood baths.

The word "culture" is no more helpful than "race" without the type of skilled analysis it has received at the hands of Raymond Williams.[8] Used in a purely subjective or political context, it can become simply a surrogate for "race." In its contemporary sense, "culture" is a product of the nineteenth

---

[4] The preceding lines of poetry are from "Runagate Runagate" and "Middle Passage" by Robert Hayden, from *Selected Poems.* Copyright © 1966 by Robert Hayden. Reprinted by permission of October House Inc.

[5] Melville J. Herskovits, *The Myth of the Negro Past* (New York: Harper, 1941).

[6] E. Franklin Frazier, *The Negro Church in America* (New York: Schocken Books, 1964), p. 82.

[7] Jacques Barzun, *Race: A Study in Superstition* (New York: Harcourt, 1937).

[8] Williams, *Culture and Society.*

century, which also fostered the present institutional connotations of such words as "industry," "democracy," "class," and "art." In response to the Industrial Revolution, certain moral and intellectual endeavors were designated the components of culture and set apart from more functional aspects of society. Thus, moral and intellectual activities were set above processes of practical social judgment and became a court of human appeal that sought an alternative to the times. This designation of culture as a body of intellectual and imaginative work created a distilled version of the word. "Culture" was primarily a response to the industrial metamorphosis; many pre-industrial social endeavors were not viable in an industrial society, and a new order had to be established. The activities of this new order were segregated under the heading of "culture," and in this version it came to represent "a whole way of life." Therefore, until the full substance of the term—culture as a whole way of life— has been reasserted, it cannot be used to discuss the differentiation between groups of people without invoking the same superstition and meaningless appendages that accompany the word "race."

Black America can justifiably say that it possesses a true culture—a *whole* way of life that includes its own standards of moral and aesthetic judgment. The black American need not engage in arguments over the superiority or the inferiority of particular attributes; he need not fight pitched battles over different bodies of intellectual and imaginative work and attempt to assess their relative worth. A body of intellectual and imaginative work reflects a whole way of life. And only that same culture can evolve the standards by which its intellectual and imaginative work is to be judged. The malaise of the black psyche has come, in part, from the attempts of white America to set both "race" and "culture" in an unreal context.

Not content with denying the black American the frontier and a share of the nation's wealth, white America has attempted to justify its denial. Race theories and the use of "culture" in a slanted manner have allowed whites to state that black men are part of an inferior race and possess no cultural capabilities. The first assertion is sheer superstition; the second is grounded on an attempt to use "culture" in a limited context. By inculcation from generation to generation, however, white America has succeeded in distorting the black psyche. This process is obvious in the realm of race theorizing; the more subtle distortions occasioned by culture theorizing, however, can be illustrated by an autobiographical example.

Culture Theorizing and Its Distortions

"God's in his heaven / All's right with the world!" was one of the first literary phrases that came from her lips and fixed itself in my mind. There were countless others, but I specifically remember being overjoyed when I could match my mother word for word in the first eighteen lines of the "General Prologue" to *The Canterbury Tales:* "Whan that Aprill with his shoures soote /

The droghte of March hath perced to the roote." I had heard her quote the words time and again, but it was not until one hot summer afternoon that I discovered they came from Chaucer. I was looking over the bookshelves upstairs; after a few minutes I pulled out *The Complete Works of Geoffrey Chaucer.* It was a moment of triumph when I was able to run downstairs and recite these lines for an admiring parent.

Looking back on that time, I remember the four or five long rows of shelves that held the family books: Rudyard Kipling, Robert Louis Stevenson, Charlotte Brontë, and a host of other white writers. I perused each of the books and looked forward to the day when I would be able to read them all with understanding.

In the meantime, there was the local "colored" library to satisfy my reading fancy. The black librarian was not a kindly old lady who steered me in the proper direction; she was quick-tempered and stern and handed over my officially charged-out volumes as though dispensing her personal property. And so every two weeks I walked or rode the bus to this august lady's library and checked out the allotted five books. I read the entire sports collection, which consisted of books about white athletes in white high schools, white colleges, or white major leagues. I read pioneering stories until the sound "Westward, ho!" rang in my ears twenty-four hours a day; all the pioneers, of course, were white; all the Indians, and even the beasts of the field, were "dark." I read biographies of American heroes and grew so inspired that I set up my own garage workshop in an attempt to emulate the performances of young Tom Edison and young Sam Morse. This was the world of the library until the great event occurred—the white library downtown was opened to "colored people"!

I walked between its grimy Ionian columns, across the shadows to the front door, and entered the lobby on tiptoe. There was an unbelievable bustle, strange after the small, cramped silences of the colored library. Here, there was light and activity, and an incredible sense of importance seemed to hang from the ceilings decorated with ancient, white figures. At the information desk, I finally attracted someone's attention and learned where the children's section was located. I tiptoed up the stairs and was greeted by a kindly white lady who smiled and asked if she could help me. "What sort of book do you want?" I told her I wanted sports stories, pioneer stories, or biographies, and she led me to the pioneer section. As she pulled out book after book, I watched this kind white lady turn redder and redder. I kept saying that I had read the books she pulled out, and she grew so incredulous that she finally submitted me to an oral examination on some innocuous story about a ten-year-old white boy who shot a mountain lion and saved his community. When I knew the answers, she slammed the book shut and simply pointed to where I could find the sports stories and the biographies. It did seem strange that the colored library and the white library had the *same* pioneer books.

Fortunately, I only had to use the children's section for a brief time. A whole new world opened to me with high school English and the works of Plato, Voltaire, and Joyce that my brother brought home from college. When I finished high school there was little doubt in my mind that I wanted to be an English major and get to know as much as possible about as many books as possible. However, the cultural bias reflected equally in the colored and white libraries was destined to recur in relation to a black college and a white graduate school. At the white graduate school, I read the *same* books that I had studied at the black college. When I asked at either school about the works of black writers, I was told that in English one need study only the "classical" works. A friend in graduate school attempted in vain to demonstrate that I should study black works since they were reflections of the whole way of life that I was living. Some time later, I did begin to deal with the works of black literature—when I was not pursuing the "classics."

My first job was teaching English—a course from Homer to Joyce. My colleagues, both old and young, knew little about black writers, and the syllabuses (like those in graduate school) were barren when it came to the names of black authors. And now, as I teach black American literature, I find few colleagues with whom I can really discuss the works that I am teaching; indeed, many of my associates think that black literature begins with Richard Wright and ends with James Baldwin.

This pattern of events seems to offer a perfect example of culture theorizing and the distortions that it occasions. Born in a racialistic and former slave state, I was bombarded with the words, images, and artifacts of the white world. My parents had been bombarded with the same images, and the black librarian was no better off. There are thousands of black men in America who have gone through similar experiences. Few of us realized that "the doctors" had bored holes in our heads, cut out part of our brains, and shot electricity through the rest.[9] All of us had been lobotomized into an acceptance of the word "culture" on the white world's terms; we failed to realize that the manner in which the white world used "culture" only helped justify its denial of the black man.

Having recovered or attempted to reconstruct that which was cut away, black Americans have now cast aside the etherizing veil; no longer can white America hide behind the culture curtain. Whites quote Matthew Arnold at blacks; they say that culture consists of the best that has been thought and said in the world. The world, of course, means the white world, and the best can only be that which is white and Western. For one to possess culture, according to whites, one has to possess a firm knowledge of the best that the white Western world has to offer, whether it is Beethoven or Brecht. That culture might stand for a whole way of life and that there might be a multitude of wholes never occurs to most white Americans. Those who have read Ruth Benedict or Margaret Mead do acknowledge that there are many cultures, but

---

[9] Etheridge Knight, "Hard Rock Returns to Prison from the Hospital for the Criminal Insane," in *Poems From Prison* (Detroit: Broadside Press, 1968), pp. 11–12.

they seldom (if ever) admit that the "best" may lie somewhere beyond the narrow bounds of the particular culture from which they spring.

In other words, culture, like race, is little more than a superstition for most whites; the word, defined in a manner that sets the idea of the great white West over actual fact, holds them all in a tight fraternity. Vested interests are certainly a part of their reluctance to move outside their narrowly defined conception of culture. For if culture means a whole way of life and if its intellectual works are only the reflections of that whole, then so-called objective and universal standards are no more than the tastes and inclinations of those engaged in one whole way of life. In this sense, the standards of white Americans are neither objective nor universal; they are simply subjective and white.

To accept this, however, would be for whites to admit that the world does not begin with Homer; they would have to realize that they are dealing with only a minute fraction of the best the world has to offer; and they would be forced—which is most to the point—to realize that the world is not composed of white supermen producing culture and nonwhite underdogs and colonial subjects attempting to equal white culture. But white literature, white art, white architecture, white philosophy, and white patterns of social organization are seldom looked upon by white intellectuals as anything but the best that has been thought and said in the world. And for countless years, as products of those weird lobotomizing machines established by whites (and exposed in Ralph Ellison's *Invisible Man*), many black men were willing to let such an evaluation stand. When we take a less slanted view of culture, however, we can see that the white world's definition will not do. In fact, it is to a great extent the culture theorizing of whites that has made for a separate and distinctive black American culture. That is to say, one index of the distinctiveness of black American culture is the extent to which it repudiates the culture theorizing of the white Western world; that such a repudiation is not made in any significant degree within the white world goes without saying; there are too many vested interests that militate against any dispersion of the fraternity made possible by white culture theorizing.

Folklore and Literature

We are brought back then to the history, to the question "What is America to me?" and to the most supportable answer the black American can give— "something apart." America as the refuge of huddled masses yearning to be free; America as a domain of boundless frontier; America as freedom's dream castle—these are the components of the white culture theorizer's perspective. The black perspective is another thing altogether. The masses are huddled in dark holds; the domain is one of endless slavery; and the domicile is one of bigotry's major fortresses. The cultures that proceed out of these differing perspectives are polarized, and the bodies of intellectual and imaginative work that reflect these different cultures—while their artistic forms merge at times—

stand in striking contrast to one another. A brief look at the literary aspect of the body of intellectual and imaginative work reflecting black American culture serves to illustrate the marked differences.

Brought to America in chains, put to the most degrading tasks imaginable, set outside the laws, and worked "from can to can't," black Americans were not likely to produce the same type of folklore that white America produced. Black folklore and the black American literary tradition that grew out of it are the products of a people who began in slavery and who, to a large extent, remain in slavery. Black folklore does not deal primarily with derring-do like that of Davy Crockett and Mike Fink; instead, we find the cunning and guise of Br'er Rabbit or the artful gymnastics of Buck or John. Black folklore reflects the Southern agrarian environment that acted as the first home of black Americans. The lore is filled with the flora and fauna of a new world as it was seen through the eyes of an enslaved people. The woods that symbolized vast wealth for white America represented a place of refuge from an irate master to blacks. To blacks, the roots and herbs that seasoned the dishes brought to white tables were a source of magic and power over the white master. And the animals of the forest, which were looked upon as game by white America, became symbols of human behavior to black Americans, who were often on better terms with the animals of the forest than with their white masters and overseers. Indeed, the first heroes of black American folklore were the animals of the surrounding forests.

Black folklore is not distinguished from other bodies of folklore in its employment of animal heroes; but the type of animal hero that emerges from black American folklore does set it apart. The chief trickster of black American folklore — Br'er Rabbit — differs significantly from the trickster animals of other lores. Br'er Rabbit was not simply another animal of the forest to black America; this trickster was not merely an entertainment for children as the early white culture theorizer Joel Chandler Harris tried to make him. Rather, Br'er Rabbit was a projection of some of the deepest and strongest drives of the slave personality. As J. Mason Brewer points out,

> The animal tales told by Negro slaves with Brer Rabbit as the hero had a meaning far deeper than mere entertainment. The rabbit actually symbolized the slave himself. Whenever the rabbit succeeded in proving himself smarter than another animal the slave rejoiced secretly, imagining himself smarter than his master. [10]

There was thus a psychological or subliminal aspect to the early animal tales of black American folklore, an aspect that was surely supplied by the slave narrator and the slave audience. That Harris[11] and subsequently Ambrose E.

---

[10] J. Mason Brewer, ed., *American Negro Folklore* (Chicago: Quadrangle Books, 1968), pp. 3–4.

[11] Joel Chandler Harris, *Uncle Remus: His Songs and Sayings* (New York: Houghton Mifflin, 1880).

Gonzales[12] tried to identify the animal tales of black America with Aesop and an old Western tradition is indicative of the differentiation between black and white culture. Any black man reading about Br'er Rabbit, any black man who knows that the rabbit tales were produced by his ancestors in slavery, realizes that this black American trickster has more to do with Denmark Vesey and Nat Turner than with Chauntecleer and Pertelote. The rabbit is a shirker of work, a master of disguise, and a cunning figure who wins contests against much larger and stronger animals. In the general American scheme of things, to state that he is a subversive figure is not to engage in overstatement. We can, in fact, see Br'er Rabbit as one of the first black American figures to repudiate the culture theorizing of whites.

To turn to the tales of Buck and John, the trickster slaves, is to again encounter repudiators of white culture theorizing. Buck and John employ daring, resourcefulness, and a type of rude wit to gain personal benefits. The wish-fulfillment aspects of the trickster-slave stories are even more obvious than the psychological identification with the Br'er Rabbit tales. Richard Dorson states that

> folktale critics who see the Rabbit as the psychic symbol of Negro resentment against the white man cannot know of the crafty slave named John. Seldom printed, the spate of stories involving John and his Old Master provides the most engaging theme in Negro lore. . . . Yet trickster John directly expresses and illuminates the plantation Negro character. No allegoric or symbolic creation, he is a generic figure representing the ante-bellum slave who enjoyed some measure of favoritism and familiarity with his owner.[13]

In other words, John and Buck are also subversive creations of black American folklore; they are bent on changing the scheme envisioned by the white culture. For them, the best that has been thought and said in the world is not the latest injunction to obedience by the white master but the clever ruse that Buck uses in order to gain his freedom.[14]

The sacred folk music of black America also contains the undercurrents of repudiation that set black American culture apart. The singing that wafted to John Pendleton Kennedy's ears on his visit to "the quarters"[15] was not the gentle outpouring of a contented slave. When black Americans sang their spirituals, Pharaoh was a very real person: he was the white master who sat on the porch, whip in hand. The River Jordan was not a mystical boundary between earth and heaven: it was the very real Ohio that marked the line be-

---

[12] Ambrose E. Gonzales, *With Aesop Along the Black Border* (Columbia, S.C.: The State Company, 1924).

[13] Richard M. Dorson, *Negro Folktales in Michigan* (Cambridge, Mass.: Harvard University Press, 1956), p. 49.

[14] Arna Bontemps and Langston Hughes, eds., *The Book of Negro Folklore* (New York: Dodd, Mead, 1958), p. 68.

[15] John Pendleton Kennedy, *Swallow Barn* (Philadelphia: Carey and Lea, 1832).

tween slave and free states. And to "steal away" was not to go docilely home to God but to escape from the Southern land of bondage. The slow and beautiful rhythms spoke not only of another world but of the real sorrow in this world; they spoke of the bare consolations offered by the American slave system, and they rejoiced that an otherworldliness was possible for men trapped in that degrading institution.

The secular folk music of the black American expresses many of the same concerns that we witness in spirituals. In black work songs, we find ironic repudiations ("pick a bale a day") of the American system, celebrations of the escaped member of a chain gang, and complaints of the inhumanity of overseers. In the blues of black America, we find the themes of injustice, poverty, and oppression expressed in one of the most important art forms that the black American has produced.[16] And when we look at the religious tales, the sermons, and the conversion stories of the black American, we find many of the same themes, though the narrators, like Paul Laurence Dunbar's preacher in "An Ante-Bellum Sermon," often claim "Dat I'm talkin' 'bout ouah freedom / In a Bibleistic way."[17]

Thus, repudiation is characteristic of black American folklore; and this is one of the most important factors in setting black American literature apart from white American literature. The basic literary works of black America are not tales of armed frontiersmen; there are no hymns to an American God; and there are few muscular and terrible heroes who save society with their boundless vigor and ingenuity. The armed frontiersman, the American God, and the ferocious hero were the ones who stood over the slave's back and ensured his continued brutalization. Out of that brutalizing experience there emerged a consummate body of folk expression. The rhythms of black music are distinctive, and it is perhaps the only unique American music. The dialect and intonation of black sermons are powerful and enthralling; they capture, as Mike Thelwell[18] has demonstrated, the ethos of their people in a way that it has never been captured by a white American. The patterns of imagery and the astute wit employed in the folk narratives are magnificent. These and other traditional forms of black expression have provided a firm, skillfully crafted base for the works of subsequent black artists.

From Paul Laurence Dunbar to Don L. Lee, black literary artists have employed the black folk base in their work, and this helps to explain the manner in which the black American literary tradition has grown. The theme of

---

[16] Ralph Ellison, "Richard Wright's Blues," in *Shadow and Act* (New York: Random House, 1964).

[17] Paul Laurence Dunbar, *The Complete Poems of Paul Laurence Dunbar* (New York: Dodd, Mead, 1968), p. 13.

[18] Mike Thelwell, "Mr. William Styron and Reverend Nat Turner," in *William Styron's Nat Turner: Ten Black Writers Respond,* ed. John Henrik Clarke (Boston: Beacon Press, 1968).

repudiation runs through Dunbar's "We Wear the Mask" and is as much present in Lee's "A Poem to Complement Other Poems." The rhythms of the music
so dominant in Langston Hughes's first volume, *The Weary Blues,* are as vital
to Ted Joans's first volume, *Black Pow-Wow.* The dialect and intonation of
black sermons and religious tales that are very much in evidence in Zora
Hurston's *Jonah's Gourd Vine* also characterize the speeches and the autobiography of Malcolm X. Building upon the unique body of folklore that grew
out of the slave's whole way of life, black literary works continue to reflect the
development of a distinctive black culture on the American continent.

Black American folklore is very different from white American folklore,
but it also differs significantly from African folklore. The same can be said
for black American literature in general; it is certainly not African, and most
assuredly—as its traditional theme of repudiation illustrates—it is not another
component in the white American literary tradition. The African hare and
Br'er Rabbit—as trickster animals—are as far apart, given the experiences
out of which they grew, as Davy Crockett and Stackolee. And the same might
be said in reference to the protagonist of Richard Wright's *Native Son* and the
narrator of Aimé Césaire's *Return to My Native Land.* Black folklore and
the black American literary tradition that grew out of it reflect a culture that
is distinctive both of white American and of African culture, and therefore
neither can provide valid standards by which black American folklore and
literature may be judged.

Recovery

Having taken a brief glimpse at only the literary aspect of the body of intellectual and imaginative work produced by black America, it is easy to see
why black Americans are now unequivocally repudiating the white culture
theorizers of our day. Black Americans have always known that race theorizing
was simply the white man's means of justifying his denial of a share of the
nation's wealth to the black man. Race theorizing by whites has led black men
to formulate plans for African colonization, separatist groups, and black na-
tionalist organizations. Unequal employment, the Ku Klux Klan, lynchings,
East St. Louis, restrictive covenants—all these tangible, felt aspects of oppression and race theorizing have been attacked by black Americans throughout their history. But only in recent decades have black Americans launched
a full-scale attack on the culture theorizing of white America: cultural nationalism has been a phenomenon of the 1950's and 1960's.

The reasons behind the emergence of cultural nationalism are too manifold
to be treated here. Certainly, an increased awareness of the invidious results
of culture theorizing has played a large part in the growth of a new mood
among black Americans. In recent years, black Americans have realized that
whites have not only deprived them of material wealth but also of the invaluable facts of their own culture. In the past, white America has taken the most

skillfully crafted and beautifully expressive artifacts of black American culture and labeled them "American"; thus jazz is viewed as "America's gift to the world." Well, that just is not so; jazz, like the rich folklore, the skilled literature, and the countless other facets of the body of intellectual and imaginative work reflecting black American culture, is simply not America's to give. Black jazz, folklore, and literature proceed out of an experience that is unknown to most white Americans; they are products of a culture that white America has chosen to ignore, misrepresent, or deny. Call it black, Afro-American, Negro, the fact remains that this culture has little if anything to do with the white American's culture, or his definition of culture. Homer, Plato, E. M. Forster, Baudelaire, and many others at the heart of what white America calls culture have only the remotest connection with black American culture.

First, black American culture was developed orally or musically for many years; the innovations of Guttenberg and Caxton, whose effects McLuhan has attacked in recent years, had little influence on the early expressions of black American culture. Second, black American culture was not characterized by the individualistic ethos of white American culture; brought to America in shackles and placed in a society where all technology and wealth were in the hands of whites, black Americans had little opportunity to participate in American dreams of rugged individualism or fantasies of individual advancement. Black American culture is characterized by a collectivistic ethos; society is not viewed as a protective arena in which the individual can work out his own destiny and gain a share of America's benefits by his own efforts. To the black American these benefits are not attained solely by individual effort, but by changes in the nature of society and the social, economic, and political advancement of a whole race of people; society, for obvious reasons, is seldom seen as a protective arena. The final point is one we have already discussed at length: black American culture is partially differentiated from white American culture because one of its most salient characteristics is an index of repudiation. Oral, collectivistic, and repudiative—each of these aspects helps to distinguish black American culture from white American culture.

There are, of course, those who insist on a unanimity of the two cultures; they say to black America, "We are all from the same land, and the *forms* of your intellectual and imaginative works are the same as ours." Yes, we are all from the same land; but, to go back to the beginning, one must realize that you came as pilgrims and I came as a "negre." Yes, the forms of our intellectual and imaginative works do coincide at points, but the experiences that are embodied in those forms are vastly different; in fact, the experiences embodied in some of the forms of black American culture explicitly repudiate the whole tradition out of which those forms grew. And there is no contradiction here. Kept illiterate for years by the laws of the land, the black American started where he could, with a few approved Western forms. But a John Coltrane solo has little to do with Western forms; LeRoi Jones's latest poems are so far from the West that white Americans just shake their heads in disbelief; and William

Kelley's *Dunfords Travels Everywheres* ends on notes that the white West is hard pressed to comprehend.

The lobotomizing is over, white America. The question "What is America to me?" has been answered by black America with a great deal of certainty in recent years. We are no longer what Calvin Hernton has called "self-riddled" blacks;[19] the sense of "twoness" that Du Bois handles so skillfully in *The Souls of Black Folk* is fast disappearing as cultural nationalism grows stronger. The doubts, speculations, and reflections are falling into a clear and ordered pattern, and we realize that America is something apart; the boundaries of our nation are marked by the color of our skin, Harold Cruse tells us,[20] and we are willing to accept his assessment. When the history is submitted to a just scrutiny, its clear and hard facts speak of the marked difference between the whole way of life of the black man and the whole way of life of the white man. Fully aware of white America's denials, fully aware that white America's talk of race differentiation is sheer superstition, black Americans are now engaged in a rejuvenating examination of the body of intellectual and imaginative work that reflects their own unique culture. The numbing electric shocks are at an end, and we are feeling completely well.

[19] Calvin Hernton, "Dynamite Growing Out of Their Skulls," in *Black Fire,* ed. LeRoi Jones and Larry Neal (New York: William Morrow, 1968), p. 84.

[20] Harold Cruse, "Revolutionary Nationalism and the Afro-American," in *Black Fire,* ed. LeRoi Jones and Larry Neal (New York: William Morrow, 1968), p. 44.

1 SUGGESTIONS FOR FURTHER READING

Barzun, Jacques, *Race: A Study in Superstition**. New York: Harcourt, 1937.
▪ A scholarly study, useful in understanding race history.

Brewer, J. Mason, ed., *American Negro Folklore.* Chicago: Quadrangle Books, 1968. ▪ A collection of folk tales with bearing on the oral tradition that developed among American slaves.

Carr, Edward Hallett, *What Is History?** New York: Alfred A. Knopf, 1962. ▪ A brief and very readable discussion of the historian's discipline and craft.

Courlander, Harold, *Negro Folk Music, U.S.A.** New York: Columbia University Press, 1963. ▪ An extensive survey of black American folk songs.

Davidson, Basil, *The African Genius: An Introduction to African Social and Cultural History.* Boston: Atlantic-Little, Brown, 1970. ▪ A recent study of the cultural heritage of at least the first generation of Afro-Americans.

Dorson, Richard M., ed., *American Negro Folktales**. New York: Fawcett, 1967. ▪ Selections from black American folklore.

Fisher, Miles Mark, ed., *Negro Slave Songs in the United States**. Ithaca, N.Y.: Cornell University Press, 1953. ▪ A valuable collection of black folk songs.

Herskovits, Melville J., *The Myth of the Negro Past**. New York: Harper, 1941. ▪ A description of West African culture and of the transmission of Africanisms to the New World.

Hughes, Langston, and Bontemps, Arna, eds., *The Book of Negro Folklore.* New York: Dodd, Mead, 1958. ▪ An imaginatively edited survey.

---

*Available in paperback edition

Johnson, James Weldon, and Johnson, J. Rosamond, eds., *The Books of American Negro Spirituals**. New York: Viking Press, 1925, 1926; combined ed., New York: Viking Press, 1940. ▪ The most complete available collection of Negro spirituals.

Quarles, Benjamin, "What the Historian Owes the Negro," *Saturday Review* 49 (3 September 1966): 10–13. ▪ An article presenting the view that the historian is obligated to reconstruct Negro history.

Stern, Fritz, ed., *The Varieties of History: From Voltaire to the Present**. New York: Meridian, 1956. ▪ A collection of excerpts from the writings of major historians, exemplifying a wide variety of historical concepts.

Szwed, John F., ed., *Black America.* New York: Basic Books, 1970. ▪ See especially Robert Blauner's article, "The Question of Black Culture," pp. 110–20.

Williams, Raymond, *Culture and Society, 1780–1950**. New York: Columbia University Press, 1958. ▪ A broad-based study that offers many useful insights.

Wish, Harvey, ed., *American Historians: A Selection**. New York: Oxford University Press, 1962. ▪ A selection of writings by major American historians. The variety of approaches and assumptions demonstrated in this book attests to the relativistic nature of the field.

2

African
Beginnings

West African Society and the Atlantic Slave Trade, 1441-1865

MARION DUSSER DE BARENNE KILSON

Marion Kilson, a scholar at the Radcliffe Institute from 1968 to 1970, is associate professor of sociology at Simmons College. Mrs. Kilson has done extensive anthropological research in West Africa. Her publications include "Towards Freedom: An Analysis of Slave Revolts in the United States" (*Phylon*, 1964) and several essays on the folklore of the Mende people of Sierra Leone and on the social system and ritual symbolism of the Ga people of south-eastern Ghana. Her first book, *Kpele Lala: Ga Religious Songs and Symbols*, will be published soon by Harvard University Press. In the following essay, Mrs. Kilson is concerned with the socioeconomic and political conditions in West Africa that permitted the rise of the Atlantic slave trade and with the impact of the trade on traditional African polity. Emphasizing that the traditional African rulers not only participated in the slave trade but in large measure controlled it, Mrs. Kilson concludes that the trade had far less radical social consequences for Africa than for America.

For four hundred and fifty years European and African entrepreneurs engaged in mutually advantageous trade along the Atlantic seaboard of the sub-Saharan African continent. During this period of intercontinental maritime trade, which began with the initial Portuguese voyages in the middle of the fifteenth century and ended with the imposition of European colonial rule in Africa late in the nineteenth century, European consumer goods were exchanged for African products. The principal African commodities sought by the Europeans varied over the years: gold was in demand during the fifteenth and sixteenth centuries; slaves, from the seventeenth century to the middle of the nineteenth century; and agricultural products, in the second half of the nineteenth century. In addition, the location of the trading centers varied during this period—partly in response to changes in the availability of the commodities on the African coast and partly in response to political and economic events on the African, American, and European continents.

Although slaves constituted the primary African export for two and a half centuries, they were exchanged throughout the era of intercontinental maritime trade. The precise number of people directly affected by the slave trade will probably never be known, but estimates range from eight million to fifty million. (The latter figure includes not only those shipped as slaves from African shores but also those who died prior to embarkation, during capture, on the journey from the interior to the coast, or in coastal factories.[1]) The majority of the slaves were taken between the end of the seventeenth century and the middle of the nineteenth. Though slaves for the Americas were obtained from ports all along the Atlantic coast of sub-Saharan Africa, the majority probably were exchanged at international ports of trade on the Lower Guinea Coast.[2]

During the era of European and African intercontinental maritime trade, then, both the volume and the provenance of the slave trade varied considerably. In this essay, I will attempt to analyze the factors that affected these numerical and geographical changes.[3] I will begin by considering the socioeconomic conditions in Africa that set the stage for the Atlantic slave trade. Then, I will examine the general sociological parameters of the trade and discuss its ramifications through time and space on the Atlantic seaboard of the sub-Saharan African continent.

The Socioeconomic Setting for the Atlantic Slave Trade

The demand for slaves from sub-Saharan Africa was slight during the early years of maritime trade between European and African entrepreneurs, but it expanded enormously in subsequent years. For example, whereas 3,500 slaves were shipped from the Upper Guinea Coast in 1506 and 4,000 from Kongo in 1536, 20,000 were shipped annually from the port of Whydah on the Slave Coast in the 1680's and from the port of Bonny on the Niger Delta a hundred

---

[1] See Basil Davidson, *Black Mother: The Years of the African Slave Trade* (London: Victor Gollancz, 1961), pp. 87–88.

[2] The geographical terms used in the literature on this subject are often confusing. In this essay, I refer to three main geographical areas: the Upper Guinea Coast, the Lower Guinea Coast, and the Central African Coast. In contemporary geopolitical terms, the Upper Guinea Coast stretches from Senegal to Liberia; and in the geopolitical terms of the era of intercontinental maritime trade, it incorporated Senegambia and the Windward Coast. The Lower Guinea Coast, in modern terms, extends from the Ivory Coast to Cameroon; in the terms of the time of the trade, it incorporated the Ivory Coast, Gold Coast, Slave Coast, Bight of Benin, Niger Delta, and Bight of Biafra. The Central African Coast covers the Atlantic shoreline of Congo and Angola.

[3] In preparing for this essay, I have been impressed by the lack of reliable information on the Atlantic slave trade in relation to African society. The need for detailed case studies of particular societies, analogous to the work of Ivor Wilks on Akwamu and Ashanti, Karl Polanyi on Dahomey, G. I. Jones on the Oil Rivers, and Jan Vansina on Central Africa, is sorely apparent. Further, apart from Basil Davidson's *Black Mother* and Daniel Mannix's and Malcolm Cowley's *Black Cargoes: A History of the Atlantic Slave Trade, 1518–1865* (New York: Viking Press, 1962), there are few, if any, synthetic treatments of this topic.

years later.[4] Correspondingly, at the terminus of the trade in the Americas, whereas the French imported 3,000 slaves annually between 1670 and 1672, they imported 29,000 to Santo Domingo in 1788.[5] The ability of African entrepreneurs to meet the rising demands of their European counterparts depended upon a number of pre-existing conditions in African society, involving the level of socioeconomic development of African society, the existence of trading networks prior to the arrival of the Europeans, and the earlier intercontinental maritime trade in gold.

The African societies encountered by European traders were territorially small-scale state systems based upon redistributive Iron Age agricultural economies. In certain instances, especially on the Lower Guinea Coast, the intercontinental maritime trade led to the development of territorially more extensive and more complex political units. However, as a rule the level of technological and societal development of African coastal societies was sufficient to enable them to meet the economic challenge offered by the Europeans, a factor that did much to facilitate the development of the trade. The second factor of importance to the development of the trade was the existence of regional and long-distance trading networks in Africa prior to European contact. Throughout sub-Saharan Africa, regional trading networks based on a system of rotating markets linked local communities both within a single polity and between different polities.[6] Although in Central Africa long-distance trade developed only in response to the stimulus of European demands,[7] societies in West Africa had participated for many centuries in the trans-Saharan trade, to which they contributed gold and slaves.[8] Moreover, societies on the Lower Guinea Coast between the Bight of Benin and the western Gold Coast probably engaged in maritime trade before their first encounter with the Portuguese, in the late fifteenth century.[9] Thus, the development of trade with Europeans on the Atlantic shores of the sub-Saharan African continent, especially on the Lower Guinea Coast, frequently meant changing the orientation of long-

---

[4] Davidson, *Black Mother,* p. 56. Karl Polanyi, *Dahomey and the Slave Trade* (Seattle: University of Washington Press, 1966), p. 138. K. Onwuka Dike, *Trade and Politics in the Niger Delta, 1830–1885* (Oxford: Clarendon Press, 1956), p. 29.

[5] Davidson, *Black Mother,* p. 72. Frank Tannenbaum, *Slave and Citizen* (New York: Alfred A. Knopf, 1947), p. 33.

[6] E.g., G. I. Jones, *The Trading States of the Oil Rivers* (New York: Oxford University Press, 1963), pp. 13–16; Paul Ozanne, "Notes on the Early Historic Archaeology of Accra," *Transactions of the Historical Society of Ghana* 6 (1962): 67; Jan Vansina, "Long-Distance Trade-Routes in Central Africa," *Journal of African History* 3 (1962): 375–76.

[7] Vansina, "Long-Distance Trade-Routes," p. 376.

[8] E. W. Bovill, *The Golden Trade of the Moors* (New York: Oxford University Press, 1958).

[9] J. D. Fage, "Some Remarks on Beads and Trade in Lower Guinea in the Sixteenth and Seventeenth Centuries," *Journal of African History* 3 (1962): 343–47. Ivor Wilks, "A Medieval Trade-Route from the Niger to the Gulf of Guinea, *Journal of African History* 3 (1962): 339.

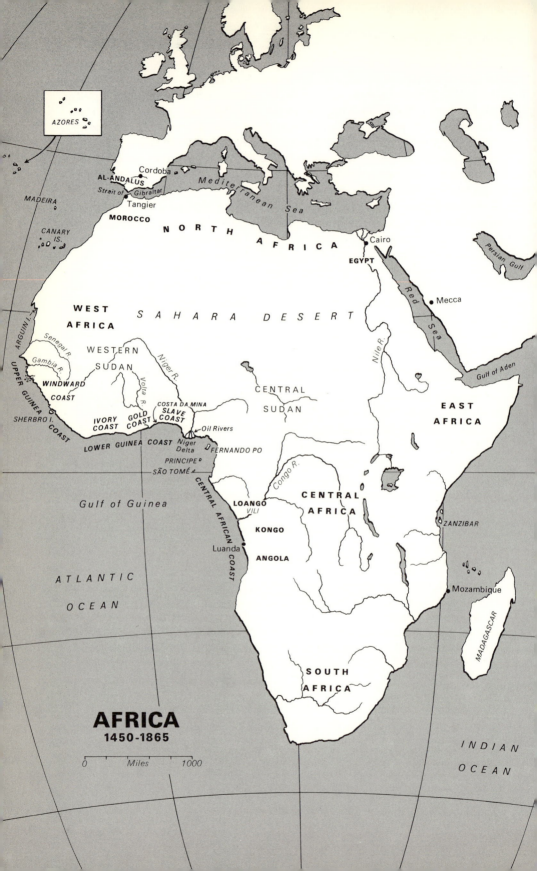

AZORES

MADEIRA

CANARY
IS.

Cordoba
AL-ANDALUS
Strait of Gibraltar
Tangier
MOROCCO   N O R T H   A F R I C A

Mediterranean Sea

Cairo
EGYPT

Mecca

Persian Gulf

WEST
AFRICA   S A H A R A   D E S E R T

Red Sea

Nile R.

Gulf of Aden

ARGUIN I.

Senegal R.
WESTERN
SUDAN

Gambia R.
UPPER GUINEA COAST
WINDWARD
COAST

Volta R.
Niger R.

CENTRAL
SUDAN

EAST
AFRICA

SHERBRO I.
IVORY
COAST   GOLD
COAST
COSTA DA MINA
SLAVE
COAST
Oil Rivers

LOWER GUINEA COAST   Niger
Delta
FERNANDO PO
PRINCIPE
SÃO TOMÉ

Congo R.

Gulf of Guinea

CENTRAL AFRICAN COAST

LOANGO
VILI

KONGO
Luanda
ANGOLA

CENTRAL
AFRICA

ZANZIBAR

ATLANTIC

OCEAN

Mozambique

MADAGASCAR

SOUTH
AFRICA

AFRICA
1450-1865

0   Miles   1000

INDIAN

OCEAN

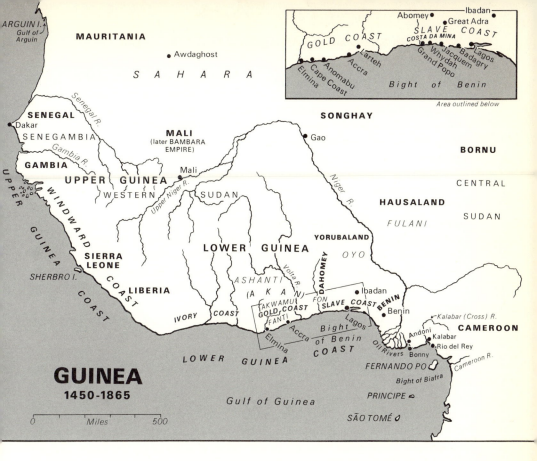

GUINEA
1450-1865

distance trade from south-north to north-south and establishing or expanding coastal termini, rather than actually initiating a commercial pattern.[10]

Finally, once the Africans had established trading relations with Europeans at ports on the African coast, the avenues for the exchange of slaves were open. It was a relatively simple matter to shift from gold to slaves as the primary African commodity.

The Sociological Parameters of the Coastal Slave Trade

Several distinctive sociological attributes characterized the coastal trade which engaged European and African entrepreneurs for almost five centuries. The trade in African products was based upon a reciprocal relationship involving European buyers and their African agents, on one hand, and African sellers and their African or European agents, on the other hand.[11] As the European

---

[10] E.g., Jones, *Trading States,* pp. 13–16; Ivor Wilks, *The Northern Factor in Ashanti History* (Legon, Ghana: Institute of African Studies, 1961), p. 10; Paul Ozanne, "Notes on the Later Prehistory of Accra," *Journal of the Historical Society of Nigeria* 3 (1964): 22.

[11] E.g., David A. Ross, "The Career of Domingo Martinez in the Bight of Benin, 1833–64," *Journal of African History* 6 (1965): 79–90.

buyers' demands for African products fluctuated both in kind and in degree and as the ability of the African sellers to satisfy these demands varied, trading centers on the African coast shifted position either temporarily or permanently. Still, the fundamental relationship between African sellers and European buyers remained constant regardless of temporal, geographical, or commercial changes.

Moreover, the locus of interaction between European and African entrepreneurs remained fixed: Europeans and Africans transacted their business at international ports of trade on the Atlantic seaboard. Except in Central Africa and on the Gambia River, African rulers did not permit European entrepreneurs to venture into the interior except under their aegis. Even in Central Africa, European entrepreneurs resided in "staples" which were located at or near the inland capitals of African rulers.[12] Consequently, the pattern of relations between ruler and European entrepreneur was analogous to that at the trade centers on the coast.

The ports of trade were under the authority of local African rulers who determined in large measure the terms of the conduct of the trade and who did not hesitate to institute economic or political reprisals when these terms were violated, as events throughout the era of intercontinental maritime trade amply demonstrate. For example, in July 1526, the king of Kongo "complained that the [Portuguese] traders were robbing the highways, kidnapping citizens, . . . and he decided to close the trade. In October . . . he reversed his decision and instituted a three-man commission which would inspect all slaves before embarkation."[13] When the Portuguese built a fort at Guinala on the Upper Guinea Coast in 1589, the local population "deliberately raised" the price of slaves.[14] At the turn of the eighteenth century, William Bosman, a Dutch trade commissioner, reported that at Anomabu on the Gold Coast "the . . . Fantyn drive a very great Trade with all sorts of Interlopers . . . in the sight of . . . the English and Dutch, neither of them daring to hinder it: For if they should attempt it, 'twould ruine them there, we not having the least power over this Nation."[15] During the first three-quarters of the eighteenth century, six French directors of the fort at Whydah "were expelled by the Fon authorities . . . on various charges arising from their resentment of Abomey jurisdiction over their Hueda [Whydah] laborers or, more frequently, from . . . attempts to prevent their European personnel from trading with Fon brokers on their own account."[16]

---

[12] Vansina, "Long-Distance Trade-Routes," p. 376.

[13] Ibid., p. 377.

[14] Walter Rodney, "Portuguese Attempts at Monopoly on the Upper Guinea Coast, 1580–1650," *Journal of African History* 6 (1965): 321.

[15] William Bosman, *A New and Accurate Description of the Coast of Guinea* (London, 1705), p. 57.

[16] C. W. Newbury, *The Western Slave Coast and Its Rulers* (Oxford: Clarendon Press, 1961), p. 24.

During the same period, Dahomean armies destroyed several European forts and factories at Whydah.[17]

The control of African rulers over the commercial activities of European entrepreneurs extended to the European commodities for which African gold or slaves were exchanged. "On the whole West African coast, slaves and other items of export were purchased by an assortment of trade goods, ranging from firearms to glass beads."[18] In the international ports of trade, European and African commodities were evaluated according to certain standards of equivalence. Though the standard employed varied from the copper manilla of the Niger Delta (a metal bracelet worn on the wrist or the arm) to the iron bar of the Upper Guinea Coast and the Gold Coast, the principle of using such a standard did not vary, and its application was limited to the intercontinental maritime trade. European commodities were utilized by indigenous coastal rulers not only for consumption but for redistribution to hinterland authorities in order to maintain the flow of commodities to the coast. Since the ports of trade were the termini of long-distance trade routes leading from the interior to the coast, the ability of the various coastal polities to keep these routes open and thereby to ensure the steady passage of goods for exchange played a major part in determining the location of trading centers on the coast. Thus, it can be said that while the demands of European buyers for African commodities initiated the trading relationship between African and European entrepreneurs, the terms and the conditions of transaction were determined primarily by African sellers.

European Buyers and African Sellers

Fundamentally, the intercontinental trade on the African coast rested on the complex interplay between European demand and African supply. During the four hundred and fifty years of the trade, various factors affected both parties to the exchange and led to significant alterations in the trading patterns. As they relate to the Atlantic slave trade, these factors are of interest to us here.

As I have already noted, the demand of European buyers for African products initiated the intercontinental trade, and the first African commodity that interested Europeans during the era of intercontinental maritime trade was gold. As a result of a shortage of gold in Europe in the fourteenth century, "European gold merchants looked to Africa for increased supplies, and their demands were felt first at the North African ports, and later, via the trans-Saharan routes, in the gold entrepôts of the Western Sudan."[19] When the

---

[17] A. F. C. Ryder, "The Reestablishment of Portuguese Factories in the Costa Da Mina in the Mid-Eighteenth Century," *Journal of the Historical Society of Nigeria* 1 (1958): 160–67.

[18] Rodney, "Portuguese Attempts at Monopoly," p. 311.

[19] Wilks, "Medieval Trade-Route," p. 337.

Portuguese set out on their voyages of exploration and trade along the Atlantic coast of sub-Saharan Africa in the latter half of the fifteenth century, yellow gold was their principal object. Then, during the sixteenth century, gold became the main African export not only for Portugal but for its European competitors as well.[20]

With the discovery of the Western Hemisphere at the close of the fifteenth century, a new phase in intercontinental maritime trade was inaugurated—the trade in slaves. From the beginning of their connection with sub-Saharan Africa, the Portuguese had taken some African slaves for sale in the Iberian Peninsula, where slavery had existed since ancient times. Anthony Luttrell, to cite one example, states that "in 1441 Antão Gonçalves inaugurated the regular flow of slaves from the African mainland to Portugal, though his were not the first slaves taken on the mainland, nor were they acquired by trade, nor—with one exception—were they Negroes."[21] However, with the discovery of the West Indian islands and later the American mainland, and with the development of pre-industrial plantation economies in the Western Hemisphere, the demand for slaves increased. "In 1515 there came the first Spanish shipment of slave-grown West Indian sugar and in 1518, . . . the first cargo of African slaves directly from Africa to the West Indies."[22] It was not until 1640, when sugar became the staple of the French and British West Indies, that the demand for slaves began to near its zenith.[23] The demand was intensified not only by the development of plantation economies in the Caribbean islands and on the mainland of the American continent but also by the discovery of gold mines in Brazil at the close of the seventeenth century.[24] From

---

[20] During the centuries of intercontinental trade on the sub-Saharan Atlantic coast, various European powers competed for commercial ascendancy. The fifteenth-century Portuguese monopoly of African trade was broken in the sixteenth century by British and French traders in Senegambia and by Dutch traders on the Gold Coast. Although representatives of several European powers (Portugal, France, England, Holland, Sweden, Denmark, and Brandenburg) competed for the trade on the Guinea coasts in the seventeenth century, the most important power during this period was Holland, which in mid-century destroyed the Portuguese presence on the Gold Coast and in the Bight of Benin. Toward the end of the seventeenth century, England began to challenge Dutch ascendancy on the Guinea coasts, and in the eighteenth century England became the most important European trading power in this region. Although Portugal lost its preeminence on the Guinea coasts, it remained the dominant European power on the coast of Central Africa throughout the era of intercontinental maritime trade.

[21] Anthony Luttrell, "Slavery and Slaving in the Portuguese Atlantic (to about 1500)," in *The Transatlantic Slave Trade from West Africa,* mimeographed (Edinburgh: Center for African Studies, University of Edinburgh, 1965), p. 67. See also Winthrop D. Jordan, *White Over Black: American Attitudes Toward the Negro, 1550–1812* (Baltimore: Penguin Books, 1968), p. 56.

[22] Davidson, *Black Mother,* pp. 62–63.

[23] J. D. Hargreaves, "The Slave Traffic," in *Silver Renaissance,* ed. Alex Natan (London: Macmillan, 1961), pp. 82–83.

[24] Pierre Verger, *Bahia and the West African Trade, 1549–1851* (Ibadan, Nigeria: Ibadan University Press, 1964), p. 5.

the middle of the seventeenth century until the beginning of the nineteenth, the demand for slaves from Africa was at its height throughout the Western Hemisphere.

At the opening of the nineteenth century, an event occurred which changed the character of the Atlantic slave trade drastically. In 1807, for a variety of socioeconomic reasons, Great Britain, which had been the major transatlantic slave-trading nation for almost two centuries, declared the slave trade illegal and attempted to impose her decision on other European slave-trading powers.[25] The slave trade was illegal north of the equator by 1815 and south of the equator after 1831.[26] Nevertheless, the transatlantic slave trade continued, especially to Brazil. In his study of the suppression of the Atlantic slave trade, Leslie Bethell states that by the mid-1820's few slaves "were being imported into the British, French, or Dutch West Indies, the new Spanish American republics or the Southern United States; but for another thirty years thousands were exported from Africa—for the most part illegally to the sugar and coffee plantations of Brazil, and it was a further ten years before the illegal slave trade to the Spanish colonies of Cuba and Puerto Rico was suppressed."[27] Concomitant with the official abolition of the slave trade was the growth of the palm oil trade on the Lower Guinea Coast, which began early in the nineteenth century and waxed as the slave trade waned, thereby initiating a new phase in the relations between African and European entrepreneurs.[28] Thus, in effect, the growth and decline of the Atlantic slave trade was coordinate with the developmental cycle of pre-industrial plantation and mining economies in the Americas. As these systems became stabilized, the necessity and consequently the demand for increased supplies of their sources of human power from Africa subsided.

Both the intensity and the legality of the European buyers' demands for slaves affected the pattern of trade on the African coast. Before the middle of the seventeenth century, when the demand for slave labor was relatively low, fairly inefficient methods of procurement could be tolerated. J. D. Hargreaves, to give one example, reports that "Nicholas Owen . . . resided in the Sherbro from 1754 until 1759. . . . His diary records no transaction involving more than five slaves."[29] (Although this case derives from a later period, it exemplifies the inefficient mode of procurement that characterized the slave trade on the Upper Guinea Coast throughout the era of intercontinental maritime trade.) During the first half of the seventeenth century, slaves were obtained primarily on the Upper Guinea Coast and on the Central African Coast. As the demand for slaves grew more intense, increasingly efficient modes of

---

[25] See Davidson, *Black Mother,* pp. 78–83.

[26] Verger, *Bahia and Trade,* p. 31.

[27] Leslie Bethell, "The Mixed Commissions for the Suppression of the Transatlantic Slave Trade in the Nineteenth Century," *Journal of African History* 7 (1966): 79–80.

[28] David A. Ross, "The Career of Domingo Martinez," p. 81. Dike, *Trade and Politics.*

[29] Hargreaves, "Slave Traffic," p. 84.

procurement were required. The societies best able to provide quickly large numbers of slaves were a succession of coastal trading states on the Lower Guinea Coast—first on the Gold Coast, subsequently on the Slave Coast, and ultimately on the Niger Delta. When the transatlantic slave trade was declared illegal, European buyers began to look for slaves in more inconspicuous spots along the African coast, especially on the eastern extremity of the Lower Guinea Coast.

Although precise knowledge of the relative contributions of different African ports may never be available, the general pattern is well documented in the existing literature.[30] During the sixteenth century, most slaves were exported from Senegambia.[31] In the seventeenth century, slaves intended for the Brazilian port of Bahia came primarily from Angola,[32] and toward the end of the century, the Ivory Coast and its hinterland were considered the best slaving area by the British Royal African Company.[33] Throughout most of the eighteenth century, European slave-trading nations concentrated on the "Mina Coast," especially the ports of Grand Popo, Whydah, Jaquem, and Apa.[34] Then, during the latter part of the eighteenth century and the first part of the nineteenth, the ports of the Bight of Benin and of Central Africa exported the largest number of slaves.[35] In further support of these general conclusions, some indication of the distribution by origin of the slaves brought into English-speaking American colonies during the eighteenth century is provided by the following table, based on Melville Herskovits' figures.[36]

Virginia, 1710–69	*South Carolina, 1733–85*	*Jamaica, 1764–88*
"Africa,"[a] 44%	"Africa," 6%	Gambia, 2%
Senegambia, 9%	Windward Coast, 18%	Windward Coast, 9%
Gold Coast, 16%	Sierra Leone–Ivory Coast, 11%	Gold Coast, 41%
Niger Delta, 20%	Gold Coast–Niger Delta, 29%	Dahomey, 12%
Angola, 9%	Congo-Angola, 35%	Niger Delta, 30%
Madagascar, 2%	East Africa, 1%	Angola, 6%

[a] Of unknown African origin.

[30] The most detailed summary of this literature is to be found in Philip D. Curtin, *The Atlantic Slave Trade: A Census* (Madison: University of Wisconsin Press, 1969).

[31] Rodney, "Portuguese Attempts at Monopoly," p. 309. Verger, *Bahia and Trade,* p. 3.

[32] Verger, ibid.

[33] Philip D. Curtin and Jan Vansina, "Sources of the Nineteenth-Century Atlantic Slave Trade," *Journal of African History* 5 (1964): 189.

[34] Melville J. Herskovits, *The Myth of the Negro Past* (Boston: Beacon Press, 1958), pp. 50–52. Verger, *Bahia and Trade,* p. 3.

[35] Curtin and Vansina, "Sources of Atlantic Slave Trade," p. 190. Verger, *Bahia and Trade,* pp. 3, 32.

[36] Herskovits, *Myth of the Negro Past,* pp. 46–48.

The more specific demands of European slave buyers varied in response to three interrelated factors: the preference for certain ethnic groups in the Americas, the price of slaves, and the supply of slaves available to the various African sellers. A consideration of each of these in turn may help to clarify some of the less obvious aspects of the operation of the European-African slave trade.

Over the years, European colonists in the New World developed various preferences for slaves originating from certain areas on the African coast. Probably these preferences arose from the initial availability of certain African peoples in different parts of the Americas, which led to the development of stereotypes about the desirable qualities of these African peoples by later generations. Be that as it may, English-speaking colonists in the Americas preferred Gold Coast slaves, especially Fanti and Ashanti, whom they considered hardy workers.[37] French West Indian planters preferred slaves from Whydah and Jaquem, who, they felt, "were probably of higher quality than the standard male slave."[38] Portuguese in Brazil preferred "Bantu" slaves from Central African ports, "because they were less independent, more submissive to slavery, . . . more talkative and adaptable than the other Negroes."[39] Nonetheless, at the close of the slave trade in Brazil, though predominantly Bantu slaves had been imported into Rio de Janeiro, Yoruba slaves constituted 90 percent of the slave population of Bahia.[40]

The price of slaves, as one would expect, varied with fluctuations in the demands of European buyers. As the overall demand for slaves escalated during the eighteenth century, prices rose accordingly. For example, the cost of male slaves at Anomabu on the Gold Coast doubled during the second decade of the eighteenth century, rising from £14–16 in 1709 to £28–32 in 1719; analogously, at Cape Coast the cost of male slaves tripled during the first half of the eighteenth century, rising from £8 in 1709 to £24 in 1749.[41]

In addition, the price of slaves varied with the bargaining skills of African sellers, which necessarily developed with experience. In the eastern Bight of Biafra, for instance, whereas in 1614 a "ship bought four boys in the area for 9 measures of wine," within fifty years the trade had been "regularized, with recognized middlemen and dues to pay at Rio del Rey and Cameroons River."[42]

---

[37] Ibid., p. 50. Marion Johnson, "The Ounce in Eighteenth-Century West African Trade," *Journal of African History* 7 (1966): 213.

[38] Johnson, "The Ounce," p. 214.

[39] José Honório Rodrigues, "The Influence of Africa on Brazil and of Brazil on Africa," *Journal of African History* 3 (1962): 55.

[40] Verger, *Bahia and Trade,* p. 32.

[41] Johnson, "The Ounce," pp. 212–13.

[42] Edwin Ardener, "Documentary and Linguistic Evidence for the Rise of the Trading Polities Between Rio del Rey and the Cameroons, 1500–1650," in *History and Social Anthropology,* ed. I. M. Lewis (London: Tavistock, 1968), pp. 104, 106.

Finally, the price of slaves was influenced by the mode of procurement employed and by the exigencies of obtaining a cargo. "Traders ashore sold slaves to the ships at a higher price than the African merchants who brought them to the coast in small batches."[43] Moreover, "occasionally a captain anxious to complete his cargo would pay prices much higher than normal."[44]

A variety of socioeconomic forces came into play in determining the African sellers' supply of slaves—the third factor that concerns us here. The slaves that were sold at international ports of trade were procured by diverse means in the African hinterland. On this subject, the only quantitative data available are found in P. E. H. Hair's study entitled "The Enslavement of Koelle's Informants." However, qualitative data from all the slaving areas suggest that Hair's figures are descriptive not only of the nineteenth century but of preceding centuries as well. The various modes of enslavement reported for the 179 slaves questioned by Koelle were as follows:[45]

> War, 34%
> Kidnapping, 30%
> Sale by relatives or superiors, 7%
> Discharge of debt, 7%
> Judicial process, 11%
> Unknown, 11%

The slaves from the interior were brought by professional traders over established routes to the coast. Although these professional traders were sometimes nationals of the coastal trading polities, such as the Vili at Loango, often

---

[43] Johnson, "The Ounce," p. 213.

[44] Ibid., pp. 213–14.

[45] P. E. H. Hair, "The Enslavement of Koelle's Informants," *Journal of African History* 6 (1965): 193–203. I am indebted to Professor Philip Curtin for a comment on the biases in Koelle's data. In a letter of February 25, 1970, he notes that "the sample is skewed, because Koelle was trying to find at least one sample of as many languages as possible. This means that his sample contains an inordinate number of single individuals from small ethnic groups, who were likely to have got into the slave trade through kidnapping or judicial process. It similarly underrepresents those who were captured in war: captives from the Yoruba wars alone made up more than half of the Sierra Leone population of that period."

Enslavement as a result of war has been noted for Senegambia (Douglas Grant, *The Fortunate Slave* [New York: Oxford University Press, 1968], pp. 47–49; Philip D. Curtin, "Ayuba Suleiman Diallo of Bornu," in *Africa Remembered: Narratives by West Africans from the Era of the Slave Trade,* ed. Philip D. Curtin [Madison: University of Wisconsin Press, 1968], p. 29); for Accra (Bosman, *New Description of Guinea,* p. 70); for Dahomey (Polanyi, *Dahomey and Trade,* p. 23; Verger, *Bahia and Trade,* p. 31; Ryder, "Reestablishment of Factories," pp. 165–66); for the Bights of Benin and Biafra (Ardener, "Documentary Evidence," p. 103; Verger, *Bahia and Trade,* p. 31); and for Luanda (Vansina, "Long-Distance Trade-Routes," p. 377). Enslavement as a result of judicial process has been documented for the Niger Delta (Dike, *Trade and Politics,* p. 40; Rodrigues, "Influence of Africa on Brazil," p. 54; D. Simmons, "Ethnographic Sketch of the Efik People," in Daryll Forde, ed., *Efik Traders of Old Calabar* [New York: Oxford University Press, 1956], p. 7); and so on.

they were not, as in the case of the Mande traders at Elmina or the Akan traders at seventeenth-century Accra.[46] The trade routes in use often traversed territory belonging to polities that were politically independent of the coastal trading states. Naturally, when the hinterland polities closed trade routes, the intercontinental trade on the coast suffered, for European buyers turned elsewhere to fill their slave quotas. Evidently, the blocking of routes by interior states was not uncommon. In 1646, the inland state of Akwamu closed the trade route through Larteh to Accra.[47] Late in the same century, Bosman observed that "the king of Great Adra, through whose Territories most of the Slaves are obliged to pass, . . . very commonly shuts up all the Passes to Fida [Whydah] by a very strict Prohibition."[48] And in 1730, "the flow of slaves to Jaquem had ceased as the Dahomeys cut all routes to the interior."[49]

The Balance of Power

As a result of this situation, the main concern of the coastal trading polities was to control the hinterland trade routes by maintaining the balance of economic and political power. In order to achieve this end, the rulers of the coastal trading states utilized either political force or economic persuasion. Usually, "political force" meant all-out war. For example, when the Akwamu closed the Larteh trade route, the Accra army successfully marched on Larteh to reopen it.[50] Similarly, Bonny and Kalabar waged frequent wars against Orika and Andoni, respectively, which lay between them and their hinterland markets.[51] "Economic persuasion" usually entailed redistributing goods obtained from European entrepreneurs to hinterland rulers.[52] On the Lower Guinea Coast, redistribution of this type appears to have precipitated the downfall of several coastal trading states and the rise of several new ones. G. I. Jones has shown that firearms were introduced successively in the Gold Coast, the Slave Coast, and the Bight of Biafra, probably in the early seventeenth, early eighteenth, and late eighteenth centuries, respectively.[53] On both the Gold

---

[46] Vansina, "Long-Distance Trade-Routes," p. 380. Wilks, *Northern Factor,* pp. 1–8. Ozanne, "Prehistory of Accra," p. 22.

[47] Ivor Wilks, "Some Glimpses into the Early History of Accra" (personal library of Ivor Wilks), pp. 5–6.

[48] Bosman, *New Description of Guinea,* p. 343.

[49] Ryder, "Reestablishment of Factories," p. 164.

[50] Wilks, "Glimpses into History of Accra," pp. 5–6.

[51] Jones, *Trading States,* p. 47.

[52] E.g., Wilks, "Glimpses into History of Accra," pp. 5–6; Vansina, "Long-Distance Trade-Routes," p. 388.

[53] Ivor Wilks, "The Rise of the Akwamu Empire, 1650–1710," *Transactions of the Historical Society of Ghana* 3 (1958): 105. Polanyi, *Dahomey and Trade,* p. 24. Jones, *Trading States,* pp. 44–46.

Coast and the Slave Coast, this was instrumental in bringing about the fall of a small, established coastal trading state (Accra on the Gold Coast, Whydah on the Slave Coast) and the rise of another coastal power (Akwamu on the Gold Coast, Dahomey on the Slave Coast). These data suggest that the large-scale introduction of firearms led to a shift in the balance of political power which favored the larger inland state over the small coastal trading state. Thus, competition for a monopoly on the intercontinental maritime trade led to the development of a succession of coastal states on the Lower Guinea Coast, each of which rose to ascendancy on the slave trade while at the same time sowing the seeds of its own destruction by redistributing arms to inland polities. The concentration of power on the Lower Guinea Coast moved progressively eastward as European buyers pushed further along the coast in pursuit of new and less tumultuous markets.

Invariably, political turmoil within the ports of trade, like conflicts along the trade routes to the interior, led to the disruption of the coastal trade. With respect to the Bight of Biafra, for instance, Jones has suggested that "one can . . . assume an oscillation of this trade between the Rio Real and the Old Calabar River, depending on which happened to be at peace and able therefore to engage in trade."[54] Analogously, A. F. C. Ryder has shown how the Dahomean attack on Whydah in 1728, which disrupted "the slave trade of the Costa da Mina for a whole year," led to the ascendancy of Jaquem, which, in turn, was destroyed by Dahomey in 1732 with a comparable dislocation of trade as a consequence.[55]

However, political unrest at the hinterland termini of the trade routes encouraged the expansion of the coastal trade, for prisoners of war constituted a major source of slaves throughout the slave-trading phase of the intercontinental trade. Thus, from the point of view of both African sellers and European buyers, turmoil at the hinterland termini of the slave routes had positive effects.[56] The wars that yielded slaves ranged from raids for the express purpose of taking prisoners[57] to wars of imperial expansion. Some of the imperial wars involved polities directly concerned with the intercontinental maritime trade, such as the wars waged in the seventeenth century by the Akwamu and in the eighteenth century by Dahomey and Ashanti, but many involved powers that had no direct interest in the coastal trade. Examples of the latter were those of the eighteenth-century Bambara kingdom of Mamari Kulubari (which contributed to the growth of the Senegambian intercontinental slave

---

[54] Jones, *Trading States,* p. 46.

[55] Ryder, "Reestablishment of Factories," pp. 163–66.

[56] E.g., Bosman, *New Description of Guinea,* pp. 70, 327.

[57] Vansina, "Long-Distance Trade-Routes," p. 385. Polanyi, *Dahomey and Trade,* p. 23. Newbury, *Western Slave Coast,* p. 26.

trade) and of the nineteenth-century Fulani state (which, with its conquests of the Hausa and Oyo kingdoms, facilitated the expansion of transatlantic slave trading in the Bights).[58]

Finally, though the destruction of a formerly great polity led to an initial period of political and economic instability, it seems ultimately to have facilitated the growth of new trade routes and trading centers. In Central Africa, the fall of the kingdom of Kongo in 1667 led within thirty years to a new pattern of trade terminating in newly important ports of intercontinental maritime trade.[59] Analogously, on the Bight of Benin, the downfall of the kingdom of Oyo and the subsequent Yoruba wars led to the growth of new slaving ports, such as Badagry and Lagos, which competed effectively with the declining Whydah.[60] Ultimately, as the demands of European buyers shifted conclusively from slaves to agricultural products, new ports arose to meet those demands, and many of the old slaving ports, such as Bonny and Kalabar, lost forever their significance as intercontinental ports of trade.[61]

Conclusion

Although the length of the era of intercontinental maritime trade between European buyers and African sellers far exceeded that of the subsequent colonial period in Africa, the impact of the trade on the politically independent African societies of our time was less significant than that of the later, political developments. In fact, intercontinental maritime trade on the African coast did not revolutionize African society. Rather, it reinforced the political and economic status quo, at least to the extent that its main beneficiaries were the traditional rulers and their subordinates. Particular state systems rose and fell, but the political and economic system as a whole remained intact. In conclusion, it can be said that the era of intercontinental maritime trade, especially its slaving phase, is significant not so much for its effect on the ordering of African society[62] as for its impact on the ordering of society in the Americas.

---

[58] Wilks, "Rise of Akwamu." Ryder, "Reestablishment of Factories," pp. 162–65. Margaret Priestley, "Philip Quaque of Cape Coast," in *Africa Remembered: Narratives by West Africans from the Era of the Slave Trade,* ed. Philip D. Curtin (Madison: University of Wisconsin Press, 1968), pp. 103–04. Curtin, "Ayuba Suleiman Diallo," p. 29. Verger, *Bahia and Trade,* p. 31. Newbury, *Western Slave Coast,* p. 35.

[59] Vansina, "Long-Distance Trade-Routes," pp. 380–81.

[60] Newbury, *Western Slave Coast,* pp. 32, 35. Verger, *Bahia and Trade,* p. 31.

[61] Jones, *Trading States,* p. 73. Cf. Vansina on rubber in Central Africa in "Long-Distance Trade-Routes," pp. 385–86.

[62] Cf. Christopher Fyfe, "The Impact of the Slave Trade on West Africa," in *The Transatlantic Slave Trade from West Africa,* mimeographed (Edinburgh: Center for African Studies, University of Edinburgh, 1965), p. 88.

Slaves or Captives?
Some Notes on Fantasy and Fact

BASIL DAVIDSON

Basil Davidson, a British writer and historian, has written numerous books and articles on the history of Africa. Among his books are *A History of West Africa to the Nineteenth Century* (Longmans, 1965) and *The Lost Cities of Africa, Black Mother: The Years of the African Slave Trade*, and *The African Genius: An Introduction to African Social and Cultural History* (Atlantic-Little, Brown, 1959, 1961, and 1970). He is the editor of *The African Past: Chronicles from Antiquity to Modern Times* (Atlantic-Little, Brown, 1964). In the following essay, Mr. Davidson dissects and attempts to dispel a number of myths that have sprung up surrounding conditions in Africa at the time of the Atlantic slave trade and before. The questions that concern him here center on African complicity in the trade: Why did Africans sell other Africans? How were they able to do so in such vast numbers? And what were the ultimate costs of their long involvement in the trade?

Marion Kilson has described the organization of the slave trade with Africa; Philip Curtin will illuminate its consequences. In between there may be room to consider another question that is relevant — perhaps highly so — to white ideas about black people and black ideas about white. This question may be variously phrased, for it relates to the analysis

---

Author's note   Since the first edition of my introduction to the consequences for Africa of the Atlantic slave trade (*Black Mother: The Years of the African Slave Trade* [Boston: Atlantic-Little, Brown, 1961]), the historiography of this little-researched subject has somewhat improved. A number of important articles have appeared in the *Journal of African History*; and in 1969 we had Philip Curtin's very important reassessment of the numbers involved and of other aspects of the trade, *The Atlantic Slave Trade: A Census* (Madison: University of Wisconsin Press). Generally, however, I find no reason to change the basic views expressed in *Black Mother*. Accordingly, this paper does not depart from them, though it develops them in one or two new directions. At the same time, recent scholarship has made it ever more apparent that the whole subject calls urgently for more research, and I hope this paper may prove a stimulus to that end.

and comparison of social structures and economic systems. Put crudely, in a shorthand we shall all understand, it is simply, Why did Africans sell Africans?

"Born to Captivity"? The "Reservoir" Theory

Few questions in history have evoked more pseudoscientific obfuscation — though not, indeed, at the beginning of the trade or for many years thereafter. Perfectly accustomed to seeing white people in Europe bought and sold, the Portuguese and their early competitors saw nothing strange — and nothing culpable — in a corresponding black commerce. Merchants in Europe had dealt in slaves for centuries, transporting them across European frontiers and selling them to Egypt and western Asia. Nothing in the records suggests that they felt any particular guilt or need for concealment — except, as quite often happened, when they sold white Christians instead of white non-Christians. Europeans sold Europeans for reasons so obvious in their age as to require no explanation and no justification: some men were free and should not be sold or bought, whereas others were not free and were therefore fair game. No doubt Europeans thought it was the same in Africa.

Probably, in fact, the question was never raised during the early years of the slave trade. Bondage was the cement of the Middle Ages — the rule rather than the exception. If most historians of Europe have said rather little on the subject, that is because they have preferred to romanticize and lend respectability to those "dear delightful Middle Ages" (as the English historian Bishop William Stubbs, recoiling from the horrors of the nineteenth century, liked to call them) and have chosen to see the Middle Ages either through the tales of kings and bishops, battles, barons and badges of ownership, or through the traditions of Christian enlightenment.[1] Like those who have written on the ancient Greeks, they have urged us to admire the soaring pinnacles of cultural achievement and to ignore the matted soil beneath. So it is that modern historians of Africa, when accused of gilding the African past, as they sometimes are accused, may perhaps be justified in thinking themselves no more at fault, and possibly less, than their colleagues in other fields.

European slavery was a thing of the past, and generally forgotten, when the slave trade with Africa got into full stride after about 1650. Even so, a sense that the trade called for justification scarcely appeared before the last decades of the eighteenth century. Then antislavery agitations, portraying Africans as the victims of European greed and violence, began in England and, later, in France. If the slave trade were stopped, said the antislavers, Africa would be much the happier. Nonsense, replied the slavers or their apologists (arguing in this instance before the British Privy Council in 1788): "There was a great

---

[1] For a review of the peculiarities of European historical writing about colonization, the reader should look at Eric Williams' entertaining study *British Historians and the West Indies* (London: Deutsch, 1964).

accession of happiness to Africa since the introduction of the trade." African kings being despotic, life in Africa unmentionably miserable and promising no improvement, it was kindness to take Africans away from their native continent and introduce them to the blessings of plantation slavery in the New World.

Such things were said and were believed. Based though they were on near-total ignorance of Africa and of black history, they came to have a certain built-in persuasiveness, even for those with no direct stake in the trade. For generations, white men saw black men primarily as slaves, and the years of slavery had their degrading effect on blacks as well as whites. It became easy to imagine that black people were somehow naturally inferior to whites: if their station was inferior in America, then it must be the same in Africa. Partly from this notion, as we know, grew the deepening wretchedness of racist prejudice.

Indeed, this wretchedness impoverished the thought of later white writers, even those who had lived or traveled in Africa. They might deplore the institutions of slavery; but, more often than not, they agreed that the "natural condition of Africa" could be held to justify the Atlantic trade. "So far as the sum of human misery in Africa was concerned," wrote in 1910 a man as liberal and well informed for his time as Sir Harry Johnston, "it is probable that the trade in slaves between that continent and America scarcely added to it. It even to some extent mitigated the sufferings of the Negro in his own home."[2]

Rooted in European thought for more than a century, this was a line of argument that now passed beyond the field of moralizing justification into the common coin of historiography. It began to be asserted as a fact that many Africans, even most Africans, had lived in slavery before and during the Atlantic trade. Africa, in other words, was no more than a great reservoir of slavery; the Atlantic trade had merely transferred slaves from one continent to another. Nineteen years after Johnston's forthright statement of the case, an outstanding French historian of the slave trade felt it quite safe to assert that "from the earliest days of the trade, the majority of Negroes were living in a state of servitude."[3] Taking up the theme in our own day, Daniel Mannix, in his *Black Cargoes,* says as something beyond discussion that "many of the Negroes transported to America had been slaves in Africa, born to captivity. Slavery in Africa was an ancient and widespread institution."[4] Along the same lines and still more recently, others have argued not only that the trade brought Africa gains as well as losses but that the losses were in all likelihood smaller than the gains. The first part of that statement may be incontestable, but the second depends on arguing, as Johnston did in 1910, that the slave trade pro-

---

[2] Sir Harry Johnston, quoted in Basil Davidson, *The African Slave Trade: Pre-Colonial History, 1450–1850* (Boston: Atlantic-Little, Brown, 1961), pp. 101–02.

[3] Father D. Rinchon, *La Traite et l'Esclavage des Congolais par les Européens* (Brussels: Hélas, 1929), p. 169.

[4] Daniel Mannix with Malcolm Cowley, *Black Cargoes: A History of the Atlantic Slave Trade, 1518–1865* (London: Longmans, 1963), p. 43.

duced no new situation in the parts of Africa it involved, but merely battened on an existing misery, and to some extent relieved it. In these pages we will take a look at this assumption and at the corresponding claim that some overall benefit came to Africa from the slave trade. Meanwhile, it may be worth pointing out that even the African peoples who gained from their rulers' involvement in slaving might have gained far more if the slave trade had never come into being and they had continued, instead, to enjoy the benefits of trade in other commodities, such as the trade with the English and the French in the sixteenth century.

Such polemics aside, one may ask whether it is in any case a fact that "the majority of Negroes were living in a state of servitude"; that many who were sold abroad had been "born to captivity"; that "slavery in Africa was an ancient and widespread institution." If these statements were true, there would of course be no need to search further for an answer to the question of why Africans sold other Africans: they would have been doing no more than tapping an existing reservoir of slaves, and nothing more would have occurred than a mere rerouting to the ocean trade of a portion of the allegedly huge number of slaves previously destined for overland export to North Africa and the East. What could have been simpler? It was purely a question of reorganizing the market in human beings—a market which, according to the apologists, dominated the economies of precolonial Africa—so as to meet a new demand.

This analysis, however, is all too simple. Certainly, if it were a true description of the case, it would point to a most peculiar situation, one never before seen or even thought possible: we should be asked to accept that economic systems described as mainly of the "subsistence" type could dispose of large quantities of forced labor, always in abundant supply. It is a comment on certain attitudes toward Africa that the inherent improbability, not to say the impossibility, of such a situation has not prevented otherwise thoughtful men from repeating the "reservoir" theory. Clearly, some re-examination of the facts, as we now have them, may lead us to a sounder answer to the central question of why Africans themselves participated in the trade.

Overland Exports: A Luxury Trade

The assertion that Africa was already a capacious reservoir of slaves when the Atlantic trade began has rested largely on certain beliefs about the overland slave trade. It is said that the overland trade was a vast business, dating at least from early Muslim times and dealing on at least as great a scale as the later Atlantic trade. We are asked to believe, on admittedly frail evidence, that the estimate that two million West Africans were exported across the Sahara as slaves every century for several centuries is probably "less than the truth."[5]

---

[5] R. Mauny, *Tableau Géographique de l'Ouest Africain au Moyen Age* (Dakar, Senegal: I.F.A.N., 1961), p. 379. This book is, in many respects, indispensable to an understanding of early West African history.

If so, the overland trade was indeed greater than the subsequent maritime trade, in the course of which, according to Professor Curtin's recent re-estimate, nine or ten million Africans were brought into the Americas as slaves. If so, again, it might well appear that West Africa truly was a "natural reservoir" of slaves, and that the institutions of slavery, and therefore of slaving, owed nothing of importance to the influences and pressures of Europeans in the Atlantic.

Now, it rests beyond doubt that the trans-Saharan slave trade with the western and central Sudan existed in some degree from ancient times. This was the route by which black servants occasionally reached Roman Europe. It is also beyond doubt that the trade grew in size with the development of large interior trading empires, such as Mali and Songhay, after the thirteenth century. Scattered evidence of varying reliability suggests that there were years in which several thousand West Africans were taken north across the Sahara. When the notable Moroccan traveler Ibn Battuta returned to North Africa in 1352 after a journey to Mali, for instance, he traveled with a caravan comprising 600 slaves.[6]

It is quite another matter, however, to suggest that the overland trade dealt on a scale even approaching two million a century. On the contrary, the evidence that can be gleaned at the northern termini of the trade routes, or the "points of reception," repeatedly leads one to the conclusion that the overland trade was much smaller than this—in fact, that in terms of large areas and long periods it was insignificantly small when compared with the later Atlantic trade.

In assessing the evidence from the north, the first point of note is that the overland slave trade was almost always a luxury trade. We know this from a great deal of incontrovertible evidence—most recently, from S. D. Goitein's vivid recapitulations of the contents and meaning of a large group of business documents conserved from medieval Cairo and known as the Geniza Collections.[7] Slaves were expensive. For the most part, only the rich man was able to purchase them. Being expensive, they were cherished as individuals; often they were regarded as irreplaceable. In the countries surrounding the Mediterranean throughout the High Middle Ages, slavery "was neither industrial nor agricultural; with the exception of the armies, it was not collective but individual. It was a personal service in the widest sense of the word, which, when the master served was of high rank and wealthy, carried with it great advantages, as well as social prestige. . . . In or out of bondage the slave was a member of the family. . . . The acquisition of a male slave was a great affair on which a man was congratulated almost as if a son had been born to him. No

---

[6] Ibn Battuta, *Travels in Asia and Africa,* ed. and trans. H. A. Gibbs (London: Routledge, 1929), p. 337.

[7] S. D. Goitein, *A Mediterranean Society,* vol. 1, *Economic Foundations* (Berkeley: University of California Press, 1967).

wonder, for a slave fulfilled tasks similar to those of a son [and] belonged, more or less, to the world of commerce and finance."[8]

To buy and maintain a single slave was thus a major investment for a relatively poor man and a considerable expense for a wealthy man. Goitein estimates that the standard cost of a slave in Fatimid Cairo (from the tenth through the twelfth century) was 20 dinars, the dinar being a gold coin which varied in value but was comparable in buying power to about $100 today. Insofar as any real comparison can be made, this means that a slave cost the equivalent of about $2,000. That was in Cairo. Elsewhere the cost could be far higher because the market was less well supplied. Writing in 1067, the Andalusian historian al-Bakri commented on the excellence of female African cooks in Awdaghost, a since vanished trading city of the western Sudan. There, he said, a good cook cost 100 dinars or more.[9] How strange, if West Africa did possess such a reservoir of slaves that it was capable of supplying the overland trade with two million every hundred years, that the cost of a cook should be some five times *higher* at the point of export in the Sudan than at the point of import in Egypt!

Other Mediterranean evidence tends the same way. Records reveal that in the richly endowed Muslim state of al-Andalus, as in Egypt, Africans from south of the Sahara were prized as soldiers, household servants, administrators, and artisans, in exactly the same way as were slaves from Christian Europe. In al-Andalus, however, they were even more expensive than in Egypt. Records from 1065 to 1067, for example, show that a black slave cost 160 mitcals (the word generally used in al-Andalus for dinars). During the same period, a house in the capital city of Cordoba was sold for an equal sum, another house for 280 mitcals, a horse for 24, and a mule for 60.[10] From these relative figures, we must conclude that any man who had several slaves must have been unusually rich. Other evidence shows that what would-be buyers of the day looked for in a slave were the qualities that would befit a reliable soldier, a good business assistant, a clever craftsman—in brief, a person valued for intelligence, skill, or enterprise.

It would be possible to extend the evidence. But let it suffice to say that none of it gives any ground for supposing that these Muslim countries, or their neighbors, ever absorbed more than a small but steady number of slaves, whether black or white. Of the large-scale use of slave labor in the countries around the Mediterranean, or in Africa, there is absolutely no evidence save for one case, and that was an exception.

---

[8] Ibid., p. 130.

[9] Abu Obeyd al-Bakri, *Al-Masalik w'al-Mamalik* [*The Roads and Kingdoms*] (Cordoba, 1067); trans. MacGuckin de Slane, in *Description de l'Afrique Septentrionale* (Algiers, 1913; reprint ed., Paris: Maisonneuve, 1965), p. 300.

[10] E. Lévi-Provençal, *Histoire de l'Espagne Musulmane,* vol. 3, *Le Siècle du Califat de Cordoue* (Paris: Maisonneuve, 1967), p. 259.

The exception was the development in southern Iraq during the ninth century of a system of cultivation on large estates which made use of forced labor from Africa. At that time, the problem was to reclaim waterlogged lands and render them fit for crops such as sugar cane. It was a problem that could not be solved by the use of Iraqi peasant labor alone, so large numbers of Africans were imported for the work. Finding themselves ill treated, they organized a great revolt which won them power in southern Iraq from 869 till 883. This episode has often been advanced as evidence that a large slave trade between Africa and Arabia existed, then or later, before the nineteenth century. But it appears certain that this was the only case of its kind, "the one big attempt on these lines,"[11] and that nowhere else was there any such effort to construct a system of plantation slavery using African labor on the eastern side of the Atlantic.[12]

And after the Middle Ages? The answer seems to be the same. There may have been some rise in the numbers of servants imported from Africa during Ottoman suzerainty over Egypt and parts of North Africa; but again, nothing suggests that it was large. In general, "the practice of slavery among the Muslims seems to have undergone no radical changes during the modern period, down to the last [the nineteenth] century."[13]

A large slave trade began along the East African coast in about 1830 and continued for half a century, centering around Zanzibar and its neighboring mainland seaboard, then dominated by the Omani of southeastern Arabia. It may be that over a number of years this trade annually involved some 20,000 slaves, taking into account those collected by Portuguese bandits in Mozambique. But the total number affected by the East Coast trade over the fifty-year period was almost certainly much smaller than one million. (This was not, of course, the total number of victims of the trade: a great many people died in slaving raids, during the march to the coast, and in slave markets before export.)

For a time, then, the East Coast trade was large—a fact which might be interpreted as pointing a priori to the existence of an inland "reservoir," were it not that the time was short. Indeed, any assumption that the "majority of Negroes" in East Africa, or even a significant minority, were "living in a state of servitude" at the time of this trade would have to depend on previous developments: slavery as a "widespread institution" cannot be the structural consequence of any brief or sudden series of events. Be that as it may, the assumption that slavery was a widespread institution in East Africa simply

---

[11] R. Brunschvig, in *Encyclopedia of Islam,* vol. 1, *A–B,* ed. H. A. Gibbs et al. (New York: Humanities Press, 1960), s.v. "'Abd" [Slave].

[12] This whole question is authoritatively discussed by Claud Cahen in *Der Islam: Vom Ursprung bis zu den Anfängen des Osmanenreiches* (Frankfurt: Fischer, 1968), p. 137 ff.

[13] *Encyclopedia of Islam,* s.v. "'Abd" [Slave].

will not fit the evidence. A small trade in slaves had undoubtedly gone on in this area since Ptolemaic times; that it remained small, even very small, is powerfully suggested by all the pre-1830 records that we have, and these are not negligible. Across the centuries many Africans reached the East as servants, where they were employed in the same semiskilled or highly skilled occupations as in Egypt. Some even reached China, where they were spoken of as doorkeepers who were sad because they were homesick. But how many doorkeepers could be absorbed even by the lords of Yüan or Ming China? On the external evidence, in short, the "reservoir" theory simply will not stand for East Africa, any more than it will stand for West Africa.

The Internal Evidence Considered

One can reach the same conclusion by asking questions of a different kind. Does the *internal* evidence, from Africa south of the Sahara, lend any serious support to the view that "slavery in Africa was an ancient and widespread institution"? Does it anywhere point to the existence of slave economies — of productive systems which made extensive use of slave labor?

In trying to answer questions such as these, as much qualitative as quantitative, we are faced with several rather severe difficulties. The first is the grave poverty of research into the productive systems and economic institutions of precolonial Africa. The available evidence is very confused and contradictory, scattered and inadequate; even so, it should be enough to enable researchers, through serious effort, to cast some light on these important matters. Evidently, this effort remains to be made. What exactly was "subsistence economy," in most of sub-Saharan Africa, after about 1300? How great a role did markets play in determining the trends of production, whether for short-distance or long-distance trade? Were artisan producers moving into some kind of cash economy, based on a medium of exchange such as cowrie shells, cottons, or metal bars? And, if so, can we descry in this development the beginnings of a wage economy? One hopes that the next generation of Africanists will give us detailed answers, for, as things stand, we can do little more than sketch general outlines in reply.

Another difficulty, scarcely less acute, results from a confusion of terms: it has not been sufficiently noted that the use of the word "slave" to mean a man with no rights and no claim to equality with other men is a fairly modern one. To all intents and purposes, the term, used in this sense, was an invention of the plantation economy in the Americas after the middle of the seventeenth century. Before that time, attitudes had been different. As John Hope Franklin writes, "there can be little doubt that the earliest Negroes in Virginia occupied a position similar to that of the white servants in the colony. They were listed as servants in the census enumerations of 1623 and 1624; and as late as 1651 some Negroes whose period of service had expired were being assigned land in much the same way that it was being done for white servants."[14] Indeed, only after about 1650 did attitudes and the system change. Then servants, if they were black, ceased to be servants and became slaves. By 1900, after three long centuries, the word "slave" had acquired quite a different meaning from that generally attached to it in 1600.

From the confusion surrounding this term have come a number of misunderstandings. Around 1900, there appeared in Europe a series of translations from the Arabic classics bearing on historical Africa. Sometimes the translators for these volumes were good Arabists with some knowledge of Africa; often they were poor Arabists who were deeply ignorant of the material they were dealing with. Always, the translators were content to render *'abd* bluntly as "slave"—lexically correct enough were the reader careful to place the word within its socioeconomic context. Unfortunately, the reader seldom did, or could do, anything of the kind. Finding frequent references to "slaves" or *esclaves* (as *'abid* was translated) in his texts, he deduced that slavery, in the sense of chattel slavery, was a "widespread institution" in Africa since ancient times. Thus in retrospect those expensive lady cooks of eleventh-century Awdaghost came to be awarded quite a different status from the one they had actually held.

In reality, as records like the Geniza documents of Fatimid Cairo convincingly show, the status of these cooks was far above chattel slavery—that is, the kind of slavery in which forced labor represents a major element of production. Like most *'abid,* they occupied a position which seems to have been somewhere between that of a dependent, or client, and that of a servant. In some respects, of course, they stood lower than dependents, for they were bound by law to their masters and could move about only with difficulty. Often, however, they held positions of crucial responsibility which supposed, and entailed, the privileges of delegated power.

The *'abid* could and did use these privileges to their own advantage. Europeans trading along the Guinea Coast during the seventeenth and eighteenth centuries found themselves dealing with men described as "slaves" who were serving as the agents of inland kings. Often the Europeans had difficulty understanding how "slaves"—persons whose status, as they understood it, appeared beneath contempt—should wield so much authority in Africa, commanding the disposal and even the consumption of considerable wealth. More than that, historical records abound with cases of "slaves" who became kings. The most powerful of the early rulers of the Mali empire, according to the great Berber historian Ibn Khaldun, was a former *'abd* who had usurped the throne from the legitimate Keita dynasty. Several centuries later, toward 1700, along the Upper Niger, the Bambara kingdom founded by Mamari Kulubari was ruled by a series of "slave generals," much in the manner of the Mamluk

---

[14] John Hope Franklin, *From Slavery to Freedom: A History of Negro Americans,* 3rd ed. (New York: Alfred A. Knopf, 1966), p. 71.

"slaves" from Turkic West Asia who had earlier formed one of Egypt's strongest post-Pharaonic dynasties. Similarly, during the nineteenth century, several of the leading officials of the Ashanti empire were men whose status was misleadingly described by the word "slave." They were in reality men of humble birth who were raised to great administrative power by kings interested in building regular civil services so as to balance the power of lineage chiefs appointed by right of heritage. To see such persons as proof of the existence of slave institutions capable of supporting a slave economy, in any meaningful sense of the term, is simply to misread the evidence.

Here and there, no doubt, such institutions came near to being born.[15] It is said that the kings of the Muslim countries Bornu and Hausaland began to establish "slave villages" for purposes of production even before 1500. Yet these fledgling systems remained at most peripheral to the economies of the kingdoms. In any case, it appears likely that the slave laborers they employed were far from being chattels. Insofar as they differed from the "free peasantry" of Bornu and Hausaland—and the quotation marks are necessary, if only because we lack the terms to express these relationships precisely—the difference lay in the slaves' greater degree of obligation to their masters and in certain restrictions on their movements.

Generally, in these Muslim kingdoms, the men who had political power counted on the work and the tribute of peasants who were subjected to them by ties of dependence, or clientage. The relationship of the peasants to their rulers in some ways resembled that of the villeins of the feudal lords of Europe: villeins were not serfs, but they were also far from being freemen. Whether tied to their land as slaves or occupying it by prescriptive right of heritage, the African peasants were obliged to deliver tribute to the rulers in the form of produce. This was true, at least in the Mali and Songhay empires, of specialist groups as well—metalsmiths, who produced lance and arrow heads; boatbuilders, who made and serviced Niger canoes; and many others were required to pay tribute in kind. So long as the vassals, or clients, were not sentenced for grave offenses in the courts or captured in war, the ties of dependence worked both ways: in return for the tribute delivered to them, the rulers protected their subjects from warlike raids and other political misfortunes. At a few points in this history—as, for instance, in sixteenth-century Gao, the capital of the Songhay empire—there seem to have been trends toward large-scale farming which may have involved an economically significant quantity of forced labor. Apart from these rare exceptions, which bulk small in the record, slavery was of no productive importance.

In the forest states of West Africa, slavery was even less significant economically. Here, the scale was smaller; even more than in the grasslands, the

---

[15] This aspect of African history, as well as other matters related to this essay, is considered more fully in Part 4 of Basil Davidson, *The African Genius: An Introduction to African Social and Cultural History* (Boston: Atlantic-Little, Brown, 1970).

farming systems called for individual enterprise. Indeed, the possible uses for enslaved labor in West Africa were practically nil, at least until the end of the nineteenth century. For the existing social systems provided for the kind of work that slaves might have done: this or that service of value to the community, such as garden clearing, porterage, or canoe ferrying, was performed by this or that age set or by some other group in the society. Only in a few cases, so far as present evidence can show, did these mechanisms prove incapable of meeting the demand for labor service. The lords of the Ashanti empire, to give one example, early in the development of their long-distance trade southward to the coast as well as northward to the Sudan, found it necessary to import men to work as porters on the trails through their country. Even so, one wonders how far these imported workers differed in status from others in the empire whose services could be commanded but whose rights were enshrined in the social code. "A slave who knows how to serve," ran the Ashanti saying, "succeeds to his master's property." The indentured servants and wage workers of contemporary Europe or America, not to speak of eighteenth-century American plantation workers, might well have been glad to exchange places with the "slaves" of Ashanti.

Like the external evidence, then, the internal evidence yields no sign that Africa had a large reservoir of slaves available for export, or that slavery on that continent had become an institution in any way comparable with the one which grew up in the New World. Whatever the slave traders may have thought they were doing, they were not transferring men and women from one state of wretchedness to another and similar state. On the contrary, they were plunging their African captives into a new and degrading form of bondage.

The Status of Disposable Persons

Having cleared the "reservoir" myth from our path, we can raise a new set of questions approaching the one that most concerns us. Millions of people were exported from Africa by way of the slave trade. If they did not come from slavery, what statuses and institutions did they come from? Who were they, and how did they get to be aboard the slave ships?

It is almost certain that from the trade's small beginnings in the 1450's to its period of major growth after 1650 the slaves came from two chief sources: either they were persons who had lost their civic rights, in the state that sold them, by sentence of the courts, or they were citizens of another state who had lost their rights through capture in war. The general situation, in short, was similar to that in medieval Europe. So long as men were citizens, they were entitled to and could expect the protection of their rulers, and they could be taken and sold only if they came into conflict with the law. But if they became prisoners of war of another state, they could be bought and sold, forced to work at whatever employment they might be suited for, given as gifts between rulers, or exchanged as items of trade. Such was the condition of the countless Slavs of eastern Europe who for several centuries, before their conversion to Christianity, were sold by the Europeans.

This meant, of course, that a certain number of men and women were always available for export. The first Europeans to sail down the Atlantic coast of Africa and reach the Guinea seaboard met institutions, so far as the possibilities of human bondage were concerned, which were not unlike their own. The Portuguese, who initially gathered their slaves in piratical raids on the seaboard populations of Mauritania and Senegal, needed only ten or fifteen years to establish mutually profitable partnerships with the rulers they found there.

The parallels between Europe and Africa run close. European rulers customarily deported their criminals, their contentious rebels, and even their rivals into the safety of slavery somewhere else; African rulers undoubtedly did the same. Courts could be accommodating, and slaving captains or other buyers were the last people to question their judgments. More than a few African princes reached the Americas as a result of the judicial process.

Further, services rendered could be repaid with slaves. The famous story of the English adventurer John Hawkins is a case in point. Knowing that black slave labor could be sold at a good profit in Hispaniola (now Haiti and Santo Domingo), he sailed to Sierra Leone in 1562, nearly a hundred years before the British took any interest in slaving as a system of trade. There Hawkins began by pillaging a Portuguese slaver, thus acquiring 210 African captives. At this point he was visited by the ambassadors of two local monarchs who sought military aid against two others. Hawkins agreed to send a contingent of his men to join their forces, and together they captured an enemy town. Hawkins was rewarded for his help in the battle by the gift of 260 prisoners. With a total of 470 captives, as his logbook says, "we set our sails and directed our course over to the India named America or the New World, there to trade with the said wares."[16]

The parallels can be taken still further. Records show that the Oba of Benin would not agree to the sale of his own citizens, and other African kings applied the same rule. One should not sell one's coreligionists: the social and the moral order were alike against it. So it was in Europe. Christians felt they ought not to enslave other Christians, or to maintain in slavery any non-Christians who accepted Christianity. Azurara's *Chronicle of the Discovery and Conquest of Guinea,* completed in 1453, makes it clear that the Portuguese applied to converted Africans the same general rule that Africans applied to captured persons who were similarly absorbed into their societies.

Once Africans were baptized, wrote Azurara, "our people . . . made no difference between them and their own free servants born in our own country.

[16] Logbook of John Hawkins, Cotton Manuscripts, British Museum; partly reproduced in Basil Davidson, *The African Past: Chronicles from Antiquity to Modern Times* (Boston: Atlantic-Little, Brown, 1964), pp. 199–200.

Those [captives] whom they took while still young they caused to be instructed in the mechanical arts, and those whom they saw fitted for managing property they set free and married to women who were natives of the land [of Portugal], making with them a division of their property, as if they had been bestowed on those who had married them by the will of their own fathers. . . . Yes, and some Portuguese widows of good family who bought some of these female slaves they either adopted or left some portion of their estate by will, so that in future they married right well, being treated as entirely free."[17] Perhaps Azurara was overstating the generosity of the Portuguese for propagandist reasons, promoting before time the illusions of Bishop Stubbs about the "dear delightful Middle Ages." Yet the latter's enthusiasm for the medieval period was not entirely mistaken, and what we know broadly of fifteenth-century Europe does bear out the probability of Azurara's description. If the Middle Ages were delightful only for a happy few, even the many could benefit from a pervasive tolerance that was to be denied those in bondage during later times of mercantile expansion.

In summary, then, it may be said that the great majority of the Africans who were given or sold to Europeans by other Africans during the early period of the slave trade were drawn from a small minority in any given population. They were persons who had lost their rights of citizenship and who, for one reason or another, had not yet been able to re-establish them. Before the discovery of the Americas, and even for a while afterwards, these Africans were taken to Europe and were there permitted to acquire new rights and to establish new ties of interdependence within this or that European society.

The opening of the Americas to European settlement changed all this, for reasons which lie outside the scope of this essay, but which are not mysterious. The social systems to which Africans were sent in the Americas had small place, and soon no place at all, for the kind of social ties supposed by a unitary social order, and thus for the establishment of citizenship rights by those who arrived in the Americas without such rights. What these systems increasingly required was a sharply differentiated social order consisting of permanent masters and permanent slaves, with a harsh and ever deepening line between the two. Of tremendous importance to subsequent developments in Africa was the fact that the numbers of "disposable persons" who were available for export from Africa proved far too few for the American enterprises now in hand. So it came about that the trickle of the early slave trade became, under persistent and determined European pressure, a mighty flood.

Our central question now grows more complex. Why did Africans sell Africans in such large numbers? Who were the African sellers, and what were their motives in responding to the heightened European demands? How did the few thousands of "disposable persons" grow into many thousands, into millions? By what stages, through what mechanisms, did this happen?

---

[17] Gomes Eannes de Azurara, *The Chronicle of the Discovery and Conquest of Guinea,* trans. C. R. Beazley and E. Prestage, 2 vols. (London: Hakluyt Society, 1896), 1:84.

The Mechanics of Partnership

Outright piracy—kidnapping, or "panyarring," as it was called—opened the taking of slaves from Africa in the fifteenth century and continued until the very end, nearly four and a half centuries later. There was never a time when kidnapping was not practiced, whether by Europeans or by Africans engaged in the trade. But soon after the first European raids on the African coast, peaceful exchange, generally free of violence (at least at the point of sale and purchase), became the order of the day.

The Venetian Ca' da Mosto, who sailed to Africa in Portuguese service in the 1450's, put the matter clearly: "Note that before this traffic was organized, the Portuguese caravels—sometimes four, sometimes more—were wont to come armed to the Gulf of Arguim [the modern Mauritanian seaboard], and descending on the land at night would assail the fisher villages and so ravage the land. Thus they took . . . both men and women, and carried them to Portugal for sale, behaving in a like manner along all the rest of the coast. . . . But for some time past all have been at peace and engaged in trade." In exchange for "disposable persons" the Portuguese offered horses, Andalusian silks, silver, and other goods. "As a result, every year the Portuguese carry away from Arguim a thousand slaves." These slaves came from many West African countries and were part of the number available for export across the Sahara.[18]

By 1500 the trade was institutionalized at several points along the Guinea Coast. "When trade was good here," Pereira, a merchant-administrator on the West Coast, reported of the years surrounding 1500, "as many as 400 slaves could be had in [the Senegal River] . . . in exchange for horses and other merchandise." At such favorable times, Pereira estimated, the trade along the Senegambian seaboard, ranging from Arguin Island in the north to the rivers of Sierra Leone in the south, could yield 3,500 slaves or more, as well as "many tusks of ivory, gold, fine cotton cloths and much other merchandise."[19]

So the trade in slaves continued for a hundred years and more—which by no means indicates that large numbers of slaves were acquired in every year, or even in most years—through European channels almost exclusively Portuguese and Spanish. As late as 1619 an English captain in the Gambia River was offered slaves and refused them. Yet by this time the English and the

---

[18] Ca' da Mosto, *The Voyages of . . . ,* trans. G. R. Crone (London: Hakluyt Society, 1937), p. 18.

[19] Duarte Pacheco Pereira, *Esmeraldo de Situ Orbis,* trans. R. Mauny (Bissau, Portuguese Guinea: Centro de Estados da Guiné Portuguesa, 1956), p. 65. Historians have not been able to agree on the precise meaning of this engaging title. One plausible translation (J. Dentinho, *Diário de Lisboa,* 21 July 1949, quoted in Mauny, *Tableau Géographique,* p. 8) suggests that it meant, at least for Pereira and his readers, merely a book "About the Seas of the Globe" or world. This gloss relies on the supposition that Pereira added the ablative of *esmeraldus* (meaning "green," derived from the feminine noun *esmeralda,* "an emerald") to the title of the well-known Roman geographer Pomponius Mela's *De Situ Orbis.* But it doesn't really matter: "the *Esmeraldo,*" for Africanists, is unique and irreplaceable as a source of late fifteenth-century information on the West African coast.

French were settling in the New World, and by 1650 they had become major slave carriers.

The institutionalizing of the slaving business proceeded at various rhythms and in various patterns, according to the circumstances of the different African regions. It came early in the Congo kingdoms (northern Angola today) by demand of Portuguese settlers on the sugar-growing islands of São Tomé and Principe. Here, too, it was unusually violent and was marked by repeated armed invasions by the Portuguese.[20] Elsewhere the process fell into two fairly distinct phases. First came the regularization of African demand for certain types of European goods, which became increasingly desirable to coastal rulers and men of power, whether for personal use or for purposes of inland trade. Abundant records show a mounting demand in Africa for such goods as iron bars and copper rings, which could supplement the generally short supply of these metals in West Africa. The metalware acquired from European traders was used by African smiths and, later, for currency and capital accumulation. Other European goods in high demand were textiles and, after 1650, guns and gunpowder.

Second, and in step with the regularization of demand for European imports, came systematic efforts in Africa to increase the supply of "disposable persons." Criminals or "subversives" failing to oblige in sufficient number, coastal rulers fell back on capture by raid and warfare. "Whydah [on the modern Dahomey coast] is the greatest trading place on the Coast of Guinea," an English captain noted in 1721, "selling off as many slaves, I believe, as all the rest together: forty or fifty sail (French, English, Portuguese and Dutch) freighting thence every year." The king of Whydah, a powerful middleman in the new ocean trade, either bought captives from his neighbors or, "if he cannot obtain a sufficient number . . . in that way, he marches an army, and depopulates. He, and the king of Ardra adjoining, commit great depredations inland."[21] In 1727 Agaja, the king of the inland Fon, put a stop to this by seizing the little coastal kingdoms of what afterwards became Dahomey, "entirely destroying our slave trade," as the English captain said. During this enterprise Agaja captured another Englishman, Bullfinch Lamb, and sent him to England to plead with the king to stop trying to export captives from Dahomey.[22] But by this time the pressures were too strong; although it seems likely that the slave trade from Dahomey diminished under Fon hegemony, it continued until late in the nineteenth century.

---

[20] The dismal story is well told by David Birmingham in his *Trade and Conflict in Angola, 1483–1790* (Oxford: Clarendon Press, 1966).

[21] John Atkins, *A Voyage to Guinea etc.,* 2nd ed. (London, 1737), p. 172.

[22] William Snelgrave, *Account of Guinea* (London, 1734). Like other sources for the Atlantic trade, this account can be found in Elizabeth Donnan's great work, *Documents Illustrative of the History of the Slave Trade to America,* 4 vols. (Washington, D.C.: Carnegie Institution, 1930–1935).

Cases of this kind of thing were numerous, as Marion Kilson has indicated in the preceding essay. The two-way pressures of the ocean trade—European demand for captives who could be sold into slavery and African demand for European goods—worked powerfully toward the institutionalization of the system. Nowhere was this clearer than in the delta of the Niger and the adjoining Cross River, the coastal borderland of one of the most densely populated regions of Africa. Over the years, many little states took shape here in response to the ocean trade; and they all embarked on the trade in "disposable persons," which meant, for the most part, the capture and sale of free men and women.

The institutionalization of the slave trade was further promoted by an increasing commercialization in the means of exchange employed. The "primitive money" of the trade's early years acquired the status of "zonal currency," and over wide areas traders began evaluating goods in terms of iron bars, copper manillas, rolls of cotton, cases of gin, or other conveniently durable or packageable articles. Thus the early ocean trade ceased to be haphazard and occasional and became, for many of the coastal rulers and afterwards for their inland overlords, a commercial system of expanding value and importance. Conceived before 1500, it was thoroughly established after 1650. And so it continued for most of another two centuries, thrusting its influence ever more deeply into coastal and near-coastal polities.

One should note at this point that the widening gap in technological power between Africa and western Europe—and, by extension, the Americas—was already having visible effects. What really separated the Africans and the Europeans after 1650 was not European superiority in military power, in cultural resilience, in the quality of civilization as expressed in moral or political values. To the contrary, there was generally no such superiority; in certain areas, indeed, as the rigors of plantation slavery, early wage employment, and the factory system began to make themselves felt, the Europeans showed distinct inferiority. What distinguished the Europeans more and more after 1650, and especially after 1750, was a slowly growing superiority in systems of production. They moved ahead into machine production while Africans continued to produce by means of hand tools. Of all the consequences of this development, the trade in firearms was undoubtedly the most dramatic.

However primitive early European firearms were when compared with the weapons of a later age, they became a major political factor along the African coast and in several near-coastal regions. Whether making wars in order to capture prisoners for sale into slavery or defending themselves against neighbors with the same ambition, coastal and near-coastal rulers found firearms indispensable to their security. They might regret, as several of them did, the need to raise the number of captives demanded of them; but each knew that failure to do so would imperil and probably halt his supply of guns and gunpowder.

As the two-way pressures intensified, it appears that there was a certain balance of regret. If the Africans deplored the ever growing European emphasis on captives, the Europeans disliked the no less pressing African demand for guns. "We sell them," William Bosman, a Dutch trade commissioner on the Gold Coast, explained to Amsterdam around 1700, "incredible quantities of muskets and carbines, in the management of which they are wonderful dexterous." Why thus give Africans "a knife to cut our throats"—equip them with a better means of resisting European encroachment? Because, this Hollander replied, any European trader who stopped supplying firearms would quickly find himself displaced by a rival.[23] And so it was that "huge quantities of firearms were poured into West Africa during the major period of the slave trade. . . . At the height of the eighteenth-century commerce, gunsmiths in Birmingham (England) alone were exporting muskets to Africa at the rate of between 100,000 and 150,000 a year."[24] It was to be much the same in East Africa during the late nineteenth century.

Further reassessment of the historical evidence will be needed to show how far firearms were a dominant factor in shaping the policies of great African states such as the Ashanti empire. Undoubtedly they did much to fasten powerful rulers, as well as weak ones, into a trading system which required the sale of captives. In the imbrication of motives and responses which composed the African-European trading partnership of those centuries, pressures such as the need for guns and gunpowder were always strong, and sometimes they were decisive.

A "Business of Kings"

It is possible, as the two companion essays in this section show, to trace the growth of the trade in captives in much greater detail from piracy through early partnership between individuals to major international trade. In the measure that the plantation wealth of the New World grew in value for western Europe, and above all for England and France, the system became more ingenious. For their part, African rulers invented the "port of trade," fencing European enterprise and interference within narrowly restricted coastal areas. The Europeans, on their side, introduced devices such as the English "trade ounce," which, in displacing outright barter, reduced the danger of bad estimates and unexpected losses. A few words about the latter may help to illustrate the shrewdness with which the whole exchange system was conceived.

The "trade ounce" consisted in a "sorting," or assortment, of export goods which could be bought in England at half the price of one ounce of gold, about

---

[23] William Bosman, *A New and Accurate Description etc.* (Amsterdam, 1704; reprint ed., with introduction by J. R. Willis and notes by J. D. Fage and R. E. Bradbury, London: Frank Cass, 1967), p. 184.

[24] Basil Davidson, *Black Mother: The Years of the African Slave Trade* (Boston: Atlantic-Little, Brown, 1961), p. 242.

40s. in the English currency of the first half of the eighteenth century. This "sorting" was then exchanged—with a hundred percent markup for transportation, losses en route, and trading profit—for West African goods valued at 80s., or the current price of one ounce of gold. Needless to say, the prices were seldom or never exact, and the actual values of the exchange goods varied greatly. But a skilled English trader could at least hope to obtain West African exports for about half their price in England.

A fairly characteristic transaction conducted at Whydah, on the Dahomey Coast, between a British slaving captain and a local African partner—not exactly dated in the records, but deriving from the first quarter of the eighteenth century—may be used to illustrate how the trade-ounce system worked.[25] A male captive was bought for ten "trade ounces" composed as follows:

Items in Purchase Price	Trade Ounces	Cost in Cash
205 Pounds of Cowries	5	160 shillings
2 Ankers of Brandy	2	30
8 Platillas	1	32
2 Siamoises	2	34

Here the "trade ounce" was evidently reckoned, not at 40s., but at 25s. 6d.[26] The total profit eventually made on this transaction is yet another matter, and we cannot go into it here: once in the Americas, captives were auctioned into slavery at prices that differed according to time and place. Of course, buying agents on the African coast had some knowledge of likely slave prices and tried to adjust their West African deals accordingly.

---

[25] Interested readers will find this transaction conveniently quoted by Marion Johnson in "The Ounce in Eighteenth-Century West African Trade," *Journal of African History* 2 (1966): 208. It is from the memoirs of John Atkins relating to the first decades of the eighteenth century (but published much later).

With respect to the items of trade, we should perhaps note that all quantities and values involved elude easy definition. An anker of brandy was a small barrel of varying capacity which was probably equal to one-sixth of a hogshead in the mid-eighteenth century. Platillas, very popular items among rich men on the Guinea Coast, consisted of lengths of close-folded white linen fabric, originally made in Silesia. Siamoises, originally, were lengths of fine silk from Siam. They were afterwards copied to some extent by European manufacturers, who also offered cotton as a substitute. Facing stiff competition from West African high-quality cottons, European sellers scoured the world market for clothing stuffs acceptable to the highly discriminating taste of West African buyers.

[26] The shillings were of course of contemporary value. If their purchasing power—at a very rough guess—was about twenty times that of the 1970 British shilling, this would make the cost of 8 platillas in this transaction equal to rather more than $70 in present-day American currency. But far more study will be needed before we can arrive at any reliable estimates of comparative value.

After 1750 the trading situation was further complicated by a shift in African demand. The extraordinary situation then arose that would-be slave buyers were required to pay in gold, the very product for which the Western world had depended on West Africa for several centuries. In 1771 an English buying agent at Cape Coast Castle (on the western seaboard of modern Ghana) could even complain that "gold commands the trade," and "there is no buying a slave [here] without one ounce of gold at least on it"—that is, included in the buying price—"and the Windward Coast [west of modern Ghana] has been so ransacked that there is no such thing as getting gold, even though you sell your goods from 40 to 50 per cent under prime cost." A year later the same agent was again complaining that "there is no buying slaves now without you give two ounces of gold on each, to procure which you must sell your goods twenty per cent under prime cost, and may think yourself happy to get it even at that rate."[27]

It was a tangled system, clearly, but a powerful one. Standing back from the trees, one can now look at the forest with a better understanding. The trade belonged to its period, a period of crude accumulation of capital in which the ties of social interdependence, so much a part of the medieval scene, gave way and finally collapsed beneath the drive of individualist ambition. Opening the way to plantation slavery, the slave trade made possible the first great experiment of the modern world in the application of massed labor. In this sense, it was the forerunner of the factory system and the wage-paid regiments of the Industrial Revolution. In this great chain of cause and effect, the slave trade—or, as we should more accurately call it, the trade in captives—became the tribute paid by economies weak in production to economies that were stronger.

The myths have presented the trade in another light: specifically, they have depicted an inferior black humanity bondaged for its own benefit, and by an almost natural process, to a superior white one. We can dismiss the myths for what they were. The trade in captives was a social phenomenon, not a racial one. The Africans who sold Africans were a privileged minority who "joined hands with the Europeans in exploiting the African masses."[28] The partnership thus launched persisted, but as Europeans grew technologically stronger, it became ever more unequal, giving rise to and continually reinforcing the mythology of "savage Africa." In large part, the persistence of the slaving partnership despite its growing inequality can be attributed to the fact that African systems and methods of production failed to make the technological advances which gave western Europe, and then North America, their power and primacy. By any objective measure, the trade in captives was a price paid by Africa for a merely technological inferiority.

---

[27] Richard Brew, *A Treatise upon the Slave Trade* (1771–1772), in Donnan, *Documents of the Slave Trade,* 2:536.

[28] W. Rodney, "African Slavery . . . on the Upper Guinea Coast in the context of the Atlantic slave-trade," *Journal of African History* 3 (1966): 434.

This conclusion, in turn, suggests yet another measure of the loss suffered by Africa during the trade, and in part because of the trade. At a time when European and American methods and systems were going through great revolutions which enormously improved their efficacy, the trade established and helped to maintain, even in the coastal polities most directly in touch with European technology, a situation in which basic systems and methods of production did not need to change and did not change. One may perhaps add that the perpetuation of African technological inferiority explains to some extent why modern Africa must remain in deep distress until productive revolutions —which must obviously be in a profound sense social revolutions—are well under way. For technological inferiority was not eliminated with the ending of the trade. Indeed, the ending of the trade led only to colonial subjection, from which Africans are only now beginning to emerge.

Old John Barbot, writing of the Guinea Coast and the slave trade early in the 1680's, really said the last word on the nature and the implications of the commerce in captives. Having roundly explained that the trade was the business of "kings, rich men, and prime merchants," he went on to say that "some men in authority here [Benin] as well as in other countries, make no scruple of oppressing their poor fellow-subjects under one pretence or another . . . provided they can fill their pockets."[29] Just as other elites in the 1960's were to be the beneficiaries of a "neocolonial" relationship with their former governors, so these kings, rich men, and prime merchants were the beneficiaries of a "paleocolonial" contract, of a pattern of raw-material export, in the form of human beings, which enabled the ruling few to reinforce their positions and their privileges at the expense of ordinary people.

---

[29] John Barbot, *A Description of the Coasts of North and South Guinea etc.,* in J. and A. Churchill's *Collection of Voyages etc.* (London, 1732), p. 364. As is often the case with the eighteenth-century accounts, one must be alert here to discrepancies in the dates of travel and the repetitious use of other travelers' material. John Barbot (as distinct from his nephew James) was agent-general of the French Royal African Company and was, according to his own writings, on the Guinea Coast twice between 1678 and 1682. Much of his material was taken from Dutch accounts, though it is likewise possible that William Bosman, cited earlier, borrowed information from Barbot. Both Bosman and Barbot, in any case, drew heavily on the accounts of seventeenth-century Dutch travelers. Nonetheless, Barbot's description of the coastal trade is on the whole quite well informed.

The Slave Trade and
the Atlantic Basin:
Intercontinental Perspectives

PHILIP D. CURTIN

Philip Curtin is professor of history at the University of Wisconsin in Madison and is the current president of the African Studies Association. He has written *The Image of Africa: British Ideas and Action, 1780–1850* and edited *Africa Remembered: Narratives by West Africans from the Era of the Slave Trade* (University of Wisconsin Press, 1964 and 1968). The statistics presented in his most recent book, *The Atlantic Slave Trade: A Census* (University of Wisconsin Press, 1969), reflect the most comprehensive research to date on the magnitude of the Atlantic slave trade. In the essay that follows, Mr. Curtin deals with the slave trade in the historical perspective of the Atlantic basin, stressing its role as the basis of the vast economic complex that constituted the South Atlantic system. As he examines the origins, the spread, and the gradual evolution of plantation slavery, Mr. Curtin contrasts the slave plantation systems that grew up in the American tropics and Latin America with the unique institution that developed in North America.

The Atlantic slave trade was the largest intercontinental migration in world history before the nineteenth century, though the importance of this migration in the great cross-Atlantic movement that repopulated the New World from the Old is sometimes obscured by the even more massive migration of Europeans in the nineteenth and twentieth centuries. Before that time, more Africans than Europeans crossed the Atlantic each year, and their migration was important not merely for its demographic results but because it lay at the heart of a broad network of commerce and production that touched every shore of the Atlantic basin. This economic complex, sometimes called the South Atlantic system, centered on the production of tropical staples in Brazil,

Adapted by permission of Longman Group Limited from an essay written by Philip Curtin for *History of West Africa,* edited by J. F. A. Ajayi and Michael Crowder, the first volume to be published in mid-1971.

the Caribbean mainland and islands, and southern North America. The system reached to Africa for labor, to Europe for managerial staff and commercial direction, to northern North America for timber, food, and shipping, and to mainland South America for monetary silver. Though it was divided into competing national spheres, each under the rule of a separate European power, its various social patterns had much in common.

The Mediterranean Origins of the South Atlantic System

The institution of the overseas plantation, producing exotic staples for a distant metropolis and relying on slave labor, began to evolve long before the discovery of the New World. When, in the wake of the Crusades, the Italian city-states like Genoa and Venice set up trading-post empires in the eastern Mediterranean, they discovered certain exotic crops and realized the possibility of growing them for the European market. Sugar, for example, was all but unknown in Europe, though it was grown throughout the Middle East and in Muslim North Africa. Christian merchants could buy it from the Muslim growers whenever trade was open, but, given the prevalence of religious warfare during the period, Christian-controlled sources of supply were more dependable. Venetians began directing some sugar production in the conquered Levant as early as the second quarter of the twelfth century. After the Muslim reconquest of the Levant, however, Cyprus became the principal source of sugar for the European market, a position it held from early in the thirteenth century until the middle of the fourteenth.

Here, the pattern of the later South Atlantic slave plantation began to emerge, as the European rulers and European merchants on Cyprus began to use old institutions in new ways. In Europe, the peasant, whether free or bound, worked the land according to the customs of the village. The seigneur held a bundle of rights over the land and the people alike, and he received a share of the total production; but he was rarely a manager who could introduce drastic changes, even if he wanted to do so. On Cyprus, however, the mixed group of Venetians, Catalans, French, and Genoese who had seized control of the land found themselves in quite a different position. If they were to produce a specialty crop for export to Europe, they had to innovate. Cane fields had to be expanded far beyond the island's domestic needs, and the yield of cane juice had to be processed for shipment. The sugar plantations that developed in response to these needs were both agricultural and industrial. Whether the planters' origins in Europe were feudal or mercantile, they found themselves in the position of early capitalists, investing in land, industrial plant, and slaves, and managing the intimate details of production through their agents.[1]

---

[1] Charles Verlinden, "Les origines coloniales de la civilisation atlantique," *Journal of World History* 1 (1953); *Précédents médiévaux de la colonie en Amérique* (Mexico City: Instituto Panamericano de Geografía e Historia, 1954).

Initially, the labor force in Cyprus was a mixture of free men from Europe, a few local serfs, and slaves captured in the Levantine wars. But the planters soon found themselves faced with a labor shortage. Sugar production was extremely labor-intensive compared to the production of wheat, wine, and olives, the other Mediterranean staples. This meant that either the existing population had to be concentrated on a small part of the available land, or labor had to be imported from somewhere else. It might have been possible to attract voluntary migrants to Cyprus, as voluntary migrants were attracted from western to eastern Germany to open up new lands during the same period. But this solution to the problem was not tried—perhaps because the institution of slavery, which had survived from Roman times, offered a cheaper means of labor supply. In the eastern Mediterranean, in any event, the need to concentrate people for new economic enterprises, whether planting or mining, was met through the already established Mediterranean slave trade.

Slaves were regularly bought and sold and transported from one part of the Mediterranean basin to another—in both the Christian and Muslim sectors. Adherents to both religions held that it was licit to enslave prisoners of war of the rival faith, and this practice was one source of slaves. Licit or not, there were also many Christian slaves in Christian lands and Muslim slaves in Muslim countries, and the sale of slaves from one religious zone to the other was not uncommon. In addition to the sources of slaves within the Mediterranean basin itself, two external sources came to be important. The earliest of these was the series of slave markets in the ports along the northern and eastern coasts of the Black Sea. These markets were opened to Latin Christians with the fall of Byzantine Constantinople in 1204, and they continued as the leading source of slaves for the whole Mediterranean, Christian and Muslim alike, until the middle of the fourteenth century.[2]

The second major external source of slaves was sub-Saharan Africa. Part of the West African slave trade was geared toward exporting to North Africa, but much of it (probably most of it) was internal. As Mungo Park noted toward the end of the eighteenth century, the long-distance trade in slaves within West Africa had a definite economic base. The price of a prisoner of war close to his home was low; he might well try to escape. The farther he was from home, the more difficult his escape would be, and slave prices varied directly with distance from the scene of capture. Slaves were often passed from one dealer to another over a considerable period before they were finally settled into a new community—or exported by way of the Sahara or the Atlantic.[3] By early in the fourteenth century, Negro slaves began to appear in Europe—first through

---

[2] Charles Verlinden, "La colonie vénitienne de Tana, centre de la traite des esclaves au xive et au début du xve siècles," *Studi en onore di Gino Luzzatto,* 2 vols. (Milan: A. Giuffrè, 1949, 1950), 2:1–25; *L'esclavage dans l'Europe médiévale: péninsule Ibérique-France* (Bruges: Da Tampel, 1955).

[3] Mungo Park, *Travels in the Interior Districts of Africa,* 2 vols. (London: John Murray, 1816), 2:443. For representative itineraries of slaves in transit, see Philip D. Curtin,

capture in cross-Mediterranean warfare and later by purchase from North Africa. When, in 1453, Constantinople fell to the Turks, the Black Sea slave trade was cut off, and Africa became the only external source of forced labor for the Mediterranean slave plantations.

Meanwhile, the sugar plantation as an economic institution had spread far to the west of its place of origin. Plantations appeared in Crete, in Sicily, and later in southern Spain and Portugal—Valencia, Málaga, and the Algarve. The management of the enterprise was becoming equally international. Capital came mainly from the complex of early capitalist trading cities in northern Italy and southern Germany. Managers and technicians were attracted from the established plantations to direct the creation of new ones. Where they went, they took the institutions to which they were accustomed. Not merely slavery but a particular form of slavery was thus transmitted to the west. The labor force were chattels, but this was not the crucial aspect of their position. What counted far more was the fact that they worked in gangs which were minutely supervised on a day-to-day, hour-to-hour basis by the owner's representative. They thus became a rural proletariat, with minimal control over their lives and actions, kept separate from the rest of society, and with no possibility of upward mobility.

The Move into the Atlantic

By late in the fifteenth century, this form of slavery was already linked with West African sources, and the plantations of this period already resembled the American plantations that were to appear later as part of the South Atlantic system. At the same time, however, there were marked differences between these early plantations and their successors. The scale of plantation production was still small, and plantation slaves still came from a variety of sources—not yet from a single region of the world, whose people were of a distinct physical type that could serve as a badge of slave origin. Another century would pass before an example of the full-blown South Atlantic system would come into existence in Brazil—and three centuries, before the system would reach its greatest size and importance.

The key to the further development of the system was a revolution in maritime technology. Over the two centuries from 1400 to 1600 or so, Europeans developed the science of navigation in a way that changed the whole geopolitical order of human societies. Shortly after 1500, European ships were able to reach any seacoast in the world. Even more important, European society, which up to this time had been relatively insignificant in comparison with the Islamic world or with China, began to achieve the combination of sails and

Africa Remembered: Narratives by West Africans from the Era of the Slave Trade (Madison: University of Wisconsin Press, 1968), and Sigismund Wilhelm Koelle, *Polyglotta Africana* (new ed., Freetown: The University College of Sierra Leone, 1963).

Portuguese caravel with galley, fifteenth century.
Courtesy of the Bibliothèque Nationale, Paris.

guns that was to give it naval dominance over any possible challenger.[4] The economic and commercial revolution that ensued may have been still more important than the relocation of military power. All the coasts of Africa were now open to European trade by sea. The isolation of the Americas also came to an end, one long-run consequence of which was to make American crops like maize, manioc, pineapple, and cocoa available to African farmers. For the future South Atlantic system, however, the crucial change was the accumulation of maritime experience, which made the sailing ship the most effective machine man had yet devised for turning natural sources of energy into usable power. The real costs of ocean transport dropped sharply throughout the sixteenth and seventeenth centuries, as more efficient ships made possible lower crew-to-tonnage ratios. It gradually became more feasible to carry bulky cargoes (both sugar and slaves came into this category) over long distances. And this change made it economically possible both to produce sugar for European consumption at a distance of four thousand miles from the market, and to supply the centers of production with labor brought some six thousand miles by sea. In short, the maritime revolution made it possible to reproduce on a gigantic scale the earlier economic system which had allowed Europeans to import cane sugar grown on Cyprus by slave labor brought from southern Russia.

The maritime revolution affected Africa by stages. Like most technological advances, this one proceeded through the accumulation of small, discrete improvements followed by a dramatic breakthrough to a new level of efficiency. This dramatic breakthrough was achieved early in the fifteenth century by Portuguese mariners whose names are not even recorded. Their problem was navigation along the Sahara coast of Mauritania. These waters were extremely difficult for early sailing ships—not because of frequent storms and rough seas, but because the northeast trade winds blow all year round in the same direction, accompanied by a strong southward-flowing ocean current. Mariners had long been able to sail against the wind by tacking back and forth, but it was much harder to make headway against both wind and current. Medieval Mediterranean ships, both Christian and Muslim, were perfectly capable of sailing south along the Sahara coast. The problem was to get back to the north of the desert.

The solution to this problem came partly as a result of the gradual improvement of the sailing ship, culminating in a type that could sail much closer to the wind than earlier vessels. By the beginning of the fifteenth century, such ships were available, with modified hulls and riggings based on sailors' experience of the Mediterranean, the Indian Ocean, and the Atlantic coasts of Europe. This development made possible a series of experimental Portuguese voyages down the coast toward Senegal. The Portuguese mariners apparently learned some-

---

[4] See Carlo M. Cipolla, *Guns, Sails, and Empires: Technological Innovation and the Early Phases of European Expansion, 1400–1700* (New York: Pantheon, 1966).

time early in the fifteenth century that they could return northward if they took advantage of a small diurnal alternation of wind direction, a slight shifting of the wind onshore during daylight and offshore at night.[5] But, even after this discovery, the coastal route northward from Senegal was too time-consuming and difficult for use as a regular trade route. The real breakthrough came with the subsequent discovery that if a ship sailed northwest from the vicinity of Dakar, keeping as close as possible into the northeast trade winds on a long tack, it would finally come to a part of the ocean, near the Azores, where winds blow from all points of the compass but mainly from the west. From there it was an easy trip back to Portugal, Spain, Morocco, or the Straits of Gibraltar. Indeed, it would be hard to overestimate the importance of this discovery, which was the necessary step to the better-publicized achievements of Columbus, Da Gama, and their successors.

This discovery also lay behind the next stages in the formation of the South Atlantic system—first, the movement of Mediterranean plantation agriculture westward into the Atlantic basin, and then the establishment of a direct link between the plantation system and West Africa by way of the maritime slave trade. The westward movement of sugar planting began even before the discovery of America. In 1449, an improved sugar press was invented in Sicily, and its use soon spread to the Atlantic islands. With the new Sicilian techniques (and often with Sicilian technicians), with Genoese capital and Portuguese maritime expertise, Madeira and then the Canary Islands began shipping sugar to Europe.[6] During exactly the same period, Portuguese ships were developing their trade with West Africa. By the 1450's they had made direct contact with the West African slave trade, buying slaves along the coast from Arguin Island southward to the Senegal and Gambia rivers and shipping them back to Europe by sea. The numbers purchased in this way were still small, only a few hundred each year, and African labor was not yet the dominant group on the plantations; but the maritime slave trade had begun.

Further steps followed in short order. In the decades immediately after 1500, Portuguese capitalists began planting sugar on the island of São Tomé in the Gulf of Guinea, using the cheap slave labor available on the nearby African coast to counterbalance the long sea route from São Tomé to the European markets. Here, for the first time, there developed a plantation system that depended solely on imported African labor.

After America was discovered, sugar planting was tried there as well. The Spanish on Hispaniola brought cane and technicians from the Canaries, and a little sugar was exported as early as 1522; then, in the second quarter of the

[5] Raymond Mauny, *Les navigations médiévales sur les côtes sahariennes antérieurs à la découverte portugaise* (Lisbon: Centre de Estudes Historicos Ultramarinos, 1960). For naval architecture, see John H. Parry, *The Age of Reconnaissance* (London: Weidenfeld and Nicolson, 1963), pp. 53–68.

[6] Verlinden, *Prècèdents médiévaux,* pp. 49–55.

sixteenth century, planting spread to Puerto Rico, Jamaica, and coastal Mexico. But none of these Caribbean experiments was an unequivocal success. The crucial problem was labor. The local Indians could be enslaved, but they died out on contact with unfamiliar European and African diseases. The Atlantic islands still dominated the European plantation system, in spite of a trickle of slaves exported from Africa to the Caribbean islands. Sugar exports from Hispaniola as late as 1560 were less than half those of São Tomé.[7]

The first outstanding boom for slave plantations in the New World came in Brazil. After a half-century of experimenting with other forms of enterprise, the Portuguese found that sugar grew well on the coastal plains of northeastern Brazil. They solved the labor problem by a combined program of raiding far and wide for native Indians and importing African slaves—a possibility more open to them than it was to the Spanish, since Portugal dominated the trade of coastal Africa until the end of the sixteenth century. By 1580, the Portuguese settlements in Brazil had already reached a population of about 57,000. Of this number, about 44 percent were European, 32 percent Indian, and 29 percent African—and the African population was steadily increasing.

By the beginning of the seventeenth century, the pattern of the South Atlantic system was established. Large sugar plantations, much larger than their Mediterranean forerunners, surrounded the principal port towns in northeastern Brazil. Their owners formed the dominant class in colonial society. Not only were they de facto rulers of their own domains, but their wealth made it possible for them to control the municipalities, which theoretically ruled the countryside as well as urban areas. The plantation as an economic unit was very different from the nearly self-sufficient manor of medieval Europe, or from the African village. Its reason for existence was a market for sugar (and later for indigo, tobacco, cotton, or coffee) many thousands of miles away. The American plantation was, in fact, an intensely specialized offshoot of the metropolitan economy. Never before in world history had agricultural enterprises on such a large scale depended so heavily on an export market. In addition the planters relied on the metropolitan power of Europe—for the defense of the trading posts in Africa, for protection of the sea lanes, and for the whole range of skills and services that could be found only in the much more diversified setting of the European cities. Plantation society in tropical America has sometimes been characterized as patriarchal, a kind of neofeudalism grown up in a new country. This may be so, to a degree, but only within the social setting of the plantation itself. The specialized production and dependence on other distant specialized suppliers through a broad commercial system was distinctively "modern" and market-oriented.

This fact explains in part why plantation slavery was so different from

---

[7] Mervyn Ratekin, "The Early Sugar Industry in Española," *Hispanic American Historical Review* 34 (1954): 1–19. For the general history of sugar planting, see Noel Deerr, *The History of Sugar,* 2 vols. (London: Chapman and Hall, 1949, 1950).

African slavery or from the slavery of the ancient Mediterranean. Here the individual slave was purchased as a labor unit and treated as a labor unit. There was little or no room for individual decision, individual initiative, or even the play of individual personality. As long as he remained a field slave on a plantation, he was merely part of the apparatus of a dehumanized economic enterprise. This is not to say, of course, that there was no escape from field work. Even within the slave caste, differentiation of status and the possibility of certain rewards existed on every plantation. Some slaves served the household of the master or his subordinate officials. Others held positions of trust and leadership over the other slaves. Still others did skilled work or were allowed to take up occupations off the plantation in return for the periodic remission of part of their earnings. These were the exceptions, however, and field work on the plantation was the norm.

The Spread to the Caribbean

Once the slave plantation was established in Brazil and its economic advantages were recognized, the system began spreading to other suitable regions in tropical America. In the process the details were changed, but the essential nature of the plantation was preserved, and, in fact, many of its features were copied directly from Brazil. The first agents of this further diffusion were the Dutch, who, by early in the seventeenth century, had displaced the Portuguese as the most efficient Europeans trading at sea and had begun to move into the African trade. Between 1630 and 1654, the Dutch West India Company seized control of a part of northeastern Brazil, where they learned how the existing plantation order operated. Then, bolstered by their superiority at sea and their understanding of the South Atlantic system, they sailed to the Caribbean islands that were already occupied by France and England and offered, in effect, a package including technical assistance in setting up sugar estates, a supply of slaves from Africa, and carrying services in taking the sugar produced to market.

Dutch assistance of this kind was contrary to the spirit of mercantilist commercial policy (and often contrary to the letter of French and English commercial law), but it was profitable. Up to this point, the Lesser Antilles—Barbados, Martinique, Guadeloupe, St. Kitts, and Antigua, in particular—had been settled by Europeans whose small farms produced tobacco and a few other crops suited to small-scale enterprise. Over the few decades from 1640 through 1660, these islands were transformed into sugar colonies: white settlers gave way to African slaves; small farms gave way to large plantations; tobacco gave way to sugar. Once the "sugar revolution" was accomplished in the Lesser Antilles, it spread westward. Jamaica and the French part of Hispaniola (the colony of Saint Domingue, or present-day Haiti) were acquired by England and France respectively before 1700. Within half a century they were the most prosperous of all the sugar islands. Thus, while Brazilian sugar production stabilized at a level near that achieved early in the seventeenth century, the system was able to meet the growing demand for sugar in Europe by expanding into new territory.

In the eighteenth century, the system continued to expand, becoming more and more diverse. Slave plantations, often built on West Indian models, were set up beyond the fringes of the Caribbean, which had by this time become the heartland of the system. Virginia with tobacco, South Carolina with rice and indigo, and, from the end of the eighteenth century, the whole of southern North America east of the Mississippi with cotton entered the system as centers of production. In North America, however, the slave plantations remained intermixed with the small farms of white settlers, most of whom owned no slaves but worked their own lands. Thus, the southern states of North America were only partially integrated into the South Atlantic system, and the northern states never entered it.

Disease and Migration

At the risk of oversimplification, it might be said that three distinct kinds of societies developed in the Americas from the seventeenth century through the nineteenth. One type was apparent in highland Peru and Mexico, where the Indians survived better than they had in the lowlands, and where relatively small cadres of Spanish officials, miners, ranchers, and planters ran a society that was predominantly Indian. A second was typical of northern North America, where the Indians were few to begin with, and where the European settlers created a new society on the model of the Old World they had left behind. Finally, there was the South Atlantic type of development, most fully exemplified by Jamaica, Barbados, and Saint Domingue during the eighteenth century, where virtually all manual work was done by slaves from Africa, and where white settlers and Indians were equally few in number.

As of 1650, Negroes outnumbered Europeans in the Americas as a whole.[8] Though the Negro population was most heavily concentrated in the societies of the South Atlantic type, both slaves and free men of African descent were to be found throughout the Americas. The very existence of large numbers of slaves in the American tropics made them available for further sale into the settler portion of society or into the true empire of Spanish America. Many Negroes were bought for use as domestic servants in northern North America. And even greater numbers were bought to labor in the silver mines of Bolivia and Mexico or the gold and diamond mines of eighteenth-century Brazil.

Just as Negroes filtered from the South Atlantic system into the other two sectors of American society, both European and Indian laborers were drawn into the South Atlantic system, at least in the early centuries. On the first Bra-

---

[8] Angel Rosenblat, *La población indígena y el mestizaje en América,* 2 vols. (Buenos Aires: Nova, 1954), 1:59.

zilian plantations, Indian slavery was important. Both England and France tried in the seventeenth century to colonize the Lesser Antilles with white settlers; but the tropical lands had a reputation for bad health conditions, and settlers without capital preferred North America. It was possible, however, to attract some settlers by authorizing shipowners to advance passage money to would-be emigrants, in return for which they signed an indenture, or labor contract, for a period of years. Once they reached America, the indenture could be sold to an employer of labor in much the same way a slave from Africa was sold to a planter. Condemned criminals were also sentenced to transportation overseas, and their labor could be purchased by planters as still another alternative to Negro slavery. For France, the official policy from 1626 until at least the 1680's was to depend on the importation of white bondsmen to populate the Antilles, and the last shipment of European laborers took place in 1763.[9] The English began their settlement of Barbados in much the same way. Indeed, as late as 1643, the working population of this island was estimated at 18,600 Europeans as compared with only 6,400 Africans.[10] Yet in each of these cases, the non-African workers were eventually replaced by Africans, and in later decades the planters throughout tropical America expressed a preference for African labor—a preference that led finally to the dominance of Negro slavery in all economic development of the South Atlantic type.[11]

At the time, the planters explained the superiority of African labor to European labor by saying that Africans could work in hot climates, whereas Europeans could not. This belief became, in time, one of the cornerstones of pseudoscientific racism. Scientists now recognize that physical type has little or nothing to do with tolerance to hot weather. (For that matter, the climate in the West Indies is not as hot as that of Ohio or Illinois in the summer.) But the planters were correct in their judgment, however wrong the reasoning behind it. The key factor in the Africans' superior ability to adapt to life in tropical America was an epidemiological one.

Students of the spread and incidence of disease now recognize that a host population will, during childhood, acquire immunity to severe attacks of the diseases endemic to their own part of the world. They also point out that disease environments differ from one region to another, since germs and viruses evolve with great rapidity, producing new diseases and new strains of diseases. In the pre-Columbian Atlantic world, disease environments were more isolated,

---

[9] Louis Vignols, "L'institution des engagés, 1624–1774," *Revue d'histoire économique et sociale* 1 (1928): 12–45; "Une question mal posée: le travail manuel des blancs et des esclaves aux Antilles," *Revue historique* (1935): 308–16. Gaston Martin, *Histoire de l'esclavage dans les colonies françaises* (Paris: Presses universitaires de France, 1948), pp. 11–24.

[10] Alan Burns, *History of the British West Indies* (London: George Allen and Unwin, 1954), p. 302.

[11] See Eric Williams, *Capitalism and Slavery* (Chapel Hill: University of North Carolina Press, 1944), pp. 9–23.

and hence far more distinct, than they are today. West Africa and Europe shared many of the diseases common to the whole Afro-Eurasian land mass, but some African diseases, such as yellow fever, were limited to the tropics. Thus there was a wider range of disease in Africa than in Europe. The Americas had been cut off for millennia from effective contact with the Old World, hence the range of disease known there was still narrower. Men who had grown up in any of these environments were protected to some extent against local diseases but were extremely vulnerable to patterns of disease away from home; and the whole of the Americas was vulnerable to a great variety of African and European diseases.[12]

With the maritime revolution, both people and diseases crossed the Atlantic. The combined force of the diseases from two alien continents wiped out most of the lowland population of the American tropics within a century. This development was of fundamental significance to the future transatlantic slave trade, since it created an immediate need for new population if there was to be any further European enterprise at all in the New World.[13] There was hardly any question of European resettlement on the African continent during this period, for Africa was deadly to outsiders. Nineteenth-century statistics (from a period before the development of modern medicine) suggest that newcomers to Africa from Europe died regularly at the rate of 400 to 600 per 1,000 during their first year of residence in the "white man's grave."[14] Likewise, Europeans died at an alarming rate in the West Indies from the malaria and yellow fever of African origin, often at ten times the normal death rate for people of the same age group in Europe—hardly more than 11 or 12 per 1,000. Africans newly arrived in tropical America also faced great peril and died at something like twice the normal African death rate; but they had the enormous advantage of coming from a disease environment where they had built up some immunity to both the tropical diseases and the common Afro-Eurasian diseases. The statistics now available suggest that their death rate was about a third as high as that of European newcomers to the Americas.[15]

The Economics of the Slave Trade

Under these circumstances, it is hardly surprising that the planters preferred workers from Africa. Whether they purchased the indenture of a European bondsman, bought the labor of a European criminal condemned to

---

[12] Philip D. Curtin, "Epidemiology and the Slave Trade," *Political Science Quarterly* 83 (1968): 190–216.

[13] Percy Moreau Ashburn, *The Ranks of Death: A Medical History of the Conquest of America* (New York: Coward-McCann, 1947).

[14] Philip D. Curtin, *The Image of Africa: British Ideas and Action, 1780–1850* (Madison: University of Wisconsin Press, 1964), pp. 483–87.

[15] Curtin, "Epidemiology and the Slave Trade."

transportation, or bought a slave from Africa, they were laying out capital in return for a claim to later labor. If the European workers died out three times as rapidly as their African counterparts, the choice was clear. An American-born worker would, of course, be accustomed to the disease environment from childhood, and the price of creole (that is, American-born) slaves was always markedly higher than that of new migrants from Africa. Creole slaves, however, were always in short supply, and prices on the American slave markets appear to have been determined mainly by the cost of bringing new recruits from Africa.

If the prices of African-born slaves had not been competitive with those of labor from other sources—native born or European—the slave trade could never have come into existence, no matter what the epidemiological consequences of movement across the Atlantic. The cost conditions of the slave trade itself were therefore equally basic to the development of the South Atlantic system.

The operations of the slave trade can be divided into three functionally and institutionally distinct segments. First, the slave had to be captured in Africa—a process equivalent to the production of some other commodity destined for use as an article of commerce. In the earliest phases of the trade, Europeans occasionally went themselves to capture people in Africa, but they soon learned that Africa was far too dangerous to their own health. Enslavement came to be a function performed by Africans alone; and, since second-generation slaves in Africa were rarely sold, the stream of people fed into the transatlantic slave trade at its point of origin were mainly captives.[16] Some were certainly captured in warfare begun for other reasons—not simply in order to acquire slaves for sale. In this case their enslavement was a by-product of a particular military action, which would have taken place in any case. In economic terms, the production costs of such by-product prisoners of war were negligible from the point of view of their captor. He could sell them at a low price and still consider that he had made a profit on the transaction. A raid mounted for the sole purpose of capturing slaves, on the other hand, was an "economic" operation requiring the allocation of scarce resources. Leaders and other voluntary participants in the raid could measure the probable yield against the danger and expense to themselves. In this case, the slave's value

---

[16] See P. E. H. Hair, "The Enslavement of Koelle's Informants," *Journal of African History* 6 (1965): 193–203. Hair shows that 34 percent of 179 individuals interrogated were captured in war and 30 percent were kidnapped, but these figures are skewed by the fact that Koelle was a linguist working in Sierra Leone in the 1850's. He chose his informants so as to represent as many different languages as possible, which would produce a sample in which individual cases of enslavement were overrepresented and mass enslavement through warfare was underrepresented. Still, the sample can be taken to indicate that *at least* two-thirds of the Africans sold into slavery were violently seized—were not people who had already been slaves in Africa, or who were sold to acquit debts or enslaved as punishment for crimes committed.

to his captor or his anticipated sale price could be expected to determine the supply of slaves delivered to the trade. Little is known about the prices of slaves within Africa, but available evidence indicates that the captors received only a small part of what would ultimately be paid for a slave once he arrived in the New World.

A larger part of the final selling price went to those who performed a second function—the transportation of captives to a coastal trading point and the accumulation of enough slaves to create an attractive market for European slave ships. The institutions for transporting captives and bulking slaves for shipment varied extremely from region to region in Africa. Only rarely were slaves purchased directly from the captor and sold to the European slaver by a single African merchant. More often they passed through several hands, as individuals or in small lots, until they were finally gathered in large groups for sale on the coast. Where a long-distance slave trade existed, as it did in the eighteenth century between the Upper Niger and the coast of present-day Guinea-Conakry or the navigable Senegal and Gambia rivers, the merchants who conducted the slaves from the interior were also involved with other commodities, such as kola nuts, salt, and textiles of both European and African origin. Almost everywhere, the state was likely to be involved—but the type and degree of involvement varied greatly. In any event, part of the ultimate selling price went to transportation costs, part to profits for the African slave merchants, and part to taxes and duties required by the African rulers.

The third and final operation of the slave trade was the shipment of the slaves by sea to the Americas. The European shipowners who managed this part of the trade normally received at least half the final sale price, which meant that theirs was the largest of the three shares. This sum, however, had to cover the cost of trade goods in Europe, the transportation of these goods to Africa, and the transportation of the slaves from Africa to America. This could be an extremely profitable trade for an individual merchant, but the risks involved were also great, and the trade was intensely competitive.

Whatever the profits to individual merchants, the trade was conducted at heavy cost to European society. At least half of all personnel sent to the African coast must have died of disease. The crews of the slave ships also had a high death toll. In a sample of 598 ships sailing from Nantes, France, to Africa between 1748 and 1792, the average crew losses were 169 per 1,000 per voyage. This compares unfavorably with the mortality rate of the slaves themselves, despite the notoriously bad conditions aboard the slavers. A similar sample of 465 slavers leaving from Nantes during the same period shows a slave mortality per voyage of only 152 per 1,000. Furthermore, the mortality rate for the slaves dropped by more than half during the period of the survey, while that of the crews remained relatively constant.[17]

---

[17] See Philip D. Curtin, *The Atlantic Slave Trade: A Census* (Madison: University of Wisconsin Press, 1969), pp. 275–86.

In spite of the number of people sharing the profits from the slave trade, in economic terms the real cost of a slave delivered in the New World was extremely low. In 1695, when the South Atlantic system was fully established in the Caribbean, a slave could be bought in Jamaica for £20 currency— roughly the value of 600 pounds of muscavado sugar sold on the London market, or the cost in Europe of 16 guns for exchange in Africa.[18] This was a low price in the islands, because a prime slave could be expected to add more than 600 pounds to the sugar production of an estate in the first year. It was also low in comparison with alternative labor prices. In the 1680's, a criminal condemned to labor in the colonies sold for from £10 to £15, and in addition the buyer had to pay for his transportation to America and assume the risk of his escape or death from disease before he even arrived on the plantation.[19]

These prices, however, are representative only of the year 1695 and of the British segment of the South Atlantic system. Prices elsewhere could be very different, reflecting the price of slaves in Africa, which fluctuated greatly from one area to another in response to conditions of supply and demand. But the trend in the system as a whole was toward rising prices. The prime cost of the goods required in exchange for one able-bodied slave in Africa rose from about £3 or £4 at the beginning of the seventeenth century to more than £20 at the end of the eighteenth.[20] This price rise represents more than merely a decrease in the value of the pound sterling. In barter terms-of-trade, the Europeans were forced over time to put down more and more goods for each slave they exported from the African coast.

Nevertheless, in 1695, 8 trade guns or 600 pounds of iron in bars represented the coastal African price of a slave. From present-day perspective, it may seem curious that an African society could capture a man and deliver him to the coast so cheaply. Too little is known about the African economies of this period to explain this phenomenon fully, but part of the answer seems clear. Europe was already progressing toward the enormous technological advances of the Industrial Revolution, while African technology was relatively backward. Many African societies could produce high-quality iron, but they could not produce it (or any other kind of iron) in large quantities without very high labor costs in gathering wood, manufacturing charcoal, mining iron ore, and building the high clay furnaces that were common at the time. Naturally, the value of iron in Africa, whether imported or not, was determined by the African production costs—not by the much lower cost in time and materials to manufacture the same iron in Europe. Measured in the light of African metal

---

[18] Kenneth G. Davies, *The Royal African Company* (London: Longmans, 1957), pp. 356, 364.

[19] Richard Pares, *A West-India Fortune* (London: Longmans, 1950), p. 9.

[20] *Report of the Lords of the Committee of Council for . . . Trade and Plantations . . . Concerning the Present State of Trade to Africa, and Particularly the Trade in Slaves . . .* (London, 1789), Part 2 (hereafter cited as *Board of Trade Report*).

technology, even 300 pounds of iron in bars, delivered to the interior and ready for use in manufacturing hoe blades or spear points, may well have been a profitable exchange for a newly captured, unskilled slave. Similar technological differences in the production of firearms and textiles and in the distilling process would tend in the same way to create a comparative advantage for the Africans as well as the Europeans who participated in the slave trade.

Firearms, however, were something of a special case. Unlike textiles and iron, which were produced in Africa as well as in Europe, firearms were a European innovation—and one that could bestow power on any African society that managed to acquire them before its neighbors did. A change in the power relations among the African states could have far greater consequences than an influx of cheap, European-made iron or a new supply of luxury goods. It is possible, in fact, that the availability of firearms set off a gun-slave cycle in which an African state used the arms to capture more slaves, to buy more arms, and so on—forcing African states to take up slave raiding in self-protection, since guns could only be bought with slaves. The importance of the gun-slave cycle, however, is still a matter of controversy among historians. It may not have counted for much before the nineteenth century. The long reloading time of earlier trade muskets made them less than universally dominant, against either the cavalry of the savanna or the bowmen, skilled with poisoned arrows, of the forest.

The Demography of Slavery

In any event, the very cheapness of slaves set up economic and demographic patterns that turned the slave trade into a permanent feature of the South Atlantic system rather than merely a brief migration for a century or so until the American tropics had been repopulated. The crux of the matter was a negative rate of natural population growth in tropical America. This came about for a variety of reasons. Initially, epidemiological factors dictated that migration was costly in human life, but this should have been a short-run influence, since creole slaves of African descent would have developed immunities to the American disease environment. The more persistent cause of the low rate of natural growth was a very low birth rate in the American tropics, and this was tied directly to the low real cost of slaves in Africa. Planters wanted more men than women on their estates, calculating that it was cheaper to buy young African men of working age than it was to import African women, who would sit idle raising families.

The slavers responded to demand conditions, normally importing two men for each woman. Since birth rate depends directly on the number of women of child-bearing age, this meant an automatic reduction of 30 percent in the potential birth rate for each group of migrants from Africa. In addition, the planters regarded female slaves as labor units and did little to encourage either a high birth rate or a low rate of infant mortality. When slave women found themselves in a situation where stable family life was impossible, where the demands of field work were constant, and where the rearing of children was difficult (if not actually discouraged), they simply had fewer children (they knew about both abortives and contraceptive techniques). The result was a low birth rate, not merely in terms of total population but also in terms of female population. Slave populations in tropical America, thus, normally experienced a net natural decrease as a result of very low fertility rates.[21] The rate of this decrease sometimes ran as high as 50 per 1,000 per annum, and 20 per 1,000 appears to have been common in the Caribbean.[22]

The failure to create a slave society with a self-sustaining population made the slave trade necessary, not merely for the expansion of the plantation regime but simply to maintain the existing slave populations of the plantations. Thus, the cheapness of African manpower led the South Atlantic system into a pattern of consuming manpower as other industries might consume raw materials. Estimates for the French colony of Saint Domingue indicate that a total of about 860,000 slaves were imported between 1680 and 1791, but its Negro population in 1791 was only about 480,000. For Jamaica, the net immigration from Africa was about 750,000 during the whole period of the slave trade, yet the Negro population upon emancipation in 1834 was only about 350,000.[23]

The planters recognized that their enterprise consumed manpower, and they also understood the link between this pattern and the low price of slaves on the African coast. As slave prices in Africa rose toward the end of the eighteenth century, some planters responded by seeking a better balance of the sexes as a way of producing a self-sustaining slave population. One study of the island of Nevis shows that such a policy was successfully put into practice as early as 1775.[24] The point at which this policy began to work to the planters' economic advantage, however, must have differed considerably from one colony to another. It appears to have been reached in Jamaica in about 1788, for example, when an able-bodied slave straight from Africa sold for £62 to £65 and a creole slave sold for £80 to £100 — roughly the cost of rearing a slave up to the age of fourteen, when he could first be used for field labor.[25] But the change to a self-sustaining population took time. Even in Jamaica, where slave imports were cut off by imperial legislation in 1808, the population did not begin to achieve a natural increase until the 1840's. On other islands, like Cuba, where the plantation system was still expanding, a high demand for

---

[21] George W. Roberts, *The Population of Jamaica* (Cambridge, Eng.: At the University Press, 1957), pp. 219–34.

[22] Roberts, *Population of Jamaica,* p. 37. Martin, *Histoire de l'esclavage,* p. 125. Elsa V. Goveia, *Slave Society in the British Leeward Islands at the End of the Eighteenth Century* (New Haven, Conn.: Yale University Press, 1965), p. 234.

[23] Curtin, *Atlantic Slave Trade,* pp. 71, 78–79.

[24] Pares, *West-India Fortune,* pp. 123–25.

[25] *Board of Trade Report,* Part 2. Roberts, *Population of Jamaica,* p. 241.

slaves from Africa and a high rate of natural decrease continued on into the nineteenth century.[26]

The Timing and Flow of the Slave Trade

These demographic peculiarities of tropical slave societies had important consequences for the timing and flow of the slave trade. Rather than rising to a peak and then declining as the American territories' need for new population was met, there was a steady increase in the number of slaves transported from Africa from the fifteenth century until the 1780's, after which the Atlantic slave trade began to decline and then, after the 1860's, died away. But the trade did not draw continuously from the same parts of West Africa, nor did it deliver slaves continuously to the same parts of the New World. Instead, the stream of migrants across the Atlantic was supplied by a series of different tributaries leading from the coast of Africa, and it branched out into a number of different parts on the American side of the ocean.

In all, between eight and eleven million Africans were delivered to the Americas.[27] Since they were brought for sale to the European colonists, their destinations in the Americas varied according to the patterns of European activity and economic development. In the first half of the sixteenth century, even before the South Atlantic system had begun to emerge, Africans accompanied the Spanish in the conquest of the great Indian civilizations. As a result, in the 1570's, when Europeans still outnumbered Africans in Brazil, Africans outnumbered Europeans in both Mexico and coastal Peru.[28] With the seventeenth-century expansion of tropical agriculture, the main flow of slaves was to Brazil. Then, in the eighteenth century, the Caribbean became the principal destination for slaves, with a trickle flowing on to North America. Finally, in the nineteenth century, after the slave trade to English- and French-speaking territories had been largely cut off, Brazil and Cuba were the only rapidly growing plantation economies that remained; hence they became the principal destinations of the trade.

Certain patterns at the origin of the slave trade—at least along the African coast—can also be traced. Whereas economic conditions in the Americas or patterns of war and peace between European powers on the Atlantic caused fluctuations in the total demand for slaves, the supply varied directly with economic and political conditions in Africa. As a matter of course, the Euro-

---

[26] Ramiro Guerra y Sanchez, ed., *Historia de la nación cubana,* 10 vols. (Havana, 1952), 4:167–81.

[27] The paragraphs that follow are based on carefully calculated estimates, the details of which are explained in Philip D. Curtin, *The Atlantic Slave Trade: A Census.*

[28] James Lockhart, *Spanish Peru, 1532–1560: A Colonial Society* (Madison: University of Wisconsin Press, 1968), p. 180. David M. Davidson, "Negro Slave Control and Resistance in Colonial Mexico," *Hispanic American Historical Review* 46 (1966): 235–53.

pean slavers directed their ships to whatever part of the coast promised to be the most secure source of slaves at the lowest prices, and no single region in Africa was a leading exporter of slaves over a long period. The slave traders tended always to be drawn to regions where political instability or the rise and fall of African states were accompanied by widespread warfare and could thus be expected to yield large supplies of slaves for sale.

The changing patterns at the origin of the slave trade in Africa explain in part why different regions of the New World were populated with different ethnic mixtures of African peoples. A country that received a large share of its slave imports late in the eighteenth century was likely to receive a high proportion of Africans from the Niger Delta and from Angola, simply because these were the major exporting areas of the time. But a country that received the largest part of its imports early in the eighteenth century might well find its slave population heavily weighted with Africans from Liberia, the Ivory Coast, and the Gold Coast. In addition, planters in various parts of the Americas developed ethnic prejudices in favor of particular African peoples. South Carolinians preferred Senegambians and Bambara from the interior of West Africa. Jamaican planters favored the Akan peoples from present-day Ghana, while the planters of Barbados disliked the Akan and preferred Africans of almost any other origin.

The United States as an Exception

Considering the Atlantic slave trade in the historical perspective of the entire Atlantic basin, it is clear that the United States formed a marked exception to the patterns of the South Atlantic system as a whole. Not merely did the North American slaves find themselves in a society where large numbers of nonslaveholding white settlers were also present, but the basic demographic pattern of the South Atlantic system was reversed in North America. Rather than showing more deaths than births, the North American slave population began to grow naturally—even in the southern states, where it was heavily concentrated—at a very early date, perhaps as early as the late seventeenth century. This meant that in the long run relatively few slave imports were required to produce a large slave population. A total immigration from Africa of only about 430,000 slaves produced a slave population of about four and a half million by 1863, the year of emancipation. In short, with less than about 5 percent of the total immigration from Africa, the United States came to have one of the largest Afro-American populations in the present-day Americas.

The striking difference between slavery in the United States and in the tropical Americas has been apparent to historical demographers for almost a century and a half, but historians of the United States are only now beginning to pay serious attention to the comparative study of New World slavery. The full implications of North America's unique place in the South Atlantic system therefore remain to be understood, but some of them are already clear. The African cultural heritage is somewhat weaker and more diffuse in North America than it is elsewhere on the continent. The peak in the importation of slaves to North America was reached during the two decades on either side of 1750. This means that the African population in this country arrived, on the whole, much earlier than did the majority of settlers from Europe. Afro-Americans have therefore had many generations in which to assimilate general American culture, and the African culture they brought with them has been diffused very widely throughout the population, both black and white, of the Southern states. In this sense, the African heritage has become the heritage of all North Americans, and the special place of the Afro-American community in the history of this country, stemming from the conditions of slavery and its aftermath, is of crucial importance to an understanding of United States society at large.

2 SUGGESTIONS FOR FURTHER READING

Bovill, E. W., *The Golden Trade of the Moors.* New York: Oxford University Press, 1958. ▪ A pioneering historical study of the trans-Saharan trade.

Cipolla, Carlo M., *Guns, Sails and Empires: Technological Innovation and the Early Phases of European Expansion, 1400–1700*.* New York: Pantheon, 1966. ▪ A detailed treatment of the technology that led directly to the development of the transatlantic slave trade.

Curtin, Philip D., ed., *Africa Remembered: Narratives by West Africans from the Era of the Slave Trade*.* Madison: University of Wisconsin Press, 1968. ▪ A collection of documents presenting recollections of Africa and of the slave trade.

————, *The Atlantic Slave Trade: A Census.* Madison: University of Wisconsin Press, 1969. ▪ A skilled and comprehensive inquiry into the number of persons directly affected by the Atlantic slave trade, and a volume that should open a new chapter in the exact study of the trade.

Davidson, Basil, ed., *The African Past: Chronicles from Antiquity to Modern Times*.* Boston: Atlantic-Little, Brown, 1964. ▪ An imaginative selection of documents.

————, *Black Mother: The Years of the African Slave Trade.* Boston: Atlantic-Little, Brown, 1961. In paperback under the title *The African Slave Trade: Pre-Colonial History, 1450–1850*.* ▪ A broad, general examination of the consequences of the Atlantic slave trade for the African societies engaged in it and victimized by it.

————, *A History of West Africa to the Nineteenth Century*.* London: Longmans, 1965; revised ed., New York: Anchor Books, 1966. ▪ A study of the area most deeply involved in the slave trade.

---

*Available in paperback edition

————, *The Lost Cities of Africa**. Boston: Atlantic-Little, Brown, 1959. ▪ A study of African civilization in the Middle Ages.

Davies, Kenneth G., *The Royal African Company.* London: Longmans, 1957. ▪ One phase of mercantilism seen in relation to a company created by the British king primarily for the purpose of dealing in slaves.

Donnan, Elizabeth, ed., *Documents Illustrative of the History of the Slave Trade to America,* 4 vols. Washington, D.C.: Carnegie Institution, 1930–1935. ▪ An invaluable sourcebook for records and memoirs of the Atlantic slave trade, and a collection that has put all students of Africa in profound debt to the editor.

Du Bois, W. E. B., *The Suppression of the African Slave Trade to the United States of America, 1638–1870**. New York: Schocken Books, 1969. Originally published in 1896. ▪ Du Bois' classic study of efforts to put an end to the Atlantic slave trade.

Hair, P. E. H., "The Enslavement of Koelle's Informants," *Journal of African History* 6 (1965): 193–203. ▪ An analysis of the demographic attributes and the mode of enslavement of the informants for Reverend Sigismund Wilhelm Koelle's *Polyglotta Africana* (new ed., Freetown: The University College of Sierra Leone, 1963), a unique nineteenth-century historical document.

Mannix, Daniel P., and Cowley, Malcolm, *Black Cargoes: A History of the Atlantic Slave Trade, 1518–1865** New York: Viking Press, 1962. ▪ An excellent secondary account of the slave trade.

Oliver, Roland, and Oliver, Caroline, eds., *Africa in the Days of Exploration**. Englewood Cliffs, N.J.: Prentice-Hall, 1965. ▪ A good collection of documents pertaining to Africa at the time of the trade.

Williams, Eric, *Capitalism and Slavery**. Chapel Hill: University of North Carolina Press, 1944. ▪ A classic of modern study and a book of key importance to understanding the economic significance of the slave trade in the development of Western industrialism and to evaluating the economic reasons for abolition.

Readers who wish to read further on the history of Africa and the trade should also look at all relevant articles in the *Journal of African History.*

3

Slavery

Patterns of Settlement of the Afro-American Population in the New World

HERBERT S. KLEIN

Herbert S. Klein, professor of Latin American history at Columbia University, is the author of *Slavery in the Americas: A Comparative Study of Cuba and Virginia* (University of Chicago Press, 1967) and *Parties and Political Change in Bolivia, 1880–1952* (Cambridge University Press, 1969). He has published many articles on Latin American history, and he is now working on a study of the South Atlantic slave trade and the settlement of Africans in Brazil in the eighteenth and nineteenth centuries. In the following essay, Mr. Klein presents a demographic analysis of the African migration to the Western Hemisphere, showing how patterns of settlement were affected by changes in the nature and the extent of New World slavery.

The Development of the Slave Labor Market

The forced migration of the peoples of sub-Saharan Africa to the New World was the direct outgrowth of a seemingly inexhaustible demand for labor on the part of the European colonizing powers. Though the Western Hemisphere contained between eighty and one hundred million Indians at the time of its discovery, this population was incapable of surviving both the initial conquest and the introduction to the continent of a whole new range of European diseases. By the end of the first century of European colonization, no more than ten million Indians were left in the New World.[1] This demographic decimation seems merely to have intensified the demand for labor in the Americas, for the production of precious metals was constantly on the increase during this period of population decline. At the same time, new colonizing empires were moving into areas so far uninhabited by the Spanish and Portuguese pioneers.

Though this movement into previously unsettled areas of the New World attracted many European settlers, they did not come in sufficient numbers to guarantee mineral and commercial-agricultural production. To the 140,000 or so Portuguese and Spanish who inhabited the hemisphere by the last third

---

[1] Henry F. Dobyns, "Estimating Aboriginal American Population . . . ," *Current Anthropology* 7 (October 1966): 395–416.

of the sixteenth century, the English, French, and Dutch added several hundred thousand more, so that by 1650 there were some 849,000 white colonists in the Americas.[2] Still, these white colonists formed a largely exploitive elite in relation to the dwindling Indian population, and the demand for labor from other sources persisted.

Because the European laborers (except those from northern Europe) proved unwilling to migrate in large numbers, and because the costs of transportation and settlement of those who did migrate were so great for the creole, or native-born, elite, it was decided by all the colonizing regimes to turn toward slave labor on a massive scale. Though only the Iberians actively practiced slavery in western Europe at this time, slavery in the Old World was an ancient institution. In the fifteenth century, Jews, Moors, Berbers, Arabs, and Eastern Europeans were all part of the slave labor force of the Mediterranean world. These traditionally enslaved peoples, however, were rapidly being replaced by the relatively unexploited African peoples. In the early part of the century, new caravan routes between North Africa and the Sudan were developed, and after the 1440's the Portuguese were able to bring African slaves to the Continent via direct Atlantic sea routes. Although Slavs, Muslims, and even Canary Islanders still formed large slave populations in the Old World during the last half of the century, the sub-Saharan black population had by that time become the predominant group in the western Mediterranean slave labor force.[3] Thus, when the New World looked to the Old for a new supply of labor, it was directed to sub-Saharan Africa, the closest source of large numbers of slaves to be obtained readily and cheaply. The result was the mass forced migration of Africans to the New World.

For the first half-century of the Atlantic slave trade, from the 1440's to 1500 approximately, Europe itself was the market for African slaves. Large numbers of slaves were imported to Portugal and Spain, where they assumed many of the social roles which they would eventually play in the New World. From the beginning, Africans were employed in both rural and urban occupations, performing both domestic and gang labor.[4] But the European slave

---

[2] Unless otherwise indicated, these and all subsequent New World population figures are taken from Angel Rosenblat, *La población indígena y el mestizaje en América,* vol. 1 (Buenos Aires: Nova, 1954).

[3] For a good summary of slavery in the Mediterranean in the fourteenth and fifteenth centuries, see Charles Verlinden, *Les origines de la civilisation atlantique* (Paris, 1966), pp. 174–75.

[4] It has been estimated that the Portuguese exported something like 140,000 slaves from Africa, primarily to Europe, between 1450 and 1505 (Vitorino Magalhães Godinho, *A economia dos descobrimentos henriquinos* [Lisbon, 1962], p. 209). In the port of Valencia on the Spanish Mediterranean coast, to give just one example of the African impact on the peninsula, about two-thirds of the slaves imported from 1489 to 1516 were African, and an average of about 250 Africans were imported annually (Vicenta Cortes, *La esclavitud en Valencia durante el reinado de los reyes católicos (1479–1516)* [Valencia, 1964], pp.

labor market had developed in response to labor shortages during an age of major economic expansion, and it was not without limits. As European populations themselves began to expand late in the fifteenth and sixteenth centuries, the need for slave labor on the Continent declined.[5]

The European experience with African slave labor and the high level of commercial organization achieved by the early Atlantic slave trade were crucial factors in the almost immediate introduction of African slave labor to the New World at the end of the fifteenth and the beginning of the sixteenth century. African slaves participated in the initial conquest of the West Indian islands and, later, in the conquest of the mainland regions.[6] Within half a century, African and creole slaves were often as numerous as the white conquistadors in the newly won lands.[7]

Since the conquered Indians were still the largest single group in the labor force of the New World, the settlement and occupational patterns of the incoming African slaves tended to reflect those of the American Indian population. In the highlands of Mexico and Peru, where Indians had survived the demographic upheaval and the several epidemics that accompanied the arrival of the Europeans, the Negro slaves were employed almost exclusively as skilled and semiskilled urban artisans or domestic servants. Where large bodies of Amerindians had not survived — primarily in the lowland and coastal regions and on the West Indian islands — the Europeans turned almost exclusively to African labor, and slaves were employed in all types of occupations, rural as well as urban.

Blacks in the Conquest and Settlement of Spanish America

During the first two centuries of American colonization, Negro slaves could be found in all parts of the New World. From the beginning, they made up half or more of the conquering armies, and they intermingled quite freely to form a new intermediate social grouping of *castas,* or people of mixed Indian, white,

---

57–60). By the sixteenth century, such central areas as Portugal and Andalusia already had large slave populations. By 1551 some 9,950 slaves were counted in Lisbon, out of a total population of 100,000, and by 1573 the whole of Portugal was said to contain over 40,000 slaves, a large number of whom were sub-Saharan African Negroes (Fédéric Mauro, *Le Portugal et l'atlantique au xviie siècle* [Paris, 1960], p. 147; Charles Verlinden, *L'esclavage dans l'Europe médiévale,* vol. 1 [Bruges, 1955], p. 837).

[5] On the population expansion of sixteenth-century Europe, see Marcel R. Reinhard and André Armengaud, *Histoire générale de la population mondiale* (Paris, 1961), pp. 84 ff.

[6] José Antonio Saco, *Historia de la esclavitud de la raza africana en el nuevo mundo . . .* (Barcelona, 1879), pp. 71 ff.

[7] Rosenblat estimates that the population of Spanish America in 1570 consisted of 118,000 whites and 230,000 Negroes, mulattoes, and mestizos. Though mestizos and mulattoes are lumped together with Negroes in this famous estimate, it seems likely that between one-half and two-thirds of the total colored population were Negro at this early date.

and Negro ancestry. As early as 1570 the Viceroyalty of New Spain, as Mexico was then called, had a Negro slave population of about 20,000, more than the Spanish and creole white populations combined. Of these 20,000, it was estimated that at least 2,000 had already become fugitives. In addition, there was a free colored population of about 2,435 in Mexico. The Negro slave population there grew slowly, and a half-century later, in 1646, it was estimated at about 35,000; the maximum level reached seems to have been under 50,000. In contrast, the free mulatto and Indian-Negro populations increased enormously during this period, numbering about 116,000 combined in 1646. Because of the Africans' greater resistance to European diseases, and because of their close contact with the Indians, it appears that mixed Indian-Negro and Afro-mestizo (African and Spanish-Indian) populations grew up rapidly, passing 600,000 combined by 1810 and thus representing 10 percent of the total Mexican population and around 25 percent of the total *castas*.[8] In Peru, too, Africans quickly came to form a substantial part of the population. It was estimated that by the 1580's there were about 4,000 Negro slaves in Peru, roughly the same as the number of whites.[9]

After the first century of rapid expansion, however, the Spanish colonies on the American continent tended to absorb fewer Africans, and their slave populations tended to stabilize at relatively low numbers—less than 50,000 in Mexico and less than 100,000 in Peru. By 1650, there were probably no more than 345,000 Negro slaves in all of Spanish America, in addition to some 135,000 mulattoes.[10]

In seventeenth-century Spanish America, the African slaves and freedmen played a crucial role in the developing creole society. Particularly in the areas of heavy Indian population, they tended to identify with white culture and were considered part of the dominant society. As far as the Indians were concerned, they were one with the conquerors, and they were treated in much royal legislation as a distinct element of the Western cultural elite. They spoke Spanish,

---

[8] Gonzalo Aguirre Beltran, *La población negra de México, 1519–1810* (Mexico, 1946), pp. 208–13, 221, 237.

[9] James Lockhart, *Spanish Peru, 1532–1560: A Colonial Society* (Madison: University of Wisconsin Press, 1968), p. 230. By 1630 there were about 30,000 Negro slaves in Lima, Peru, as compared with some 25,000 whites (Rosenblat, *La población indigena*, p. 225).

[10] These figures are derived from Rosenblat's estimates in *La población indigena*. From his total figure of 857,000 Negroes in the New World, I have subtracted 122,000, the estimated number of North American and Brazilian blacks in the population, as well as 390,000 for the black population of the Dutch, English, and French West Indies. This leaves 345,000 for the population of the Spanish empire, about 10,000 of whom probably inhabited the Spanish islands. I have estimated the mulatto population at 130,000 for continental Spanish America, plus 5,000 for the Spanish Antilles. Given the fact that the majority of the mulattoes were listed as freedmen in almost all available census records, it would seem reasonable to suppose that there was a free colored population of at least 67,500 in Spanish America by 1650.

learned European skills and crafts, and often exploited the Indians as mercilessly as did the whites.[11]

This type of slavery within the context of an Indian peasant economy was largely urban-oriented. (Slaves in this category included truck farmers and some mine laborers, as in the north of South America.) The classic type of plantation slavery was slow to develop in Spanish America, where it was not to make its major appearance until the second half of the eighteenth century, after certain basic economic changes had taken place. The early lack of importance of plantation agriculture in the Spanish empire was largely due to the fact that the Spaniards concentrated on exploiting the great mineral wealth of the New World along with the free labor of the Indian masses. They therefore tended to settle in urban centers, and primarily in the major areas already inhabited by the Amerindians, leaving the future plantation areas for the most part as wasteland.[12]

The Evolution of Plantation Slavery

In contrast, when the other European colonizing powers arrived in the New World, they found these two vital sources of immediate wealth closed to them. The Spanish had preempted almost all the easily accessible mining areas and almost all Indian populations native to these regions. The Indians who remained, those who made their homes outside the Central American and Peruvian centers, were not peasant village agriculturalists but seminomadic peoples or simple village agriculturalists, accustomed to a subsistence economy and unaccustomed to a stratified multicommunity state. Hence they found it impossible to adapt to a life as slave laborers, or even dependent rural laborers, and thus to integrate themselves into colonial society. Indeed, they were unable even to survive the initial encounter with the Europeans. When the colonizing powers, finding themselves with neither mines nor a dependent peasantry, sought to develop commercial agricultural products for European consumption and began experimenting with Indian labor, disease and the lack of technological and social development drove the Indians to virtual extinction.

---

[11] Time and again the Spanish Crown ordered that Negroes and mulattoes be forbidden to mingle with the Indians in the communities, "because they help the Indians toward drunkenness and other evil customs" (from the Law of 1540, reprinted in Richard Konetzke, ed., *Colección de documentos para la historia de la formación social de Hispanoamérica, 1493–1810,* vol. 1 [Madrid, 1953–1962], p. 213). In 1554, for example, the Crown acknowledged complaints from persons in the Indies that the Negroes of Peru were robbing and exploiting the Indians and called for royal officials to protect the Indians from such mistreatment (ibid., p. 321).

[12] Many of the ideas in this and the following paragraphs grew out of insights presented in two major works: Silvio A. Zavala, "Relaciones historicas entre indios y negros en Iberoamérica," *Revista de las Indias* 28 (1946): 55–65; and Charles Gibson, *Spain in America* (New York: Harper, 1966).

The Europeans, left without a labor base for their society, since they themselves were too few in number to develop large-scale plantation economies, turned to Africa for a new supply of slaves. Whereas the Africans brought into the central areas of Spanish America had been drawn into the cultural elite of the plural societies developing there, those brought into the new colonies, as well as into the marginal areas of Spanish America, found themselves in the bottom half of a two-part, racially segmented regime. Here there were no Indians to fill the bottom positions of unskilled labor or to make possible the emergence of a third major social group such as the *castas* of Peru and Mexico. Precisely because of the large Indian population in these older regimes, especially in Mexico, the Negro had found it far easier to enter into colonial society, transforming it into a multiracial creole society in which the Afro-mestizo population was virtually indistinguishable from the mestizo population. There, too, where the Indians made up the exploited element of the society, the colonial patterns of prejudice and oppression would have a much milder effect on the Negroes than in societies where they alone made up the agricultural and urban masses. Though the creole societies that formed in the newer colonies in the Americas would eventually contain tripartite color groupings of Negroes, mulattoes, and whites (in all areas except continental North America), the Africans in these societies would take the place of the exploited Indians, and the process of lower-class integration into a multiracial community would be considerably slower.

Whereas the slaves of sixteenth- and seventeenth-century Spanish America were primarily miners, truck gardeners, and urban and domestic laborers, the slaves brought into the colonies of the new imperial powers were almost exclusively employed in plantation agriculture. Though a host of crops—including cotton, indigo, tobacco, and rice—would eventually become important colonial agricultural products, the primary export crop during the early years of New World expansion was sugar. A product that was fast becoming a European staple, sugar had been developed as a plantation crop in the eastern Mediterranean by the twelfth century and had then spread to Cyprus and Sicily in the thirteenth century and to the southern Iberian peninsula by the fourteenth. Finally, in the middle of the fifteenth century, it reached the Madeira islands. When these Atlantic islands became the center of European sugar production, it was inevitable that the Spanish and Portuguese should transport the crop to the new world.[13]

Thus sugar came to be grown throughout the Spanish Caribbean area, though there it remained a relatively minor crop. The Portuguese, however, made it a major crop in the second half of the sixteenth century, when they decided to exploit their Brazilian holdings to the fullest. In this they had the support of a key group of merchants, the Flemish and Dutch traders. The pro-

---

[13] Charles Verlinden, *Précédents médiévaux de la colonie en Amérique* (Mexico, 1954), pp. 45–52.

duction of sugar was one of the most capital-intensive industries then known to European agriculture and industry. Aside from the huge sums of money needed to purchase slave labor, the producer had to invest in expensive processing machinery and in mills to extract the sugar, in even its crudest form, from the cane. The Flemish and Dutch merchants had the required capital, and it was they who provided everything from the slaves and the boilers needed to get production under way to the ships used for transporting the finished product to market. In fact, the very first *engenhos*, or sugar mills, established in Brazil early in the sixteenth century were built with the assistance of Flemish and Dutch capital.

At the beginning of the sixteenth century, when Spain first began to issue *asientos*—monopoly grants to merchants for supplying slaves to the Spanish Indies—the Flemish and Dutch merchants came away with the prime contracts and subcontracts. By the end of the sixteenth century, the Dutch merchant marine had become the largest in Europe and was already actively engaged in the transatlantic carrying trade, bringing slaves from Africa to the Americas and carrying American products to Europe.[14] While the Spanish Indies were reasonably well served in these early years by a national merchant marine and so were able to retain control of their own commerce, the Portuguese with their overextended Asian empire had few resources left for supplying the New World. They therefore adopted a policy of semifree trade as far as Brazil was concerned, and this permitted the Dutch to make major inroads in the New World. Antwerp and later Amsterdam became the principal importing ports for Brazilian sugar.[15]

Sugar production in Brazil was concentrated in the famous northeastern region of Bahia and Pernambuco, with a minor center in the south at Rio de Janeiro. By 1580 production had reached such dimensions that Brazil had replaced the Madeira islands as Europe's chief source of sugar.[16] With this firm base in sugar, the Portuguese were able to turn Brazil into a prosperous commercial farming or plantation colony, the first exclusively agricultural colony created in the New World. By the end of the sixteenth century Brazil was the world's largest producer of sugar and already had a slave labor force roughly estimated at between 13,000 and 15,000.[17]

---

[14] C. R. Boxer, *The Dutch Seaborne Empire: 1600–1800* (New York: Alfred A. Knopf, 1965), pp. 20 ff. Though Dutch merchants were thus involved in the slave trade from the beginning, the Dutch did not dominate the trade until the last part of the seventeenth century. (See Chapter 2 of Rolando Mellafe, *La esclavitud en Hispanoamérica* [Buenos Aires, 1964].)

[15] Sergio Buarque de Holanda, ed., *Historia geral da civilização brasileira*, 5 vols. to date (São Paulo, 1963–   ), Tomo 1, vol. 1:235–36, Tomo 1, vol. 2:204. Celso Furtado, *Formación económica del Brasil* (Mexico, 1962), pp. 18–19.

[16] Fédéric Mauro, *Le xvie siècle européen: aspects économiques* (Paris, 1966), p. 151.

[17] Mauro, *Le Portugal et l'atlantique*, p. 179.

But Brazil's leading role as a sugar producer was eventually to be challenged by a series of external circumstances centering around events in Europe. In 1580 Portugal became subject to Spain, under Philip II. In the same period, the Dutch provinces of the Low Countries united to begin a long rebellion against Spanish domination. Because of their preeminence at sea, the Dutch concentrated on attacking the overseas Iberian empire. In 1594 a Dutch fleet sailed to the East Indies, and in 1598 Philip II retaliated by confiscating all Dutch shipping in the Portuguese empire. However, while the Dutch and the Portuguese were in active competition in East Asia, their interests in Brazil were at this point too closely connected and too profitable for them to cease cooperating. Thus, despite the bans of Philip II, Dutch-Portuguese sugar trade continued and even increased, until by 1609 the Dutch were carrying from half of two-thirds of all Brazilian exports to Europe.

This trade by special agreement could not long survive the conflicts of interest between the two countries in Europe and East Asia, however. In 1621 the Dutch created the West Indies Company for colonization and trade in both the New World and Africa. In 1630, after several abortive attempts, the Dutch finally gained control of large sections of northeastern Brazil, thus acquiring title to Europe's largest source of sugar. From 1630 to 1654 the Dutch controlled most of northeastern Brazil, centering around Recife in Pernambuco, and, in Africa, the Costa da Mina, the island of Fernando Po in the Bight of Biafra, and Angola, which they also captured from the Portuguese. Thus they were able to control the major sources of slave labor as well as the major sources of sugar.[18] But the Portuguese, after breaking away from Spanish domination in 1640 and losing a large part of their East Asian empire in the Dutch wars in the first half of the century, still had more energies to concentrate on retaking Brazil; and since the planters in the northeast had remained Portuguese during the period of Dutch dominion, it was relatively easy to overthrow the Dutch with direct aid from Lisbon. By the middle of the century the Brazilians had succeeded in expelling the Dutch from Brazil.[19]

But the departure of the Dutch was to prove disastrous to Brazil's position as the world's foremost sugar producer. Though Angola and the African islands were recaptured from the Dutch, the crucial link with European markets was now broken. Equally important, the Dutch now took their capital, their technology, and their commercial expertise to the West Indies, becoming the crucial middlemen in the establishment of the sugar empire of the French and

---

[18] Buarque de Holanda, *Historia geral,* Tomo 1, vol, 1:235 ff.

[19] One of the leading captains in the war against the Dutch was the colored freedman Henrique Dias, who led an army of several hundred ex-slaves and freedmen and was eventually rewarded by the Portuguese Crown with a title of nobility (see José Antonio Gonsalves de Mello, *Henrique Dias, governador dos pretos, crioulos e mulatos do estado do Brasil* [Recife, 1954]).

English in the New World.[20] From the middle of the seventeenth century on, the West Indies gained ground in terms of world sugar production, while the Brazilian industry receded into a secondary position.

The first surge of the new development in sugar-plantation agriculture came in the British West Indies. By 1650 the small island of Barbados was producing both tobacco and sugar and was well on its way toward the creation of a large plantation system with over 20,000 slaves.[21] When Jamaica was taken by the British under Cromwell in 1655, this hitherto marginal island was rapidly brought into sugar production and quickly came to challenge the leadership of Barbados. By 1700 Jamaica had some 45,000 slaves and had become the single largest producer of sugar in the world; and by the middle of the eighteenth century, the British West Indian islands as a group had become the great center of plantation agriculture.[22]

This position of dominance was very soon challenged by the French. By 1700, the French had imported some 16,000 slaves into the small island of Martinique alone, and they had brought another 20,000 into the just developing Saint Domingue (present-day Haiti). The plantation system on both islands expanded rapidly thereafter, but Saint Domingue far outstripped Martinique and the other French possessions within the next fifty years. By 1750 its slave population had risen to over 230,000, a phenomenal increase, and it was rapidly surpassing Jamaica as the world's leading sugar producer.[23] By the 1780's all the unoccupied islands in the West Indies had been brought into cultivation, and this famous plantation region had reached the apogee of its production. At that time, the French and British islands together held over a million slaves and some 47,000 freedmen.[24]

Blacks in the Settlement of North America

Meanwhile, during the seventeenth century, a new stronghold of slavery was established as the North American continent was settled by British col-

---

[20] On the role of the Dutch in introducing sugar cultivation and slaves to the West Indies, see Arthur Percival Newton, *The European Nations in the West Indies, 1493–1688* (London, 1933), pp. 196 ff.

[21] Ibid., p. 197.

[22] Frank W. Pitman, *The Development of the British West Indies, 1700–1763* (New Haven, Conn.: Yale University Press, 1917), p. 373.

[23] Lucien Peytraud, *L'esclavage aux Antilles françaises avant 1789* (Paris, 1897), pp. 237–39.

[24] Of these million slaves, the French held some 673,500 (ibid., p. 139) and the English, some 465, 276 (Sir William Young, *The West-India Common-Place Book* [London, 1807], p. 3). Of these, Saint Domingue and Jamaica respectively had 452,000 and 256,000 slaves. In addition, there were 36,400 free colored in the French islands and 10,569 in the English possessions.

onists. Here, as in the other English and French colonies, Dutch traders proved to be vital suppliers of both capital and slave labor. The first shipment of African slaves to British North America, arriving in 1619, was carried from the West Indies by a Dutch vessel. Of course, the climate in the continental colonies was more temperate than in the other English colonies, so sugar was not a feasible crop there. Further, the northern colonies were a greater risk for capital investment, and the funds needed to develop a commercial crop economy were not available. As a result, the colonists were initially forced to develop crops that were not capital-intensive for export to Europe. Fortunately for the inhabitants of Virginia, tobacco proved an ideal crop in both ecological and economic terms. Virginia leaf quickly became an effective competitor to the Cuban tobaccos, which were of better quality but limited in supply, and the capital generated by this export was sufficient to finance the importation of slave labor on a major scale.

Thus, for the first time in the New World, tobacco became a plantation crop worked by slave labor in a gang system. Along with tobacco, the southern colonies of continental British America were soon producing rice, some sugar, and finally cotton on plantations worked by slaves. By 1790, when the colonial period ended, British North America held over 757,000 Afro-American slaves and freedmen.[25] Still, this was only about two-thirds the number of Afro-Americans in the French and British West Indian islands. Thus, while the thirteen continental colonies were becoming a major slave and plantation zone by the end of the eighteenth century, they were still not comparable to the great production zones of the West Indies.

Black Settlement Patterns in the Eighteenth Century

The North American colonies were not the only continental area to develop plantation and slave economies in the eighteenth century. The Spanish Crown, in the second half of that century, heavily subsidized sugar, indigo, cacao, rice, and cotton plantations in such areas as Guatemala, Colombia, Venezuela, and Ecuador. It also promoted its previously neglected West Indian islands, Cuba and Puerto Rico, and after 1789 replaced the granting of monopoly contracts with free trade in African slaves, thus promoting massive immigration to these islands. The net result was that by the end of the eighteenth century, Spanish America contained a colored population of about two million, including both slaves and freedmen.

In Brazil, where the first plantation economy had developed, an entirely new pattern of slave labor was to appear in the eighteenth century with the opening up of the mines in the hinterland. Beginning in the 1690's, when gold was first discovered in Minas Gerais, slaves poured into the Brazilian interior,

---

[25] These and all subsequent figures on United States populations are taken from the Bureau of the Census, *Negro Population, 1790–1915* (Washington, D.C., 1918).

and a new mining economy based on colored slave labor began to develop. While mining had been practiced with slave labor in Colombia, Mexico, and Peru, the majority of mine workers throughout the Spanish empire were still Indians.[26] In Brazil, however, all mine workers were colored, and Minas Gerais and Goias became major new centers of colored population and of a whole new mining–slave-labor economy.[27]

The basic system of slave labor—plantation, urban, and mining—which had been elaborated by the end of the eighteenth century was to remain unchanged till well after abolition. There would be major shifts in crops and in the plantation centers during the nineteenth century as new areas came into sugar production or as such staples as indigo were replaced by other products, but the economic, social, and legal structures that were to prevail in the Americas had all been roughly established by the time the colonial period ended.

Black Settlement and Plantation Society in the Nineteenth Century

Unquestionably the single most important event to affect the postcolonial plantation system occurred late in the eighteenth century. This was the Haitian revolution of the 1790's—a revolution with a profound impact, for not only did it serve as a terrifying example to slave masters throughout the New World, but it helped to reorder the centers of plantation agriculture in the Caribbean. From the 1750's to the 1790's Haiti—or Saint Domingue, as the French then called it—was the world's leading producer of high-grade, low-cost sugar. The efficiency and the productivity of the French plantations were proverbial, and French West Indian sugar dominated the European market, driving the higher-priced English and Brazilian products out from all but their protected metropolitan markets.[28] However, with the uprising led by Toussaint L'Ouverture and the eventual destruction of the Haitian slave regime, there was a mass exodus of planters and capital from the island. Just as the Dutch exodus from

---

[26] Alexander de Humboldt, *Political Essay on the Kingdom of New Spain*, 4 vols. (London, 1811), 1:124–26, 3:246–47. Of the major mining areas, the two largest, Mexico and Peru-Chile, used virtually no colored slave labor. Among the secondary mining regions, Venezuela had a large colored slave force but also a large force of slave and free Indians. Further, Venezuelan mines were exhausted by the eighteenth century and ceased to employ significant numbers of slaves (Federico Brito Figueroa, *La estructura economica de Venezuela colonial* [Caracas, 1963], pp. 80 ff.). Only in Colombian mines were colored slaves used extensively throughout the colonial period, and even there Indian labor was also used (Aquiles Excalante, *El negro en Colombia* [Bogota, 1964], pp. 121–27).

[27] C. R. Boxer, *The Golden Age of Brazil, 1695–1750: Growing Pains of a Colonial Society* (Berkeley: University of California Press, 1969), and Sergio Buarque de Holanda, *Historia geral*, Tomo 2, vol. 1, are the best available studies of Minas and Goias colonial mining society.

[28] Eric Williams, *Capitalism and Slavery* (Chapel Hill: University of North Carolina Press, 1944), pp. 113–14, 122–23.

Pernambuco over a century earlier was followed by a relocation of the production centers, the Haitian loss of capital and technological and commercial knowledge worked to the gain of other regions in the New World—especially the traditional sugar regions of northeastern Brazil and the island of Cuba, which eventually replaced Haiti as the world's largest producer of cane sugar.[29]

With Haitian capital at its disposal, and with the effective elimination of Haitian competition in sugar production, by the first decades of the new century Cuba was fast becoming a major slave plantation economy. Beginning with a slave population of only about 44,000 in 1774, Cuba by 1861 had a slave population of 399,000 and a total colored population of 613,000.[30] By the middle of the nineteenth century, it had taken the lead in world sugar production and had over 150,000 slaves engaged in sugar production alone.[31]

An even more important outgrowth of the Haitian revolution was a shift in the centers of coffee production. Until the 1790's Haiti had also been the largest producer of coffee in the New World. When the old regime was brought to an end, many French coffee planters shifted their operations to Cuba, where some 50,000 slaves were employed in coffee production in the 1830's. Cuban coffee interests, however, soon faced mounting competition from growers in Rio de Janeiro.

The exportation of Brazilian coffee on a major scale began in the 1820's, and by the 1830's the famous coffee boom was on. First growing up in the area around Rio de Janeiro, the coffee plantations spread to the southwest down the Paraíba valley and then, by the middle of the nineteenth century, into the flat highlands surrounding the city of São Paulo. In the West Paulista plains, as these highlands were called, coffee thrived with a vigor unknown, until then, to any crop in Brazil.[32] The São Paulo area thus became a center for coffee production, and the slave population in the area increased rapidly.

Despite these developments, however, the old mining region of Minas Gerais continued throughout the nineteenth century to have the largest slave population of any state in Brazil. Though the famous gold mines of this area had been seriously declining since the middle of the eighteenth century, Minas Gerais was able to develop a thriving, diversified economy built upon cattle raising, sugar and coffee production, and truck gardening—all of which had absorbed some 370,000 slaves by the 1870's. The south-central states of Rio de Janeiro and São Paulo had also developed major slave populations by this

---

[29] Roland T. Ely, *Cuando reinaba su majestad el azúcar* (Buenos Aires, 1963), pp. 77 ff.

[30] Herbert S. Klein, *Slavery in the Americas: A Comparative Study of Cuba and Virginia* (Chicago: University of Chicago Press, 1967), Table 2, p. 202.

[31] Jacobo de la Pezuela, *Diccionario geográfico, estadístico, histórico de la isla de Cuba*, 4 vols. (Madrid, 1863–1866), 1:61.

[32] Klein, *Slavery in the Americas*, p. 152. Stanley Stein, *Vassouras: A Brazilian Coffee County, 1850–1900* (Cambridge, Mass.: Harvard University Press, 1957). Affonso de E. Taunay, *Historia do Cafe no Brazil*, 15 vols. (Rio de Janeiro, 1939–1943), especially vols. 3–5.

time, whereas the slave populations of Pernambuco and particularly Maranhão—both in the old northeast—had dropped considerably. Despite the relative decline of the northeastern states as slave centers, however, the Afro-Brazilian population did not shift as radically as one might suspect over the nineteenth century, for the rapidly increasing free colored population remained geographically immobile. Thus, by the first census of 1872, taken when slavery still flourished in Brazil, the old northeastern region plus the coastal state of Bahia contained over 2,900,000 colored persons, making up 51 percent of the total Afro-Brazilian population of 5,700,000.[33]

In the United States, the settlement patterns that had evolved by the end of the eighteenth century were to change slowly as the American population moved inland from the Atlantic seaboard. In 1790, 92 percent of the black population was located in the South Atlantic states—Virginia being the leader with over 300,000 persons. Following technical innovations in the picking of cotton in the 1790's and the increasing mechanization of the English textile industry during the same period, cotton production expanded dramatically in the United States, and cotton became far and away the largest slave labor crop on the North American continent. With the Louisiana Purchase and the War of 1812, the key Gulf Coast states of Alabama, Mississippi, and Louisiana were opened up to cotton, and by the 1840's the cotton kingdom of the South was in full operation. By this time, the total Afro-American population of the United States was 2,800,000 persons, 92 percent of whom lived in the southern states. Of these, almost half a million inhabited the Alabama-Mississippi region.

In the next two decades, as slavery further expanded into the new southwestern states, the center of the black North American population, which by then stood at 4,400,000 persons, shifted westward. By 1860 the South Atlantic seaboard states held less than half of the total slave labor force in North America, and the eastern south-central states—Arkansas, Louisiana, Oklahoma, and Texas—held just under one-fourth of the total slave population. Thus the shift was from the Upper South toward the Deep South and the Southwest. Though Virginia was still the largest slave state in 1860, with a population of some 548,000 slaves, the geographical center of the black population was now located in northwestern Georgia, well over four hundred miles to the southwest of its center in Virginia in 1790.

The Abolition of Slavery in the New World

In all of continental America except the United States, however, slavery was on the decline by the nineteenth century. Late in the eighteenth century mining went into a serious depression in Peru, Mexico, and the Colombia-Venezuelan

---

[33] Herbert S. Klein, "The Colored Freedmen in Brazilian Slave Society," *Journal of Social History* 3 (Fall 1969): 35–36.

regions, thereby eliminating a major market for slave labor. At the same time such thriving plantation crops as indigo, which was the major export crop of Guatemala, began to lose ground in the face of serious competition from artificial dyes in Europe. To the changing resources and changing market conditions was finally added the holocaust of civil war. In Venezuela, to take an extreme example, the plantations, though they suffered because of the decline in the market for indigo, continued to absorb large numbers of slaves until 1810. But the long-drawn-out wars for independence from Spain, which began in 1810 and lasted over a decade, brought the wholesale arming and freeing of slaves as well as the devastation of the plantation areas. As a result, by 1825 there were half as many slaves in the country as there had been just fifteen years earlier, when the struggle for independence began.[34] In peripheral slave regions such as Ecuador, Uruguay, and Colombia, the course of events was much the same.[35] Thus by the 1820's, slavery, although it was still legal in most areas, had become virtually obsolete, and the vast majority of the colored population were freedmen.[36] With several forces working against it — the decline of plantation agriculture, the chaos of war, and the fervent liberalism of the independence period in general — slavery became a moribund institution in continental Spanish America by early in the nineteenth century.

Indeed, by the 1830's, on the eve of British abolition, slavery was a vital institution only in the West Indies, Brazil, and the United States, and it was shortly to expire in the British and French islands. Also by this time, the trans-

---

[34] Federico Brito Figueroa, *Ensayos de historia social venezolana* (Caracas, 1960), pp. 254–55. Whereas there were an estimated 87,000 slaves in Venezuela in 1810, only 49,782 remained after the wars of independence (ibid., p. 238. Federico Brito Figueroa, *La estructura social y demográfica de Venezuela colonial* [Caracas, 1961], p. 58). However, it should be pointed out that a succession of slave rebellions and an extremely serious problem with the *cimarrones,* the runaway slaves, had begun to undermine the Venezuelan slave regime even before independence was declared (see Miguel Acosta Saignes, *La vida de los esclavos negros en Venezuela* [Caracas, 1967], pp. 297 ff.). Further, the indigo crisis at the end of the eighteenth century had disrupted plantation society and contributed to the formation of a very large free colored class — by 1800, there were something like 407,000 free mulattoes and 33,362 free Negroes in Venezuela (Brito, *La estructura social,* p. 58).

[35] The crisis of the slave regime in Colombia toward the end of the eighteenth century is described in Jaime Jaramillo Uribe, "Esclavos y señores en la sociedad colombiana del siglo xviii," *Anuario Colombiano de Historia Social y de la Cultura* 1 (1963): 50–55.

[36] Though data on the free colored population of Spanish America toward the end of the eighteenth century is scarce, the rapid rise in the number of freedmen is clearly documented for many areas. In Montevideo, Uruguay, in 1778, there were already 594 freedmen in a total colored population of 1,304; by 1781, the number of freedmen had risen to 1,103 (Ildefonso Pereda Valdes, *El negro en el Uruguay, pasado y presente* [Montevideo, 1965], p. 125). In the classically marginal area of Puerto Rico, the free colored already outnumbered the slaves 16,414 to 13,333 by 1802 (Luis M. Diaz Solar, *Historia de la esclavitud negra en Puerto Rico, 1493–1890* [Madrid, 1953], p. 110). And in Quito and Guayaquil, provinces of Ecuador, in 1781, there were already 17,528 freedmen compared with 4,684 slaves.

atlantic slave trade had almost ceased to operate in all areas except Cuba and Brazil. To these two areas, however, the slave ships would bring the largest annual number of Africans in their history, until the close of the Brazilian trade in 1850 and the Cuban trade a decade later. Alone among the major slave states in the Western Hemisphere during the nineteenth century, the United States did not engage in an international slave trade. In 1808 the international trade was effectively terminated, and the result was the full-scale development of slave breeding and of an internal slave trade unmatched in any other New World society. Thus, although a total of only about 427,000 slaves were imported into the region of the United States—only about 5 percent of the total number of Africans imported into the New World[37]—there were 4,400,000 Afro-Americans in the United States when the Civil War broke out.

Even in Cuba and Brazil, where it flourished long after it had ceased to exist in most parts of the New World, slavery had begun to lose its foothold by the middle decades of the nineteenth century. Especially in Cuba, there was a general awareness of the inevitable coming of abolition well before the final decrees of the 1880's. As early as the 1840's Cuban planters began to import alternative groups of laborers, including Yucatan Indians and Chinese coolies, and by the 1860's over one hundred thousand East Asians had been introduced into the island, not to mention other labor groups. In addition, the planters began to shift from classic plantation slavery to various forms of sharecropping and other agricultural labor systems, especially after the North American Civil War. By the end of the first Ten Years War (1868–1878), Cuba's first attempt to win independence, slavery was no longer the vital labor system it had been; freedmen made up the majority of the colored population, and only the most backward plantations still relied exclusively on slave labor.[38]

Although Brazilian sugar and coffee planters refused to experiment with nonslave labor until the late 1870's, even in Brazil slavery was fading by the 1850's. By this time at least 50 percent of the total colored population were freedmen, and when the first national census was taken in 1872, over 70 percent of the colored population of 5,700,000 were free.[39] The coffee planters were the last to give up their slaves, but they too were finally forced to concede defeat; in the 1880's they turned to massive Italian immigration to solve their labor problems. During the last years of slavery in Brazil, the Brazilian army and the urban population encouraged the mass defection of slaves. The planters could put up no effective resistance to abolition when it finally came in 1888.

Like the Brazilian coffee planters, slaveowners in the United States tried to resist the change of their labor force from a slave status to a free status.

---

[37] Philip D. Curtin, *The Atlantic Slave Trade: A Census* (Madison: University of Wisconsin Press, 1969), p. 88.

[38] Klein, *Slavery in the Americas,* Chapters 7, 9.

[39] Klein, "The Colored Freedmen," p. 36.

Southern planters made no attempts to set up sharecropping systems, to employ free labor, or to encourage the immigration of European or Asian contract labor. Here slavery was a profitable enterprise to the end, and since the Cuban and Brazilian slave empires had survived the French and English manumission of slaves in the first half of the century, the Southerners felt no external threat to their slave labor system. It was only the effective rise of abolitionism within the United States, heavily supported by the British abolitionist movement, which finally brought about the destruction of the slave regime. When North American slavery was finally terminated in 1863, the end of the regimes in Cuba and Brazil was inevitable.

Post-Abolition Settlement Patterns

The demise of these great slave regimes in the last half of the nineteenth century did not seriously affect the settlement patterns of black Americans anywhere in the New World. In no state did abolition bring the payment of reparations to the former slaves. With neither land nor capital and with no way of acquiring new skills, the ex-slaves were forced into sharecropping or debt-peonage systems and thus remained bound to the old plantation economies. For the most part, the freed black laborers remained on their plantations or in their old plantation regions. "Free" sugar, cotton, and, to a lesser extent, coffee were now produced throughout the New World by the same black workers as before abolition. Thus, until well into the twentieth century, the black settlement patterns that emerged during the eighteenth and nineteenth centuries persisted, and major black belts remained in all the old plantation areas. Not surprisingly, it would take revolution, industrialization, and the end of large-scale European immigration to finally break up these pre-abolition concentrations of black population.

When the historic settlement patterns were last interrupted, masses of blacks began to move toward the rising industrial centers in the Americas, especially the cities in the northern United States and the southern Brazilian towns of São Paulo and Rio de Janeiro. International migrations also took place as large West Indian colored populations sought greater economic opportunity in areas as diverse as Panama and other Central American states and the northern cities of the United States. These great shifts of national populations, along with the very different rates of growth among the various black American populations, had led by the middle of the twentieth century to significant alterations in the settlement patterns in the Americas. Thus by 1950—the time of the last major census for most Latin American countries—the Afro-American population was distributed in the following manner: the area north of Mexico contained 31 percent of the total colored population; the West Indies contained some 20 percent of this total, continental Spanish America contained some 12 percent; and Brazil contained some 37 percent, still the greatest single national concentration. Indeed, as can be seen in the table opposite, the three greatest centers of black American population in 1950 were still the old plantation areas—Brazil, the United States, and the West Indies—though colored populations could still be found in all American nations.

The Colored Population of the Western Hemisphere in 1950
(in thousands of persons)

Nation and Region	Negroes	Mulattoes	Total Colored	Colored as a Percentage of Total Population
Canada	22	(Included under "Negroes")	22	. . [a]
United States	14,894	(Included under "Negroes")	14,894	10%
	14,916		14,916	
British Antilles [b]	1,800	480	2,280	86
French Antilles	150	390	540	93
Dutch Antilles	70	70	140	88
Puerto Rico	50	500	550	25
Haiti	2,800	280	3,080	99
Dominican Republic	130	1,500	1,630	77
Cuba	670	800	1,470	27
Virgin Islands	20	4	24	92
	5,690	4,024	9,714	
Mexico	60	60	120	05
Guatemala	4	4	8	. .
British Honduras	23	11	34	56
Honduras	25	25	50	33
El Salvador	. . [c]	. .		. .
Nicaragua	45	55	100	09
Costa Rica	15	15	30	04
Panama [d]	95	95	190	22
	267	265	532	
Colombia	440	2,477	2,917	26
Venezuela	120	1,500	1,620	32
British Guiana	149	35	184	47
Dutch Guiana	22	80	102	47
French Guiana	2	20	22	76
Ecuador	90	240	330	10
Peru	30	80	110	01
Bolivia	7	5	12	. .
Paraguay	5	5	10	01
Uruguay	10	50	60	03
Chile	. .	3	3	. .
Argentina	5	10	15	. .
	880	4,505	5,385	
Brazil	7,000	10,529	17,529	33
TOTAL	28,753	19,323	48,076	15%

[a] Indicates less than 01%.
[b] Includes Bermuda and the Bahamas.
[c] Indicates less than 1,000 persons.
[d] Includes population of the Panama Canal Zone.

Adapted from Angel Rosenblat, *La población indígena y el mestizaje en América*, vol. 1 (Buenos Aires: Nova, 1954), Table 1 and pages 145–46. In the latter pages, Rosenblat miscalculated the West Indian Negro population estimates for 1950; I have corrected this in the above estimations.

The Daily Life of
the Southern Slave

KENNETH M. STAMPP

Kenneth M. Stampp is Morrison Professor of American History at
the University of California, Berkeley. He is the author of numerous
books and articles, notably *And the War Came: The North and the
Secession Crisis, 1860–1861* (Louisiana State University Press,
1950), *The Peculiar Institution: Slavery in the Ante-Bellum South*
(Alfred A. Knopf, 1956), *The Causes of the Civil War* (Prentice-
Hall, 1959), and *The Era of Reconstruction, 1865–1877* (Alfred
A. Knopf, 1965). The following essay is an adaptation and abridg-
ment of Chapter Eight from *The Peculiar Institution,* the work generally considered the definitive description of slavery in the United
States. In it, Mr. Stampp draws on a wide variety of contemporary
sources to describe as precisely as possible the daily life of a slave
in the American South.

Paternalism in the Slave System

In the life of the Southern slave the crucial fact was that slavery was above
all a labor system. Wherever in the South the master lived, however many
slaves he owned, it was his bondsmen's productive capacity that he generally
valued most. The great majority of slaves toiled from dawn to dusk on farms
and plantations cultivating cotton, tobacco, rice, sugar, hemp, and food crops.
The rest worked in cities and towns as skilled and unskilled laborers and domestics; on railroads, docks, and river boats; in mines, quarries, and fisheries;
and in textile mills, tobacco factories, and iron foundries.

Though the average slave's work day was long and his labor hard, though
he was subjected to a fairly rigid discipline, though his standard of living was
usually at the subsistence level, an old and by no means altogether discredited
legend holds that Southern slavery was essentially a paternalistic institution.[1]

---

[1] For early and recent statements of this point of view see Ulrich B. Phillips, *American Negro
Slavery* (New York: Appleton, 1918), and Eugene D. Genovese, *The World the Slaveholders Made* (New York: Pantheon, 1969).

Slaveholders themselves created the legend, giving it both its kernel of fact (by their numerous kindnesses toward slaves) and its texture of fancy (in their proslavery polemics). In judging the day-to-day relationships of masters and slaves, the kernel of fact—the reality of ante-bellum paternalism—needs to be separated from its fanciful surroundings and critically analyzed. How much paternalism was there? Under what circumstances did it occur? What was its nature?

A South Carolinian once described the kinds of slaves who aroused paternalistic impulses in their owners. There was the "faithful and kind old nurse" who watched over her master in his infancy; the body servant who cared for him during sickness and anticipated all his wants; and the "faithful and devoted" field hand who earned his regard "by implicit obedience to all his command[s]."[2] Harriet Martineau wasted little of her charity upon slaveholders, but she did acknowledge that some showed deep gratitude for such services from bondsmen. "Nowhere, perhaps, can more touching exercises of mercy be seen than here," she confessed.[3] A former slave, in recalling his life on a Louisiana plantation, thought it was but "simple justice" to observe that his owner had been a "kind, noble, candid, Christian man, . . . a model master, walking uprightly, according to the light of his understanding."[4]

Visitors often registered surprise at the social intimacy that existed between masters and slaves in certain situations. A Northerner saw a group of Mississippi farmers encamped with their slaves near Natchez after hauling their cotton to market. Here they assumed "a 'cheek by jowl' familiarity . . . with perfect good will and a mutual contempt for the nicer distinctions of colour."[5] Domestics moved freely among the whites at social functions and sat with them in public conveyances. On a train in Virginia Frederick Law Olmsted saw a white woman and her daughter seated with a Negro woman and her daughter. The four of them talked and laughed together, while the girls munched candy out of the same bag "with a familiarity and closeness" which would have astonished and displeased most Northerners. As an infant a master might have been nourished at the breast of one of his female chattels. Olmsted concluded, "When the negro is definitely a slave, it would seem that the alleged natural antipathy of the white race to associate with him is lost."[6]

From such close associations an owner might develop a deep affection for a slave. An Alabama mistress wrote with great tenderness about the death of a nurse who had been the playmate of all her children: "When I saw that Death had the mastery, I laid my hands over her eyes, and in tears and fervor prayed

---

[2] "Judge of Probate Decree Book, 1839–1858," May term, 1841, Abbeville District, S.C.

[3] Harriet Martineau, *Society in America,* vol. 2 (New York, 1837), p. 107.

[4] Solomon Northup, *Twelve Years a Slave* (Buffalo, N.Y., 1853), p. 90.

[5] Joseph H. Ingraham, *The South-West. By a Yankee,* vol. 2 (New York, 1835), p. 26.

[6] Frederick Law Olmsted, *A Journey in the Seaboard Slave States* (New York, 1856), pp. 17–18.

that God would cause us to meet in happiness in another world. I knew, at that solemn moment, that color made no difference, but that her life would have been as precious, if I could have saved it, as if she had been white as snow."[7] A South Carolinian mourned the loss of his "old man Friday," who had known three generations of his family: "He seemed like a connecting link between me and grand-father and grand-mother . . . for he could . . . tell me of the actings and doings of them and others of the olden time."[8]

These were the facts "out of real life" from which grew the legend of racial harmony in the Old South—the facts which proslavery writers enlarged into a generalized picture of bondage as a patriarchal institution. Many of the best illustrations of paternalism were drawn from small establishments where absentee ownership was rare, where overseers were seldom employed, and where contacts between masters and slaves were numerous. Here the discipline tended to be less severe and the system generally less rigid. Only a minority of the slaves, however, lived in holdings so small that the master was more or less constantly in close association with them. Moreover, while there were numerous exceptions, most small slaveholders tried to operate their agricultural enterprises in an efficient, businesslike way and were not easygoing patriarchs.

On the plantations the master's intimate personal contacts were confined almost exclusively to household servants; rarely was he more than casually acquainted with the mass of common field hands. For instance, when a personal attendant died, a South Carolina planter wrote a sentimental tribute to him and affirmed that his loss was "irreparable." But he recorded the deaths of more than a hundred other slaves with no comment at all.[9] In 1844, James H. Hammond was saddened by the loss of his gardener and plantation "patriarch," who had been a "faithful friend" and "one of the best of men." But the deaths of two other slaves in the same year stirred no deep emotions: "Neither a serious loss. One valuable mule has also died."[10]

Plantation paternalism, then, was in most cases essentially a form of leisure-class indulgence of family domestics. In these households, an English visitor observed, "there are often more slaves than are necessary for the labor required of them, many being kept for state, or ostentation." Since the domestics were continually in the presence of the master and mistress and their guests, they were usually treated with great liberality.[11]

---

[7] Journal of Sarah A. Gayle, 4 May 1834, Southern Historical Collection, University of North Carolina, Chapel Hill.

[8] Diary of David Gavin, 13 September 1856, Southern Historical Collection, University of North Carolina, Chapel Hill.

[9] Keating S. Ball, "Record of Births and Deaths," South Caroliniana Library, University of South Carolina, Columbia.

[10] Diary of James H. Hammond, 29 April 1844, 22 June 1844, South Caroliniana Library, University of South Carolina, Columbia.

[11] James S. Buckingham, *The Slave States of America,* vol. 1 (London, 1842), p. 200.

A planter sometimes whimsically selected a slave or two for special pets. He pampered them, consulted them with mock gravity about large matters, and permitted them to be impertinent about small. The guest of a Georgia planter told of a coachman who suddenly stopped the carriage and reported that he had lost one of his white gloves and must go back to find it. "As time pressed, the master in despair took off his own gloves, and . . . gave them to him. When our charioteer had deliberately put them on, we started again."[12] A neighbor told Fanny Kemble "with great glee" that his valet had asked him for his coat as a loan or gift. This, she thought, furnished a good example of the extent to which planters "capriciously permit their favorite slave occasionally to carry their familiarity."[13]

This kind of paternalism (Fanny Kemble likened it to "that maudlin tenderness of a fine lady for her lapdog"), which often arose from the master's genuine love for his slave, gave its recipient privileges and comforts but made the slave into something less than a man. The most generous master, so long as he was determined to *be* a master, could be paternal only toward a fawning dependent; for slavery, by its nature, could never be a relationship between equals. Ideally it was the relationship of parent and child. The slave who had most nearly lost his manhood, who had lost confidence in himself, who stood before his master with hat in hand, head slightly bent, was the one best suited to receive the favors and affection of a patriarch. The system was in its essence a process of infantilization—and the master used the amiable, irresponsible Sambos of tradition, who were the most perfect products of the system, to prove that Negroes were a childlike race, needing guidance and protection but inviting paternal love as well. "Oh, they are interesting creatures," a Virginian told Olmsted, "and, with all their faults, have many beautiful traits. I can't help being attached to them, and I am sure they love us."[14]

It was typical of an indulgent master not to take his slaves seriously, but to look upon them as slightly comic figures. He made them the butt of his humor and considered them fair game for a good-natured practical joke. He tolerated their faults, sighed at their irresponsibility, and laughed at their pompous pretensions and ridiculous attempts to imitate the whites. Even the most sensitive master called slave men "boys" and women "girls," until in their old age he made them honorary "aunties" and "uncles." In addressing them, he never used titles of respect such as "Mr.," "Miss," and "Mrs."; and, except in Maryland, he seldom identified them by family names.

Clearly, to enjoy the bounty of a paternalistic master, a slave—even a pampered domestic—had to give up all claims to respect as a responsible adult, all pretensions of independence. He had to be a Sambo in fact, or, as was probably more often the case, he had to play the role of Sambo with sufficient skill

---

[12] Fredrica Bremer, *The Homes of the New World,* vol. 1 (New York, 1853), pp. 391–92.

[13] Frances Anne Kemble, *Journal of a Residence on a Georgian Plantation in 1838-1839* (New York, 1863), pp. 67–68.

[14] Olmsted, *Seaboard Slave States,* pp. 45–46.

to establish his childlike nature. He had to understand the subtle etiquette that governed his relations with his master: the fine line between friskiness and insubordination, between cuteness and insolence. A nurse might scold the white child under her care; a cook might be a petty tyrant in her kitchen; an old servant might gravely advise on family affairs; a child pet might crawl on master's lap and sleep in his bedroom; a field hand and a small farmer might work together and eat from the same frying pan. These were the hallmarks of paternalistic regimes, but under the best of circumstances the basic relationship remained that of master and slave. Between paternalistic master and submissive slave there still remained a formidable barrier that prevented either from being entirely candid with the other. A slave was always reticent, never entirely at ease, except in the company of other slaves.

Caste and Class in Slave Communities

The ante-bellum South had a class structure based to some extent upon polite breeding but chiefly upon the ownership of property. Superimposed upon this class structure was a caste system which divided those whose appearance enabled them to claim pure Caucasian ancestry from those whose appearance indicated that some or all of their forebears were Negroes. Members of the Caucasian caste, regardless of wealth or education, considered themselves innately superior to Negroes and mulattoes and therefore entitled to rights and privileges denied to the inferior caste. They believed in white supremacy, and they maintained a high degree of caste solidarity to ensure it.

The slaves were caste-conscious too, and despite the presence of some "white man's Negroes," they showed remarkable loyalty toward one another. It was the exception and not the rule for a slave to betray a fellow slave who "took" some of the master's goods, or shirked work, or ran away. In Tennessee, for example, Jim killed Isaac for helping to catch him when he was a fugitive, and in so doing clearly had the sympathy of the other slaves. At Jim's trial the judge observed that "Isaac seems to have lost *caste*. . . . He had combined with the white folks . . . no slight offense in their eyes: that one of their own color, subject to a like servitude, should abandon the interests of his *caste,* and . . . betray black folks to the white people, rendered him an object of general aversion."[15] Former slaves testified that when a newly purchased chattel was sent to the quarters he was immediately initiated into the secrets of the group. He was told what he "had better do to avoid the lash."[16]

Although slaves were generally loyal to their caste, they, like the whites, had their own internal class structure. Their masters helped to create a social

---

[15] Helen T. Catterall, ed., *Judicial Cases Concerning American Slavery and the Negro,* vol. 2 (Washington, D.C., 1926–1937), pp. 522–23.

[16] Frederick Douglass, *My Bondage and My Freedom* (New York, 1855), p. 269. Benjamin Drew, *North-Side View of Slavery — The Refugee: or the Narratives of Fugitive Slaves in Canada* (Boston, 1856), p. 199.

hierarchy among the slaves by giving them specialized tasks for the sake of economic efficiency, and by isolating domestics and artisans from the field hands as a control technique. But the stratification of slave society also resulted from an impelling force within the slave themselves—a natural yearning for some recognition of their worth as individuals, if only from those in their own limited social orbit. To them this wholly human aspiration was, if anything, more important than it was to the whites. Each slave cherished whatever shreds of self-respect he could preserve.

The bondsmen, of course, were cut off from the avenues which led to success and respectability in white society. In slave society, therefore, success, respectability, and morality were measured by other standards, and prestige was won in other ways. The resulting unique patterns of slave behavior amused, dismayed, or appalled the whites and convinced most of them that Negroes were innately different from other racial groups.

Many domestics did adopt part of the white pattern of respectability, were proud of their honesty and loyalty to the white family, and frowned upon disobedient or rebellious behavior. Some bondsmen at times seemed to fear or disapprove of a troublemaker lest he cause them all to suffer the master's wrath. But most of them admired and respected the bold rebel who challenged slave discipline. The strong-willed field hand whom the overseer hesitated to punish, the habitual runaway who mastered the technique of escape and shrugged at the consequences, each won personal triumphs for himself and vicarious triumphs for the others. The generality of slaves believed that he who knew how to trick or deceive the master had an enviable talent, and they regarded the committing of petty larceny as both thrilling and praiseworthy. One former slave recalled with great satisfaction the times when he had caught a pig or chicken and shared it with some "black fair one." These adventures made him feel "good, moral, [and] heroic"; they were "all the chivalry of which my circumstances and conditions of life admitted."[17]

The unlettered slaves rarely won distinction or found pleasure in intellectual or aesthetic pursuits. Theirs was an elemental world in which sharp wits and strong muscles were the chief weapons of survival. Young men prided themselves upon their athletic skills and physical prowess and often matched strength in violent encounters. Having to submit to the superior power of their masters, many slaves were extremely aggressive toward each other. Slave foremen were notoriously severe taskmasters and, when given the power, might whip more cruelly than white masters. Fanny Kemble discerned the brutalizing effects of bondage in the "unbounded insolence and tyranny" which slaves exhibited toward each other.[18] "Everybody, in the South, wants the privilege of whipping somebody else," wrote Frederick Douglass.[19]

---

[17] Josiah Henson, *Father Henson's Story of His Own Life* (Boston, 1858), pp. 21–23.

[18] Kemble, *Journal,* p. 239.

[19] Douglass, *My Bondage,* pp. 69–72, 74–75, 129–32.

Each community of slaves contained one or two members to whom the others looked for leadership because of their physical strength, practical wisdom, or mystical powers. It was a "notorious" fact, according to one master, "that on almost every large plantation of Negroes, there is one among them who holds a kind of magical sway over the minds and opinions of the rest; to him they look as their oracle. . . . The influence of such a Negro, often a preacher, on a quarter is incalculable."[20] A former slave on a Louisiana plantation remembered "Old Abram," who was "a sort of patriarch among us" and was "deeply versed in such philosophy as is taught in the cabin of the slave."[21] On a Mississippi plantation everyone stood in awe of "Old Juba," who wore about his neck a half-dozen charms and who claimed to have seen the devil a hundred times.[22] On Pierce Butler's Georgia plantation, a slave named Sinda prophesied the end of the world, and for a while no threat or punishment could get the hands back to work.[23] A Louisiana planter noted angrily that "Big Lucy" was the leader who "corrupts every young negro in her power."[24] These were the self-made men and women of slave society.

Slaves who lacked the qualities which produce rebels or leaders had to seek personal gratification and the esteem of their fellows in less spectacular ways. They might find these rewards simply by doing their work uncommonly well. Even some of the field hands, though usually lacking the incentive of pecuniary gain, were intrigued by the business of making things grow and enjoyed reputations as good farmers. Similarly, the well-trained domestic might obtain a pleasant feeling of self-importance from the tactful performance of his services. A first-rate plantation cook wallowed in admiration; a personal servant who could humor his master and bandy innocuous pleasantries with him possessed the rare talent of a diplomat. Most domestics were proud of their positions of responsibility, of their fine manners and correct speech, and of their handsome clothing and other badges of distinction. They were important figures in their little world.

Indeed, the domestics, artisans, and foremen constituted the aristocracy of slave society. "I considered my station a very high one," confessed an ex-slave who had been his master's body servant.[25] Many visitors to the South commented on how the domestics flaunted their superiority over "the less favored helots of the plough"—"their assumption of hauteur when they had occasion

---

[20] *Southern Cultivator* 9 (1851): 85.

[21] Northup, *Twelve Years a Slave,* pp. 186–87.

[22] Joseph H. Ingraham, ed., *The Sunny South; or, The Southerner at Home* (Philadelphia, 1860), pp. 86–87.

[23] Kemble, *Journal,* p. 84.

[24] Edwin A. Davis, ed., *Plantation Life in the Florida Parishes of Louisiana, 1836–1846. As Reflected in the Diary of Bennet H. Barrow* (New York: AMS Press, 1943), p. 191.

[25] John Thompson, *The Life of John Thompson, A Fugitive Slave* (Worcester, Mass., 1856), pp. 24–25.

to hold intercourse with any of the 'field hands.'"[26] And former slaves described the envy and hatred of the "helots" for the "fugleman" who "put on airs" in imitation of the whites.[27]

Thus, ironically, a slave might reach the upper stratum of his society either through intimate contact with the master—through learning to ape his manners and rendering him personal service—or through being a rebel or a leader of his own people. And a bondsman, in his own circle, was as highly sensitive to social distinctions as ever his master was. In a society of unequals—of privileged and inferior castes, of wealth and poverty—the need to feel superior to some group takes on a desperate urgency. In some parts of Virginia even the field hands who felt the contempt of the domestics could lavish their own contempt upon the "coal pit niggers" who were hired to work in the mines.[28]

The Slave Family

In Africa the Negroes had been accustomed to a strictly regulated family life and a rigidly enforced moral code. But in America the disintegration of their social organization removed the traditional sanctions which had encouraged them to respect their own customs. Here they found the whites organized into families having great social and economic importance but regulated by different laws. In the quarters they were usually more or less encouraged to live as families and to accept white standards of morality.

But it was only outwardly that the family life of the mass of Southern slaves resembled that of their masters. Inwardly, in many crucial ways, the domestic regimes of the slave cabin and of the "big house" were quite different. The most obvious difference lay in the legal foundations upon which the slave family and the white family rested. In every state, white marriages were recognized as civil contracts which imposed obligations on both parties and provided penalties for their violation. Slave marriages had no such recognition in the state codes; instead, they were regulated by whatever rules the owners saw fit to make and enforce.

A few masters arbitrarily assigned husbands to women who had reached the "breeding age"; but ordinarily they permitted slaves to pick their own mates and required only that they ask permission to marry. On the plantations, most owners refused to allow slaves to marry away from home, preferring to make additional purchases when the sexes were out of balance. Still, it was not infrequent on both large and small estates for husbands and wives to belong to different masters. Sometimes, when a slave wished to marry the slave of another owner, a sale was made in order to unite them.

---

[26] Ingraham, ed., *Sunny South,* p. 35.

[27] Austin Steward, *Twenty-Two Years a Slave* (Canandaigua, N.Y., 1856), pp. 30–32.

[28] Frederic Bancroft, *Slave-Trading in the Old South* (Baltimore: J. H. Furst, 1931), pp. 153–55.

Having obtained their master's consent, the couple might begin living together without further formality; or their master might hastily pronounce them man and wife in a perfunctory ceremony. But more solemn ceremonies, conducted by slave preachers or white clergymen, were not uncommon even for the field hands, and they were customary for the domestics. The importance of the occasion was sometimes emphasized by a wedding feast and gifts to the bride.

Divorce, like marriage, was within the master's jurisdiction. He might permit his slaves to change spouses as often and whenever they wished, or he might establish more or less severe rules. A Louisiana master granted a divorce only after a month's notice and prohibited remarriage unless a divorcee agreed to receive twenty-five lashes.[29] James H. Hammond inflicted one hundred lashes upon marriage partners who separated and forced them to live singly for three years.[30] In contrast, there were slave masters who maintained a veritable regime of free love—of casual alliances and easy separations. Inevitably the rules on a given estate affected the family life of its slaves.

Not only did the slave family lack the protection and the external pressure of state law, it also lacked most of the centripetal forces that gave the white family its cohesiveness. In the life of the slave, the family had nothing like the social significance that it had in the life of the white man. The slave woman was first a full-time worker for her owner, and only incidentally a wife, mother, and homemaker. She spent a small fraction of her time in the house; she often did no cooking or clothesmaking; and she was not usually nurse to her husband or children during illness. Parents sometimes had little to do with the raising of their children; and children soon learned that their parents were neither the fount of wisdom nor the seat of authority. Lacking autonomy, the slave family could not offer the child shelter or security from the frightening creatures in the outside world.

The slave family had no greater importance as an economic unit. Parents and children might spend some spare hours together in their garden plots, but, unlike rural whites, slaves labored most of the time for their masters in groups that had no relationship to the family. The husband was not the director of an agricultural enterprise; he was not the head of the family, the holder of property, the provider, or the protector. If his wife or child was disrobed and whipped by master or overseer, he stood by in helpless humiliation. In an age of patriarchal families, the male slave's only crucial function within the family was that of siring offspring.

Indeed, the typical slave family was matriarchal in form, for the mother's role was far more important than the father's. Whatever significance the family did have rested in responsibilities which traditionally belonged to women,

---

[29] J. Carlyle Sitterson, *Sugar Country* (Lexington: University of Kentucky Press, 1953), p. 58.

[30] James H. Hammond, "Plantation Manual," Hammond Papers, Library of Congress, Washington, D.C.

such as cleaning house, preparing food, making clothes, and raising children. The husband was at most his wife's assistant, her companion, and her sex partner. He was often thought of as her possession ("Mary's Tom"), as was the cabin in which they lived. It was common for a mother and her children to be considered a family without reference to the father.

Given these conditions—the absence of legal marriages, the family's minor social and economic significance, and the father's limited role—it is hardly surprising to find that slave families were highly unstable. Lacking both outer pressures and inner pulls, they were also exposed to the threat of forced separations through sales. A slave preacher in Kentucky united couples in wedlock "until death or *distance* do you part."[31] Thus every slave family had about it an air of impermanence, for no master could promise that his debts would not force sales or guarantee that his death would not cause divisions.

Some of the problems that troubled slave families, of course, had nothing to do with slavery—they were the tragically human problems which have ever disturbed marital tranquillity. One such domestic dilemma involved a slave whose wife did not return his devotion. "He says he loves his wife and does not want to leave her," noted the master. "She says she does not love him and wont live with him. Yet he says he thinks he can over come her scruples and live happily with her."[32] For this slavery was not the cause nor freedom the cure.

But other kinds of family tragedies were uniquely a part of life in bondage. A poignant example was the scene that transpired when an overseer tied and whipped a slave mother in the presence of her children. The frightened children pelted the overseer with stones, and one of them ran up and bit him in the leg. During the ruction the cries of the mother were mingled with the screams of the children, *"Let my mammy go—let my mammy go."*[33]

The Beginnings of an Afro-American Culture

What was there in the lives of slaves besides work, sleep, and procreation? What filled their idle hours? What occupied their minds? What distinguished them from domestic animals? Much will never be known, for surviving records provide only brief glimpses into the private life of the slave quarters. But much can be learned from Negro songs and folklore, from the recollections of former slaves, and from the observations of the more perceptive and sensitive whites.

The average bondsman, it would appear, lived more or less aimlessly in a bleak and narrow world. He lived in a world without schools, without books,

[31] J. Winston Coleman, Jr., *Slavery Times in Kentucky* (Chapel Hill: University of North Carolina Press, 1940), pp. 58–59.

[32] Gustavus A. Henry to his wife, 11 December 1839, Henry Papers, Southern Historical Collection, University of North Carolina, Chapel Hill.

[33] Douglass, *My Bondage,* pp. 92–95.

without learned men; he knew less of the fine arts and of aesthetics than he had known in Africa; and he found few ways to break the monotonous sameness of all his days. His world was the few square miles of earth surrounding his cabin—a familiar island beyond which lay strange places (up North where people like him were not slaves), frightening places ("down the river" where overseers were devils), and dead places (across the ocean where his ancestors had lived and where he had no desire to go). His world was full of mysteries which he could not solve and forces which he could not control. And so he tended to be a fatalist and a futilitarian, for no other philosophy could reconcile him to his life.

When the Negroes left Africa they carried with them a knowledge of their own complex cultures. Some elements of their cultures—or at least some adaptations or variations of them—were planted somewhat insecurely in America. These surviving "Africanisms" were evident in the slaves' speech, in their dances, in their music, in their folklore, and in their religion. The extent to which their African heritage carried over to their life in America varied with time and place. More of the African past was evident in the eighteenth century, when a large proportion of the slaves were native Africans, than in the mid-nineteenth century, when the great majority were second- and third-generation Americans. Field hands living on large plantations in isolated areas, such as the Sea Islands off the South Carolina and Georgia coasts, doubtless preserved more "Africanisms" than slaves who were widely dispersed in relatively small holdings or who lived in their masters' houses as domestics. How substantial and how durable the African heritage was is a question over which students of the American Negro have long disagreed.

The disagreement, however, has been over the size of what was admittedly a fragment; few would deny that by the ante-bellum period slaves everywhere in the South had lost most of their African culture. In bondage, the Negroes lacked cultural autonomy—the authority to apply rigorous sanctions against those who violated or repudiated their own traditions. Instead, they were put under considerable pressure to learn and accept whichever of the white man's customs would help them to exist with a minimum of friction in a biracial society. Before the Civil War, American Negroes, with rare exceptions, developed no cultural nationalism, no conscious pride in African ways. At most they unconsciously preserved aspects of their old culture that bore a direct relevance to their new lives, or they fused remnants of Africa with things borrowed from the whites.

In many respects, the Negro slave existed in a kind of cultural void. He lived in a twilight zone between two ways of life, neither of which now afforded him much opportunity to develop the attributes which distinguish man from beast. Olmsted noted that slaves normally acquired, by example or compulsion, some of the external forms of white civilization; but this was poor compensation for "the systematic withdrawal from them of all the usual influences which tend to nourish the moral nature and develop the intellectual faculties, in savages as well as in civilized free men."[34] Indeed, the development of a true Afro-American culture had to await the end of slavery.

What, then, filled the leisure hours of the slaves? Not surprisingly, these culturally rootless people devoted much of their free time to the sheer pleasure of being idle. Such activities as they did engage in were the simple diversions of a poor, untutored folk — activities that gave them physical pleasure or emotional release. Slaves probably found it more difficult to find satisfying amusements on the small farms, where they had few comrades, than in the cities and on the plantations, where they could mix freely with their own people.

"I have no desire to represent the life of slavery as an experience of nothing but misery," wrote a former bondsman. In addition to the unpleasant things, he remembered "jolly Christmas times, dances before old massa's door for the first drink of egg-nog, extra meat at holiday times, midnight visits to apple orchards, broiling stray chickens, and first-rate tricks to dodge work." Feasting, as this account suggests, was one of the slave's chief pleasures, one of his "principle sources of comfort."[35] He looked forward to a feast not only at Christmas but when crops were laid by, when there was a wedding, or when the master gave a reward for good behavior.[36] "Only the slave who has lived all the year on his scanty allowance of meal and bacon, can appreciate such suppers," recalled another ex-bondsman.[37]

Occasions such as Christmas or a corn shucking were times not only for feasting but also for visiting with slaves on nearby establishments. In Virginia a visitor observed that many bondsmen spent Sundays "strolling about the fields and streets," finding joy in their relative freedom of movement.[38] On holidays they dressed in bright-colored clothes which contrasted pleasantly with their drab everyday apparel. The slaves seemed to welcome each holiday with great fervor, for they found in it an enormous relief from the boredom of their daily lives. "All are brushing up, putting on their best rigging, and with boisterous joy hailing the approach of the Holy days," noted an Arkansas master at the start of one Christmas season.[39]

Dancing was one of the favorite pastimes of the slaves, on Saturday nights as well as on special holidays. The jigs and double shuffles that the slaves delighted in were once described as "dancing all over"; they revealed an apparent capacity to "agitate every part of the body at the same time."[40] Such dances

---

[34] Frederick Law Olmsted, *A Journey in the Back Country* (New York, 1860), pp. 70–71.

[35] Henson, *Father Henson's Story*, pp. 19–20, 56.

[36] Northup, *Twelve Years a Slave*, pp. 213–16.

[37] Steward, *Twenty-Two Years a Slave*, pp. 28–31.

[38] Journal of J. Milton Emerson, 19 September 1841, Duke University Library, Durham, N.C.

[39] Diary of John W. Brown, 25 December 1853, Southern Historical Collection, University of North Carolina, Chapel Hill.

[40] *De Bow's Review* 11 (1851): 66.

were physical and emotional orgies. Fanny Kemble found it impossible to describe "all the contortions, and springs, and flings, and kicks, and capers" the slaves accomplished as they danced "Jim Crow."[41] A vistor at a "shake down" in a Louisiana sugar house found the dancers in a "thumping ecstasy, with loose elbows, pendulous paws, angulated knees, heads thrown back, and backs arched inwards—a glazed eye, intense solemnity of mien."[42] Slaves danced to the music of the fiddle or the banjo, or they beat out their rhythm with sticks on tin pans, by clapping their hands, or by tapping their feet.

Other holiday amusements included hunting, trapping, and fishing. And in spite of legal interdictions, slaves gambled with each other and with "dissolute" whites.[43] But some found both pleasure and profit in using their leisure time to pursue various handicrafts. Among the articles made by slaves were brooms, mats, horse collars, baskets, boats, and canoes. These "sober, thinking and industrious" bondsmen scorned those who wasted time in frivolities or adopted the white man's vices.[44]

A few things in the lives of the slaves belonged to them in a more intimate and personal way. Generally, these were the product of the peculiar blending of African traditions with new experiences in America which characterized the Negro slave, and which would ultimately form the basis of a unique Afro-American culture. For instance, folklore was important to the slaves, as it has always been to preliterate peoples, and they carried on a distinct oral tradition. Some of the folk tales that were passed from one generation of slaves to the next preserved legends of their own past; some explained natural phenomena or described a world peopled with spirits; and some told with charming symbolism the story of the endless warfare between black men and white men. The tales of Br'er Rabbit, in all their variations, made virtues of such qualities as wit, strategy, and deceit—the weapons of the weak in their battles with the strong. Br'er Bear had great physical power but was a hapless bumbler; Br'er Fox was shrewd and crafty as well as strong but, nonetheless, was never quite a match for Br'er Rabbit. This was a scheme of things which the slave found delightful to contemplate.[45]

The bondsmen had ceremonial occasions of their own, and they devised special ways of commemorating the white man's holidays. At Christmas in eastern North Carolina, they begged pennies from the whites as they went "John Canoeing" (or "John Cunering") along the roads, wearing outlandish

---

[41] Kemble, *Journal,* pp. 96–97.

[42] William H. Russell, *My Diary North and South* (Boston, 1863), pp. 258–59.

[43] Guion G. Johnson, *Ante-Bellum North Carolina* (Chapel Hill: University of North Carolina Press, 1937), pp. 555–57.

[44] Douglass, *My Bondage,* pp. 251–52.

[45] Mason Crum, *Gullah: Negro Life in the Carolina Sea Islands* (Durham, N.C.: Duke University Press, 1940), p. 120. Benjamin A. Botkin, ed., *Lay My Burden Down: A Folk History of Slavery* (Chicago: University of Chicago Press, 1945), p. 2. Richard M. Dorson, ed., *American Negro Folktales* (New York: Fawcett, 1967).

Slave handiwork. Top photo includes rice panner and wooden pestle reminiscent of African implements. Bottom photo includes a shoe tree, shoes, and a wooden last, sample ironwork, and a wooden pattern for ironwork. From the Old Slave Mart Museum, Charleston, S.C. Photos courtesy of Negro History Associates.

costumes and masks, blowing horns, tinkling tambourines, dancing, and chanting

> Hah! Low! Here we go!
> Hah! Low! Here we go!
> Hah! Low! Here we go!
> Kuners come from Denby![46]

[46] Johnson, *Ante-Bellum North Carolina,* p. 553.

Virginia slaves had persimmon parties, where they interspersed dancing with draughts of persimmon beer and slices of persimmon bread. At one of these parties the banjo player sat in a chair on the beer barrel: "A long white cowtail, queued with red ribbon ornamented his head, and hung gracefully down his back; over this he wore a three-cocked hat, decorated with peacock feathers, a rose cockade, a bunch of ripe persimmons, and . . . three pods of red pepper as a top-knot."[47] On some Louisiana sugar plantations, when the cutters reached the last row of cane they left the tallest cane standing and tied a blue ribbon to it. In a ceremony which marked the end of the harvest, one of the laborers waved his cane knife in the air, "sang to the cane as if it were a person, and danced around it several times before cutting it." Then the workers mounted their carts and triumphantly carried the last cane to the master's house, where they were given a drink.[48]

Rarely did a contemporary write about slaves without mentioning their music, for this was their most splendid vehicle of self-expression. Slave music was a unique blend of "Africanisms," of Protestant hymns and revival songs, and of the feelings and emotions that were a part of life in servitude.[49] The Negroes had a repertory of songs for almost every occasion, and they not only sang them with innumerable variations but constantly improvised new songs besides. They sang spirituals which revealed their conception of Christianity and testified to their religous faith. They sang work songs (usually slow in tempo) to break the monotony of toil in the tobacco factories, in the sugar houses, on the river boats, and in the fields. They sang protest songs whose nuances may well have been lost by the white men who belatedly collected them. They sang whimsical songs telling little stories or ridiculing human frailties. And they sang nonsense songs, such as "Who-zen-John, Who-za," sung by a group of Virginia slaves as they "clapped juber" to a dance:

> Old black bull come down de hollow,
> He shake hi' tail, you hear him bellow;
> When he bellow he jar de river,
> He paw de yearth, he make it quiver.
>   Who-zen-John, who-za.[50]

Above all, they sang plaintive songs about the sorrows and the yearnings which they dared not, or could not, more than half express. Music of this kind could hardly have come from an altogether carefree and contented people. "The singing of a man cast away on a desolate island," wrote Frederick Douglass, "might be as appropriately considered an evidence of his contentment and happiness, as the singing of a slave. Sorrow and desolation have their

---

[47] *Farmers' Register* 6 (1838): 59–61.

[48] V. Alton Moody, "Slavery on Louisiana Sugar Plantations," *Louisiana Historical Quarterly* 7 (1924): 277 n.

[49] A valuable collection of slave songs is Miles Mark Fisher, ed., *Negro Slave Songs in the United States* (Ithaca, N.Y.: Cornell University Press, 1953).

[50] *Farmers' Register* 6 (1838): 59–61.

songs, as well as joy and peace."[51] In their somber and mournful moods the bondsmen voiced sentiments such as these: "O Lord, O my Lord! O my good Lord keep me from sinking down"; "Got nowhere to lay my weary head"; "My trouble is hard"; "Nobody knows the trouble I've seen"; and "Lawd, I can't help from cryin' sometime." The Gullah Negroes of South Carolina sang:

> I know moon-rise, I know star-rise,
>> Lay dis body down.
> I walk in de moonlight, I walk in de starlight,
>> To lay dis body down.
> I'll walk in de graveyard, I'll walk through de graveyard,
>> To lay dis body down.
> I'll lie in de grave and stretch out my arms;
>> Lay dis body down;
> I go to de judgment in de evenin' of de day,
>> When I lay dis body down;
> And my soul and your soul will meet in de day
>> When I lay dis body down.[52]

One final element helped to make pleasant the leisure hours of numerous slave men and women: alcohol in its crudest but cheapest and most concentrated forms. To be sure, these bibulous bondsmen were indulging in a common vice in an age of hard liquor and heavy drinkers; but they, more than their masters, saw the periodic solace of the bottle as a necessity of life. In preparing for Christmas, slaves somehow managed to smuggle "fresh bottles of rum or whisky into their cabins," for many thought of each holiday as a time for a bacchanalian spree.[53] Indeed, recalled a former bondsman, to be sober during the holidays was "disgraceful; and he was esteemed a lazy and improvident man, who could not afford to drink whisky during Christmas."[54] No law, no threat of the master, ever kept liquor out of the hands of slaves or stopped the illicit trade between them and "unscrupulous" whites.[55] Some masters furnished a supply of whisky for holiday occasions or winked at violations of state laws and of their own rules.[56]

There was little truth in the abolitionist charge that masters gave liquor to their slaves in order to befuddle their minds and keep them in bondage. On the other hand, many bondsmen used intoxicants for a good deal more than an occasional pleasant stimulant, a mere conviviality of festive occasions. They found that liquor provided their only satisfactory escape from the indignities, the frustrations, the emptiness, the oppressive boredom of slavery. Hence,

---

[51] Douglass, *My Bondage,* pp. 99–100.

[52] Thomas Wentworth Higginson, *Army Life in a Black Regiment* (Boston, 1870), p. 209.

[53] Daniel R. Hundley, *Social Relations in Our Southern States* (New York, 1860), pp. 359–60.

[54] Olmsted, *Seaboard Slave States,* pp. 75, 101–02.

[55] Diary of William C. Adams, 29 December 1857, Duke University Library, Durham, N.C.

[56] Douglass, *My Bondage,* pp. 251–52.

when they had the chance, they resorted to places that catered to the Negro trade or found sanctuaries where they could tipple undisturbed. What filled their alcoholic dreams one can only guess, for the dreams at least were theirs alone.

Religion

Most slaves took their religion seriously, though by the standards of white Christianity they sinned mightily. In Africa the Negro's world was inhabited by petulant spirits whose demands had to be gratified; his relationship to these spirits was regulated by the rituals and dogmas of his pagan faith. Some of this was in the corpus of "Africanisms" brought to America. But most of it was lost within a generation, not only because of the general decay of Negro culture but also because new problems and experiences created an urgent need for a new kind of religious expression and a new set of beliefs. What the slave needed now was a spiritual life in which he could participate vigorously, which transported him from the dull routine of bondage and which promised him that a better time was within his reach. Hence, he embraced evangelical Protestantism eagerly, because it so admirably satisfied all these needs.

"The doctrine of the Savior comes to the negro slaves as their most inward need, and as the accomplishment of the wishes of their souls," explained a visitor to the South. "They themselves enunciate it with the purest joy. . . . Their prayers burst forth into flame as they ascend to heaven."[57] On many plantations religious exercises were almost "the only habitual recreation not purely sensual," Olmsted noted; hence slaves poured all their emotions into them "with an intensity and vehemence almost terrible to witness."[58] A former slave recalled the ecstasy he felt when he learned that salvation was *"for every man"* and that God loved black men as well as white. "I seemed to see a glorious being, in a cloud of splendor, smiling down from on high," ready to "welcome me to the skies."[59]

Like the whites, many slaves alternated outbursts of intense religious excitement with intervals of religious calm or indifference, for both races participated in the revivals that periodically swept rural America. At the emotional height of a revival, most of the slaves in a neighborhood might renounce worldly pleasures and live austere lives, without the fiddle, without dancing, and without whisky. But this could not last forever, and gradually they drifted back to their sinful ways.[60] And their masters often drifted with them; for although many used religion as a means of control, many others neglected it between revivals.

---

[57] Bremer, *Homes of the New World,* 2:155.

[58] Olmsted, *Back Country,* p. 106.

[59] Henson, *Father Henson's Story,* pp. 28–29.

[60] Susan Dabney Smedes, *Memorials of a Southern Planter* (Baltimore, 1887), pp. 161–62. Henry Watson, Jr., to his mother, 7 July 1846, Henry Watson, Jr., Papers, Duke University Library, Durham, N.C.

In the North, Negroes organized their own independent churches; but in the South, except in a few border cities, the laws against slave assemblies prevented them from doing so before the Civil War. Thus many slaves attended the white-controlled churches or were preached to by white ministers at special services. Doubtless this inhibited them and limited both the spiritual and emotional value of their religious experience, because there was an enormous gap between a congregation of slaves and even the most sympathetic white clergyman. Yet it was from white preachers that the slaves received their indoctrination into Christianity. To many bondsmen affiliation with a white church was a matter of considerable importance, and they did not take lightly the penalty of being "excluded from the fellowship" for immorality or "heathenism."[61] Some white clergymen preached to them with great success. And it was not uncommon to see whites and slaves "around the same altar . . . mingling their cries for mercy" and together finding "the pearl of great price."[62]

Even so, most bondsmen received infinitely greater satisfaction from unsupervised religious meetings which they held secretly, or which their masters tolerated in disregard of the law. At these gatherings slaves could express themselves freely and interpret the Christian faith to their own satisfaction, even though some educated whites believed that their interpretation contained more heathen superstition than Christian doctrine. The slaves, observed Olmsted, were "subject to intense excitements; often really maniacal," which they considered to be religious; but "I cannot see that they indicate anything but a miserable system of superstition, the more painful that it employs some forms and words ordinarily connected with true Christianity."[63]

The practice of voodooism, which survived among a few slaves in southern Louisiana, as well as a widespread belief in charms and spirits stemmed in part from the African past.[64] Frederick Douglass learned from an old African (who had "magic powers") that if a slave wore the root of a certain herb on his right side, no white man could ever whip him.[65] Slave conjurers accomplished wondrous feats with "root work" and put frightful curses upon their enemies.[66] A Louisiana master once had to punish a slave because of "a phial which was found in his possession containing two ground puppies as they are called. The negroes were under some apprehension that he intended to do mischief."[67]

[61] "Flat River Church Records" (Person County, N.C.), Southern Historical Collection, University of North Carolina, Chapel Hill.

[62] W. P. Harrison, *The Gospel Among the Slaves* (Nashville, 1893), pp. 199–201.

[63] Olmsted, *Seaboard Slave States,* p. 114.

[64] Sitterson, *Sugar Country,* p. 102.

[65] Douglass, *My Bondage,* p. 238.

[66] Diary of James H. Hammond, 16 October 1835, Hammond Papers, Library of Congress, Washington, D.C.

[67] Diary of Henry Marston, 25 November 1825, Henry Marston, and Family, Papers, Department of Archives, Louisiana State University, Baton Rouge.

But slave superstitions did not all originate in Africa; in fact, it would be difficult to prove that most of them did. For the slaves picked up plenty of superstitious ideas from "the good Puritans, Baptists, Methodists, and other religious sects who first obtained possession of their ancestors." (Indeed, it is more than likely that Negroes and whites made a generous exchange of superstitions.) There is no need to trace back to Africa the slave's fear of beginning to plant a crop on Friday, his dread of witches, ghosts, and hobgoblins, his confidence in good-luck charms, his alarm at evil omens, his belief in dreams, and his reluctance to visit burying grounds after dark. These superstitions were all firmly rooted in Anglo-Saxon folklore. Of course, the identification of superstition is a highly subjective process; and Southern whites tended to condemn as superstition whatever elements of slave belief they did not happen to share, just as they condemned the sectarian beliefs held by fellow whites.

The influence of Africa could sometimes be detected in the manner in which slaves conducted themselves at their private religious services. In the Sea Islands, for example, a prayer meeting at the "praise house" was followed by a "shout," which was an invigorating group ceremony. The participants "begin first walking and by-and-by shuffling around, one after the other, in a ring. The foot is hardly taken from the floor, and the progression is mainly due to a jerking, hitching motion, which agitates the entire shouter, and soon brings out streams of perspiration. Sometimes they dance silently, sometimes as they shuffle they sing the chorus of the spiritual, and sometimes the song itself is sung by the dancers." This, a white witness believed, was "certainly the remains of some old idol worship."[68] Olmsted reported that in social worship the slaves "work themselves up to a great pitch of excitement, in which they yell and cry aloud, and, finally, shriek and leap up, clapping their hands and dancing, as it is done at heathen festivals."[69]

But again, one suspects that the slaves learned much of their "heathenism" in the white churches and at white revival meetings. One Sunday morning, in Accomac County, Virginia, a visitor attended a Methodist church where the slaves were permitted to hold their own services before the whites occupied the building. "Such a medley of sounds, I never heard before. They exhorted, prayed, sung, shouted, cryed, grunted and growled. Poor Souls! they knew no better, for I found that when the other services began the sounds were similar, which the white folks made; and the negroes only imitated them and shouted a little louder."[70] In short, though there were differences, the religion of the slaves was, in many fundamental ways, strikingly similar to that of the poor, illiterate white men of the ante-bellum South.

---

[68] Guion G. Johnson, *A Social History of the Sea Islands* (Chapel Hill: University of North Carolina Press, 1930), pp. 149–51.

[69] Olmsted, *Seaboard Slave States,* pp. 449–50.

[70] Journal of J. Milton Emerson, 26 September 1841.

The Problem of the White Man

Since the masters kept diaries and wrote letters, books, and essays, it is relatively easy to discover their various attitudes toward the slaves. But what the slaves thought of their masters (and of white people generally) is infinitely more difficult to find. Not only did slaves and ex-slaves write a good deal less than whites, but most of them seemed determined that no white man should ever know their thoughts. As Olmsted observed, the average slave possessed considerable "cunning, shrewdness, [and] reticence."[71]

Several points, however, are clear: (1) slaves did not have one uniform attitude toward whites, but a whole range of attitudes; (2) they gave much attention to the problem of their relationship with whites; and (3) they found the "management of whites" as complex a matter as their masters found the "management of Negroes." Every slave became conscious of the "white problem" sometime in early childhood; for in a society dominated by whites, Negro children have always had to learn, more or less painfully, the meaning of caste and somehow come to terms with it. In bondage, they also had to learn what it meant to be property.

During the first half-dozen years of their lives, neither caste nor bondage had meaning to the children of either race, and blacks and whites often played together without consciousness of color. But it was not long before the black child, in some way, began to discover his peculiar position. Perhaps his mother or father explained his status to him and told him how to behave around the master and other whites. ("My father always advised me to be tractable, and get along with the white people in the best manner I could," recalled a former slave.[72]) Perhaps the slave child saw a white playmate begin to assume an attitude of superiority prior to their separation. Perhaps he first encountered reality when the authority of the master or overseer began to supersede that of his parents—or, in a more shocking way, when he saw the master or overseer reprimand or punish one of his parents. Thus the young slave became conscious of the "white problem," conscious that the white man was a formidable figure with pretensions of omniscience and omnipotence. As he became involved with white men, the slave gradually developed an emotional attitude toward them.

This attitude, while perhaps seldom one of complete confidence, was frequently one of amiable regard, and sometimes one of deep affection. Such an attitude was by no means limited to those whom slavery had turned into childlike Sambos. It was only normal for a slave who lived close to a warm, generous, and affectionate master to reciprocate these feelings, for the barriers of bondage and caste could not prevent decent human beings from showing sympathy and compassion for one another—slave for master as well as master

---

[71] Olmsted, *Back Country,* p. 384.

[72] Drew, *North-Side View,* p. 358.

for slave. Thus the domestic's proverbial love for the white family was by no means altogether a myth.

Other slaves, in dealing with whites, seemed coldly opportunistic; they had evidently concluded that it was most practical to use the arts of diplomacy, to "keep on the right side" of their masters, in order to enjoy whatever privileges and comforts were available to them in bondage. So they flattered the whites, affected complete subservience, and generally behaved like buffoons. When Olmsted was introduced to a slave preacher, he shook the Negro's hand and greeted him respectfully; but the latter "seemed to take this for a joke and laughed heartily." The master explained in a "slightly humorous" tone that the preacher was also the driver, that he drove the field hands at the cotton all week and at the Gospel on Sunday. At this remark the preacher "began to laugh again, and reeled off like a drunken man—entirely overcome with merriment." Thus, remarked Olmsted, the preacher, who had apparently concluded that the purpose of the interview was to make fun of him, "generously" assumed "a merry humor."[73] This slave, like many others, seemed willing enough to barter his self-respect for the privileges and prestige of his high offices.

Still other slaves exhibited toward whites no strong emotion either of affection or hatred, but rather an attitude of deep suspicion. Many contemporaries commented upon their "habitual distrust of the white race" and noted that they were "always suspicious." When this was the Negro's basic attitude, the resulting relationship was an amoral one which resembled an unending civil war; the slave then seemed to think that he was entitled to use every tactic of deception and chicanery he could devise. Many ex-slaves who spoke of their former masters without bitterness still recalled with particular pleasure the times when they had outwitted or beguiled them ("'cause us had to lie").[74]

To a few slaves this civil war was an intense and serious business, because they felt for their masters (sometimes for all whites) an abiding animosity. In speaking of the whites, such bondsmen used "the language of hatred and revenge";[75] on one plantation the slaves in their private conversations contemptuously called their master "Old Hogjaw."[76] Externally these slaves wore an air of sullenness. "You need only look in their faces to see they are not happy," exclaimed a traveler; instead, they were "depressed" or "gloomy."[77] Field hands often gave no visible sign of pleasure when their master approached; some made clumsy bows, but others ignored him entirely.[78]

The poor whites were the one group in the superior caste for whom the

---

[73] Olmsted, *Seaboard Slave States,* p. 451.

[74] Olmsted, *Back Country,* p. 114. Bremer, *Homes of the New World,* 1:292. Botkin, ed., *Lay My Burden Down,* passim.

[75] Northup, *Twelve Years a Slave,* p. 114.

[76] Russel, *Diary,* pp. 133, 146–47, 258, 262.

[77] James Stirling, *Letters from the Slave States* (London, 1857), p. 49.

[78] Buckingham, *Slave States,* 1:62–63.

slaves dared openly express their contempt, and the slaves did so in pictur-
esque terms. Masters often tolerated this and were even amused by it.[79] However, it is likely that some slaves were thereby expressing their opinion of the
whole white race. A transparent example of the malice that a portion of the
slaves bore the whites occurred in St. Louis when a mob tarred and feathered
a white man. "One feature of the scene I could not help remarking," wrote a
witness: "the negroes all appeared in high glee, and many of them actually
danced with joy."[80]

But the predominant and overpowering emotion that whites aroused in the
majority of slaves appeared to be neither love nor hate, but fear. "We were
always uneasy," an ex-slave recalled; when "a white man spoke to me, I would
feel frightened," another confessed.[81] In Alabama, a visitor who lost his pocket-
book noted that the slave who found it "was afraid of being whipped for theft
and had given it to the first white man he saw, and at first was afraid to pick
it up."[82] A fugitive who was taken into the home of an Ohio Quaker found it
impossible to overcome his timidity and apprehension. "I had never had a white
man to treat me as an equal, and the idea of a white lady waiting on me at the
table was still worse! . . . I thought if I could only be allowed the privilege of
eating in the kitchen, I should be more than satisfied."[83]

The masters themselves provided the most vivid evidence of the fear they
inspired in the minds of many slaves. When they advertised for runaways, the
owners were uncommonly candid in describing not only the external appearance but the character and behavior of their human property. Thus, inadver-
tently, they frequently revealed the full strain of the relationship between the
two races, a relationship that must have been for some slaves an emotional
nightmare. In their advertisements no descriptive phrases were more common
than these: "stutters very much when spoken to"; "speaks softly and has a
downcast look"; "has an uneasy appearance when spoken to"; "speaks quickly,
and with an anxious expression of countenance"; "a very down look, and easily
confused when spoken to"; "stammers very much so as to be scarcely understood." Indeed, if one were to attempt a profile of an average Southern slave,
the result would not be an easygoing, carefree Sambo; it would be an anxious
man with a downcast look.

"I feel lighter,—the dread is gone," affirmed a Negro woman who had escaped to Canada. "It is a great heaviness on a person's mind to be a slave."[84]

---

[79] Drew, *North-Side View,* pp. 156–57.

[80] J. Benwell, *An Englishman's Travels in America* (London, n.d.), p. 99.

[81] Drew, *North-Side View,* pp. 30, 86.

[82] Diary of Henry Watson, Jr., 1 January 1831.

[83] William W. Brown, *Narrative of William W. Brown, A Fugitive Slave* (Boston, 1847),
pp. 102–03.

[84] Drew, *North-Side View,* p. 179.

The Social Consequences
of Slavery

STANLEY M. ELKINS

Stanley M. Elkins is professor of history at Smith College. His book
Slavery: A Problem in American Institutional and Intellectual Life
(University of Chicago Press, 1959) is one of the most original and
provocative books on slavery published in recent years. In this
controversial work, very generally, Mr. Elkins compares the experience of the slaves in the United States to that of the concentration
camp prisoners in Nazi Germany, contending that both groups
suffered dehumanization, the loss of initiative, and confusion of
identity as a result of victimization by a viciously repressive system.
Following are two essays that were appended to the second edition
of *Slavery* in 1968. In the first, Mr. Elkins sets forth his ideas on the
way in which law and custom combined in the Southern United
States to fasten the slave into a rigid pattern of dependence. In the
second, he looks at possible historical explanations for the differences between slavery in Latin America and in North America. The
essays are introduced with a statement by the author that is original to this volume.

The two short essays that follow date from 1961 and 1967 respectively.
They first appeared as a pair in Appendix C of *Slavery,* Second Edition,
where they were intended to supplement points made in the body of the
text and, in some ways, to indicate the directions my own thought had taken
since *Slavery* was originally published in 1959. Now they are being made to
serve yet another purpose—that of illuminating a particular aspect of vital
importance in the slave experience.

If there is a single theme uniting these two essays, it is the extraordinary
rigidity that fastened itself upon virtually every aspect of American slavery.
The legal codes, the plantation etiquette, the racial assumptions that defined
in so many ways the social and individual status of the slave—all these went
together, it seemed to me, with a kind of hardness of fit that left few spaces
within which even the most gifted black man could fully realize himself, either
as an autonomous individual or as a responsible member of a community. And
with rigidity of structure went rigidity of mind. A society that prided itself on

its ingenuity, on the "pragmatic" spirit in which it addressed so many of its problems, proved starkly unimaginative in facing the moral and human problems of chattel slavery. In the era prior to the Civil War such otherwise humane and enlightened men as Jefferson and Lincoln, despite their deep aversion to slavery, found it quite impossible to envision a state in which free blacks and whites might live side by side in equality and peace.

In reaching the conclusions presented in these essays, I was fully aware of the many exceptional cases in the annals of American slavery. The self-employed workman, the skilled artisan, the trusted house servant, the valued but stubborn field hand whom it was easier to indulge than to punish—all managed in their way to circumvent some of the crushing physical and psychic coercions of the system. But what claimed my attention far more forcibly was the inflexible determination of white society to set limits on both the private and group resources of black men everywhere, and the degree to which, as I thought, it succeeded.

Recent scholars have argued, however, that the resources were nonetheless there. There has been increasing interest in what might be called the "underground culture" of slavery: the music, the folk tales, the techniques of resistance, often highly subtle—a black folk culture, in short, behind which a slave might protect his human integrity despite the overwhelming power of the master and of the white world that surrounded him. And with this has come a steady shift of emphasis from helplessness and passivity to independence of spirit, cooperation, even militancy. The result has been a growing inclination to regard American slavery, for all its repressions, as somehow less debilitating psychologically, less destructive of the slave's essential humanity, than was once supposed.

As to this, I would prefer for the moment to reserve judgment. The movement to explore black folk culture is in itself an exciting and salutary development which promises much in the way of lighting up the past. In the interests of conceptual mobility, however, I wonder how exclusively it ought to be tied to the problem of resistance to slavery. The two are certainly related. But there should also be a way of allowing for the ebb and flow of folk culture over time, and of discovering whether there may be conditions under which such culture and the range of its expression flourishes, and other conditions which tend, relatively speaking, to inhibit it.

At any rate, it was something of this sort that I had in mind in the closing paragraphs of the first essay which follows. I was guessing, in other words, that it was with Emancipation—in the transition between two very different kinds of group experience, slavery and Reconstruction—that the real upsurge in the historical development of black culture might be found. Nor do I think it well to flatten out the contrasts between these experiences, and between the conditions in which they occurred. Despite the subsequent bitter disappointments and unfulfilled promises, the mere removal of slavery's restraints that Emancipation represented must in itself have had the profoundest consequences. Such a possibility, I now feel, warrants a far more comprehensive exploration than I was able to give it in this brief statement, and I shall be pleased if the reprinting of these essays proves an impetus to further investigation of this topic.

Negro Slavery in North America:
A Study in Social Isolation

Considering how ferociously the South had defended slavery throughout the thirty years prior to Appomattox, one is sometimes tempted to think that defeat on the battlefield is not quite enough to explain the surprising ease with which the South gave up slavery in 1865. For all the intransigent bitterness of the South in the years immediately after the war, and for all the South's resistance to Northern occupation and reconstruction, the one result of the war that most Southerners did accept in good faith was Emancipation: for practical purposes you could not have found any public person after May 1865 seriously willing to claim that the South wanted slavery back. Hostile moral feeling from the rest of the world apparently had imposed its burden on the South after all—a burden that had actually become intolerable and that the South by 1865, in spite of everything, was relieved to be rid of.

But there was one dominant, central aspect of slavery that the South did not and could not rid itself of, because it quite literally did not know how. The reasons go far beyond mere wrongheadedness, and in some ways even beyond color. A society in which the mass of Negroes would live and work as free men and women was not only outside the average Southerner's experience, it was almost beyond his imagination. The Southern press, in the months after the war, was filled with stories of death and demoralization among the Negroes—stories not without some basis—and many people seriously doubted that the newly emancipated slaves would be capable of surviving physically without the care and assistance of their former masters. The crux of the matter was that the South simply could not picture the Negro as an adult, and it was this aspect of slavery that no amendment to the Constitution, even when ratified in all good faith by the Southern conventions themselves, could do very much to alter. The South's incapacity to imagine the Negro in any role but that of a helpless dependent would influence, for years, every effort of the white community to establish a new and stable relationship with its former slaves.

To some extent, of course, the South was a victim of its own propaganda. Southern polemicists had carefully fostered the image of the childlike, depen-

Reprinted by permission from Stanley M. Elkins, *Slavery: A Problem in American Institutional and Intellectual Life,* Second Edition (Chicago: The University of Chicago Press, 1968), pp. 239–45. © 1959, 1968 by The University of Chicago. All rights reserved. Originally presented as a paper at the annual meeting of the American Historical Association, December 1961.

dent Negro whose inborn helplessness made it absolutely essential that he have a master to guide and direct him. No anti-abolitionist argument was more effective than this. It allowed the strongest emphasis to be placed on the paternalistic character of the plantation and its connections with the values and sentiments of family life. Thus the master's deep sense of responsibility for his slaves—generated in part by their very dependence on him—guaranteed the slave against the kind of exploitation regularly experienced by the "wage slaves" of the North. At least this was the argument. Respectable Southern society presumably had no place for the planter who abused his slaves, whereas the Northern factory owner was free to take whatever advantage he pleased of his workers without social censure. The genial side of the plantation picture did have enough basis in fact that even outsiders were in many a case impressed, finding it hard to imagine that the average Negro was unhappy as a slave.

By the 1850's the South had become so profoundly committed to its own image of the helpless, dependent Negro that it was unwilling—and probably unable—to consider any evidence to the contrary, such as, for example, the relative vitality of the free Negro community in Virginia. The Virginians themselves continued to insist that free Negroes, removed from their "natural" state of slavery, were lazy, dishonest, and degraded.

But the South's conviction that the Negro lacked even the rudimentary sort of initiative and self-reliance normally associated with American adulthood cannot be explained entirely on the basis of its extreme proslavery ideology. The picture was deeply rooted in Southern experience. Both the traditional legal structure of American slavery and the social character of ante-bellum plantation life did tend to produce slaves who were in fact helpless, dependent, and lacking in initiative. As isolating mechanisms, law and custom, precisely in their most genial form, functioned with an efficiency so thorough that perhaps no one could have foretold or understood the entire web of consequences.

Latin American scholars have long been aware of the striking differences between the slave systems of North and South America. Latin law and custom allowed the slave a wide range of rights and privileges unknown in the North: manumission was encouraged, the authorities were legally responsible for a slave's welfare, slaves could hold property, and the marriage ties of a slave were as binding as those of his master. In the United States, on the other hand, manumission was discouraged by both law and tradition. The slave had no civil rights; he could neither hold property nor make contracts; he could not testify in court, inherit, or even buy and sell without his master's permission. He had virtually no legal recourse against abuse, and his marriage connections had no status in law whatever.

Of course the harshest features of the slave codes were often mitigated in practice. Many a master allowed certain of his slaves to hold limited amounts of property, encouraged them to make stable marriages, and even assisted them in getting around the laws that forbade manumission. But one feature of American slavery is clear: the slave's welfare depended entirely on the good will of the master, and whatever rights and privileges he had could be withdrawn at a moment's notice. Since the bulk of American slaves worked as field hands, their labor could be easily coerced; few had even the limited bargaining power of a skilled worker; and thus they had little to offer a master that he was not in a position to take at will.

So, although the curtain of isolation which the law drew between the Negro population and society at large was not perfect, the holes that did appear in it from time to time were not put there by society as such. Those openings could only exist through the paternal auspices of individual masters, as it suited their inclinations and convenience, which meant that the dependency relationship did in effect remain all but perfect.

The daily etiquette and usages of plantation life rendered it all the more so. The process whereby all the true attributes of manhood were systematically isolated and placed well beyond reach truly bears the marks of great subtlety. A mature male Negro was called "boy" until he was old enough and helpless enough to qualify for the title of "uncle." Any evidence of real self-assertion brought upon him the wrath of the whole system: the one thing which the most humane master, as the father of the establishment, could not tolerate was the slightest challenge to his authority. It was thus altogether consistent and logical that even on plantations where stable marriages were encouraged, the slave's rights as husband and father, unrecognized in law, should not be recognized (in the ways that really mattered) in plantation custom either. He had no real authority over his wife and children, and he was not responsible for either their welfare or their behavior. He could be "boy" or "uncle," but never "father"; *that* role, from the viewpoint of the system and its well-being, was not only superfluous but disruptive.

For the Negro male community, the isolating function (as I am calling it) of this situation can hardly be overstressed. A meaningful relationship between fathers and sons was simply not possible; the only real father figure on the plantation was the master. The psychological implications for the young boy growing up in such a system should thus be obvious. It is extremely difficult to be a man, any time, anywhere, if there are no acceptable male models to pattern yourself after. In short, there was no reliable way—either psychologically or socially, either through law or through custom—to break the ring of helplessness and dependence.

It is true that there were exceptions, even on the most rigidly organized plantations. The status of family servants, and of skilled workers such as carpenters, masons, or blacksmiths, allowed them a degree of personal autonomy not available to the ordinary field hand. But this was not something that could be built upon over more than one generation. In the absence of a meaningful family unit, neither the skills, the status, the standards, nor the psychological leeway that a talented father might have acquired could very readily be transmitted to his sons. In this sense there was very little that was cumulative in the life of a slave. The key to this, as with everything else, lay in the hand of the master. The chances of real talent emerging on a plantation without the direct cooperation of the master, or one of his family, were all but negligible.

Another apparent exception to the rigid pattern of dependence was the special position enjoyed by certain slave women, especially the valued family servant. The Southern "mammy" may be an annoying stereotype for the 1960's, but she was never a figure of contempt. She was normally allowed far more latitude than any male. Southern custom did not require that the "mammy" be defined as a perpetual "girl"; there was no need to deny her womanhood in quite the way that manhood was denied the male slave. So it is no accident that whatever real authority existed within the slave community tended to be exercised by women rather than men, or that most of the strong slave personalities in plantation reminiscences were female rather than male. But this authority also was the product of isolation—of relationships entirely abnormal for the adult world as society at large defined it. And over it all still presided the master, upon whom *all* women in Southern society, white as well as black, were implicitly and explicitly dependent.

If the slave had any hopes of escaping the deeper effects of personal helplessness, it was pretty much essential that he get away from the plantation. His best opportunity, especially if he were a skilled artisan, would lie in the cities and towns. Any degree of control over the conditions under which he worked automatically made the slave that much less than a full dependent. His master might see good reasons for allowing him special privileges and a degree of liberty. There were cases, despite the law, in which a slave might be allowed by his master to hire himself out in exchange for a fixed monthly or yearly payment to the master. The slave would provide his own food and lodging and manage his own affairs, so that except for the payments he was virtually a free man.

Yet even here, barriers of isolation were erected about him. It was precisely at such a point as this, where the slave was best prepared to assume the full responsibilities of freedom, that he faced the most difficult obstacles to further progress. His very skill and independence made him that much more valuable to his master when it was a question of parting with him for good. For a slave to hire himself out was one thing; but buying himself—to say nothing of buying his family—was something else again, something that was made truly formidable not only by law and custom but also by the market price for healthy slaves. And in any case, most Southern states required a newly manumitted slave to leave the state within a year.

By 1850 the status of the free Negro had grown sufficiently precarious that there was less and less incentive for the skilled and ambitious slave to join their numbers. In some sections where the free Negroes were able to win a place for themselves in the community's life—that is, where the economic interests of their employers guaranteed them a degree of protection—their position could be more or less tolerable. But in most places the restrictions on their economic and social life made the pressures fairly chronic. It was made clear to them in a hundred ways that going North, or choosing a master and returning to slavery, or emigrating to Africa would suit the white community best of all—that society at large would like nothing better than to be rid of them entirely.

It could very well be argued, then, that in the long run the cruelest feature of our slave system, when compared with that of Latin America, was not physical harshness but the virtual absence of channels for recognizing talent, energy, and ambition. Despite examples of successful Negroes in every state in the South, their numbers were so small as to make them in every way exceptional. Nor did moving North, even when possible, constitute much of a solution. The free Negro's position was not substantially better there than it was in the South. It is small wonder, therefore, that initiative and self-reliance —the prime values of nineteenth-century American society—were so rarely found within the ante-bellum Negro community, slave or free. Deliberately or not, consciously or otherwise, the larger society used every resource it had to discourage them.

Coming back again to Emancipation—the point at which I began—it is perhaps clearer what we mean when we use the term "the legacy of slavery." Lack of prior preparation made an initial state of demoralization inevitable as Negroes wandered about the countryside. Southerners shocked by the resulting disorder, and by the hardship experienced by both the former slaves and their former masters, could hardly help having their doubts about the advantages of freedom for the Negroes.

But to emphasize this side of the case unduly is to draw attention away from the profound significance and profound consequences which the experience of Emancipation did have. The very fact of slavery, and later the social reaction of the 1890's, make the short-lived era of Reconstruction only that much more valuable to us as a historical "laboratory." For if a social and psychological "leap forward" ever was made by the Negro community, the first phase of it came exactly here. It would be well to consider not the limiting features of this experience, but rather, at least for the moment, its liberating functions.

The observer in 1865 who was impressed only by the dislocation and aimlessness he saw among the Negro population was missing the profound psychological implications of freedom for even the most humble field hand. That humble field hand could now move if he chose (and he did); he could work alone rather than in a gang; he could bargain with an employer; he could live with his family on the land he farmed; he could control his own leisure time and social life to an extent never before conceivable. This man might appear unchanged to such an observer, but he was not the same person who had been utterly dependent on the will of his master a few short months before.

Perhaps the most dramatic change that followed Emancipation was the wide range of expression—not necessarily from our point of view, but from his

—that was now open to talent and initiative. All sorts of limitations on economic activity were removed; there was limited but real opportunity for an elementary education; there were unique channels for self-expression in the new churches, clubs, and societies being organized within the Negro community; and there was a chance to play roles of leadership formerly reserved to the whites. The results may occasionally have struck the white observer as ludicrous, but if so he failed to appreciate the deeper impact of what was taking place. Here, for the first time, large masses of Negroes were being allowed to live and act like full-fledged adults.

The experience of Reconstruction, moreover, served to widen and deepen that impact. The Union League clubs organized by Republican carpetbag politicians to win the support of the Negro voters may have been crassly exploitative, but they offered the former slave his first taste of organized community action in which *he* made a difference. Although the songs, oaths, and rituals may have struck the outsider as droll mumbo-jumbo, they simply added depth and color to a new and moving experience. The political offices given to Negroes of ability offered opportunities for self-realization once enjoyed only by white leaders. And the general effect was to enrich and broaden the range of experience now open to the Negro and to limit still further the influence of his former master.

Why, then, the reaction later on? That, unfortunately, is a story too complex to begin here. But the theme of isolation does, once again, have something to do with it and serves to underline once more the manner in which energy, initiative, even personality itself, must be supported by the very structure and basic arrangements of society if there is to be anything cumulative and permanent in them. For in virtually every case which I have just enumerated, it was not the larger society, properly speaking—Southern, or even Northern—that took the initiative in bringing the Negro into the life of the general community, but rather the federal government.

Slavery and Its Aftermath in the Western Hemisphere

Lyndon B. Johnson in his address at Howard University in June 1965 called upon his fellow Americans to support a program of special assistance to the American Negro community. It was the first time any President had suggested that a minority group needed anything more than equal opportunity in order to take its rightful place in the society at large. Mr. Johnson justified what

Reprinted by permission from A. V. S. de Rouck and Julie Knight, eds., *Ciba Foundation Symposium on Caste and Race: Comparative Approaches* (London: J. and A. Churchill, 1967), pp. 192–203.

amounted to a major shift in official policy by declaring that among the experience of all other American social and ethnic minorities, that of the Negro had been unique. Merely to end discrimination, the President insisted, was not enough: "Much of the Negro community is buried under a blanket of history and circumstances." It required positive action to overcome "the heritage of centuries" and to repair the profound damage done by "ancient brutality, past injustice, and present prejudice." Americans were in effect being asked to accept responsibility not only for their own sins but for those of their fathers.

In so speaking, Lyndon Johnson knowingly or not entered a historical debate that has gone on since the beginning of the present century. What precisely *were* the sins of our fathers? Were they the same sins that might be referred to by a political leader of any of the Latin countries of the Western Hemisphere that had also experienced Negro slavery? Some of them might be, yet it is hard to imagine the speech itself, or anything like it, being made anywhere in Latin America, even though slavery was at one time as widespread and as well known there as it was in British North America.

Cruelty and merciless exploitation can hardly be taken as a measure of difference. The brutality of life on the Cuban sugar plantation of the nineteenth century could be as frightful as that of the worst absentee-owned cotton plantation in Mississippi, and much the same could be said of slave life in colonial Brazil. Nor was race discrimination unique to the planting areas of North America. Castilian pride of race in the Spanish colonies made it inevitable that social inferiority should go hand in hand with color; the blacker a man was, the lower in the social scale he would be, and there, with few exceptions, he would remain. Similar conditions applied in Portuguese Brazil. Of course there was a vast difference, as everyone is now aware, between the ways in which color prejudice was socially managed in North America and in the Latin countries, and I shall return to this point. But suffice it to say for the moment that the prejudice itself was present everywhere.[1]

If I were to identify the worst of our fathers' sins in the matter of slavery, it would not be cruelty or exploitation or even prejudice. It would be rigidity of mind, a lack of inventiveness, and an almost incredible absence of social imagination. For all the sins of the Latins, I do not believe that these—at least with regard to the workings of slavery—were foremost.

The gross differences between Latin and North American slavery, thanks to the work of Frank Tannenbaum, Gilberto Freyre, and others, are by now familiar enough for me to refer to them only in passing. In most places in Latin America a slave could own property, and husbands and wives could not be

---

[1] For more evidence of both brutality and prejudice, see C. R. Boxer, *Race Relations in the Portuguese Colonial Empire, 1415–1825* (New York: Oxford University Press, 1963); Eric Williams, *Capitalism and Slavery* (Chapel Hill: University of North Carolina Press, 1944); and Charles Wagley, *An Introduction to Brazil* (New York: Columbia University Press, 1963).

separated. In some areas a slave was guaranteed a fixed number of holidays during which he might work for himself, and in others he could have his price declared so that he might, if able to accumulate the necessary money, buy his own freedom. It was far easier, in other ways as well, to become a free man in Brazil or Spanish America than was the case in the British colonies or later in the United States. Manumission in most places was socially approved; in British America it was legally discouraged. And once a man had become free, a wide variety of occupations was open to him.

To return to the rigidity with which men thought about slavery in North America, this is nowhere better seen than in the extremely unsubtle and unimaginative way in which they defined "race." From earliest colonial times, a man was either Negro or white, and a single Negro great-grandparent—in some instances great-great-grandparent—made him a Negro. The single category "mulatto" served for everything in between, but it carried no special legal or social distinctions for either the mulatto slave or the mulatto freedman; all, legally, were "Negroes."[2]

In Latin America, on the other hand, a complex terminology was developed to account for an almost infinite variety of gradations in color from pure white to pure black. In addition, these gradations involved social and economic privileges. More important still, they were sufficiently flexible that wealth, education, or political influence could, in effect, alter a man's color as well as his position in society. In Brazil there was an old folk saying, "Money whitens." Even in the Spanish colonies a man might purchase a "certificate of whiteness" that allowed him access to the highest social and political circles. Thus, although prejudice existed here as well as in North America, there were a variety of subtle, flexible, and essentially humane techniques for circumventing and absorbing it.

Beside the rigidity with which race was defined in North America was a parallel rigidity in the definition of slave status. The only satisfactory category into which a slave could be fitted was that of property. Somehow the English were tyrannized by their own logical abstractions: they seemed unable to imagine any intermediate status between a species of property and full human citizenship; somehow it had to be either one or the other. It was logically intolerable, moreover, that other statuses could coexist with that of property. How could the law permit to such a being the status of husband or father? American jurists might solemnly deplore the need to separate families in the disposition of slave property, but they declared, more solemnly still, that the logic of the law admitted of no choice.

---

[2] "An extensive search in the appropriate sources—diaries, letters, travel accounts, newspapers, and so on—fails to reveal any pronounced tendency to distinguish mulattoes from Negroes, any feeling that their status was higher and demanded different treatment." Winthrop Jordan, "American Chiaroscuro: The Status and Definition of the Mulattoes in the British Colonies," *William and Mary Quarterly* 19 (April 1962): 183–200.

Such stark and rigorous alternatives would have seemed peculiarly unreal amid the rich complexities of Latin society. There, the master of a Negro slave certainly had a form of property right in him. But the status of slave was only one of a number of other statuses such a man might have. He could be a husband, a father, a communicant of the Church (which defined him as an immortal soul), an owner of property, and for some purposes a recognized member of the community with recognized rights and privileges.

It is ironic to note that the very stratification of Latin American society with its many levels of status—a stratification which still exists to plague those countries at the present day—was a powerful factor in mitigating the inhumanities of slavery. Manumission, for example, could be freely and regularly encouraged as a socially approved act and a Christian duty with little danger of disturbing the social structure as a whole. For Latin Americans accustomed to a steady leakage of manumitted slaves into the community, psychologically the thought of such persons as a challenge to the status quo and a threat to the white elites would have seemed exceedingly far-fetched. Indeed, even when general emancipation finally came to these countries in the nineteenth century, it occurred with relatively little strain on the social system.

The question of manumission in North America, on the other hand, offers still another example of the extreme rigidity of the English colonial mind on all matters concerning slavery. There, the starkness of contrast between "black" and "white" seemed to require a distinction equally stark between "slave" and "free." For example, neither the English colonists nor their American descendants two hundred years later were ever really able to conceive a workable status for the free Negro. This dilemma has been nicely expressed by Louis Hartz:

> In a bourgeois community where the Negro is either an item of property or an equal human being, a free Negro under conditions of slavery is an enormous paradox. How can an object of property be "free"? Or if it can be free, it must be human and hence all Negroes must be free.[3]

It was almost necessary to argue that the free Negro was invariably an irresponsible, demoralized being who was a danger to both himself and the community. By the 1850's there was actually a strong movement throughout the Southern states to force the free Negro either to choose a master or to leave the region. Such a state of things in Latin America would have been unthinkable.

I have been speaking of the "sins of our fathers." But were all our fathers sinners? Were all of them equally rigid, equally without imagination? What about the Father of Independence, Thomas Jefferson? It appears that Jefferson, the man of good will, the man who deplored slavery, was in the most fundamental sense as rigid as any of them. One of the most socially inventive of

---

[3] Louis Hartz, *The Founding of New Societies* (New York: Harcourt, 1964), p. 55.

America's political leaders somehow found his imagination quite blocked when he turned his attention to the problem of slavery. His mind was frozen at the outset by the suspicion that the Negro was a different order of being from the white man. He found it all but impossible to visualize a community in which this questionable race might, as free men, live side by side with the rest of mankind. He declared, indeed, that the white men of Virginia would never stand for such an arrangement. For Thomas Jefferson, the happiest of all solutions was emancipation followed by immediate colonization in Africa or Central America. The great educator, in short, could think of no way to educate slaves for freedom. He would deal with the problem simply by eliminating it, by getting rid of the Negro altogether.[4]

For that matter, the most humane and imaginative political leaders that America produced over the next two generations—such men as James Madison, Henry Clay, and Abraham Lincoln—never really got beyond Jefferson's "ideal" solution. As late as 1864, Lincoln was still talking about the extreme difficulty of whites and Negroes living peacefully in the same community, and about the great attractiveness of colonization as a solution for everything.

As might be expected, the most extreme version of American rigidity in all such matters, amounting to a virtual paralysis of all thought, was to be found in the ante-bellum South. Here, in the midst of a society which as a whole took extravagant pride in both its social flexibility and its openness to technological innovation, the Southern planters clung stubbornly to a system of slave labor that was becoming more and more inefficient and uneconomic. With a narrow fixity of mind that parallels that of the present-day Communist ideologists in dealing with the problems of collective farms, the planters refused to consider any systems of individual incentives—such as sharecropping, money payments, or the extensive use of Negro overseers—which might have raised lagging productivity. Instead, they clung to an inefficient system of gang labor, cursed the irresponsibility of the shiftless Negro, and insisted that any change in the existing system would lead directly to its total collapse.[5]

This rigidity extended into every aspect of ante-bellum Southern life. The use of Negro slaves in factories was discouraged, a slave's hiring out of his own time and services was similarly frowned upon, and any step that might elevate a slave beyond the condition of his fellow slaves—education, special training, unusual responsibilities—was seen as a threat to the entire system. A society that congratulated itself on the rewards it offered to individual initiative and energy was totally incapable of experimenting with such drives and exploiting them within a system of slavery.

---

[4] See Saul K. Padover, ed., *The Complete Jefferson* (New York: Tudor, 1944), pp. 661–66.

[5] An extremely able and persuasive account of the weaknesses of the American ante-bellum slave economy is given by Eugene D. Genovese in *The Political Economy of Slavery: Studies in the Economy and Society of the Slave South* (New York: Pantheon, 1965), especially pp. 41–144.

In the various Latin American countries, mobility for the man of color — through slavery and up into various levels of career and social achievement — could hardly be represented typically as anything but slow and carefully graded. But by the same token, it was possible; it could occur undramatically, without disruption and without crippling psychological tensions. In the United States of the nineteenth century, the dramatic opportunities open to ambitious whites, the dazzling careers built by exceptional men of energy, were counterbalanced by the utter absence of almost any form of opportunity for any man of color, of any shade.

How is one to account for all this? To characterize the American mind as rigid and the Latin as flexible is not the way one normally assigns these qualities where problems of social change are concerned. It is usually the reverse, and, for a good many purposes, properly so. But not for this particular purpose; not for questions involving slavery and color. Why? What sorts of historical conditions might explain this difference?

One general explanation is that offered by Louis Hartz. It was quite natural, according to Hartz, that the Latin American cultures, with their basically feudal origins and their commitment to a carefully stratified society, should have been able to find a place for everyone — slaves, Indians, freedmen, mixed breeds of every kind — within their social structure. The English, consisting largely of what Hartz calls "a bourgeois fragment" of European civilization, saw society very differently. A man was either a member of it, in which case he was entitled to all its rights and privileges, or else he was outside it, and entitled to nothing. It was this "either-or" quality that characterized the English mind as it confronted the Negro and slavery. Remove slavery, and in law and logic nothing remained to prevent a black man from doing anything and being anything that any white might do or be, in the same circumstances and in the same community.[6]

Other historical explanations, more specific than Hartz's, have also been suggested. One rests on legal history alone. The English common law, for practical purposes, had no categories and no body of precedent for dealing with slavery, and American slave law, unencumbered by the softening influence of time and custom, was fashioned in direct response to what seemed the brute needs of the occasion. The Spanish and Portuguese slave codes were based on centuries of development, the origins of which reached back to Roman law. This development occurred at a time when property rights of masters — in the exclusive sense in which Anglo-Saxons think of "property" — tended to be generally of less concern than were the human rights of slaves. To the extent that these were enforced in the New World, the Negro slave was guaranteed a range of protection not to be found in the slave codes of British America.

Another explanation, having again to do with color but in a somewhat

---

[6] Hartz, *Founding of New Societies,* pp. 49 ff.

different sense from those already mentioned, concerns the actual historical experience that the Iberians had had with dark-skinned peoples. In the case of the English, the first experience involving such people in substantial numbers and in any close connection had been with Negroes from Africa. A black skin and uncivilized savagery must, to them, have amounted to much the same thing, and to think of such beings in terms of human equality required a leap in imagination that was quite beyond them. The Spanish and Portuguese had experienced centuries of domination by the Moors. Despite their own intense national and cultural pride, their conceptions of power, of individual character, even their standards of physical beauty, could not have failed to be profoundly modified by such an experience.

To account for the contrasts in still another way, the numbers of white women in the respective colonial empires—relatively high, for example, in Virginia and drastically lower in Brazil and the Spanish colonies—have been noted by various authorities. Unions between white and black, of course, occurred everywhere. But the frequency of these in the Latin countries was dramatically higher, and the children of such unions were of necessity accorded a status in the community that differed quite sharply from that of the degraded offspring of miscegenation in Virginia or the Carolinas.

I myself have in other writings placed much emphasis on the presence in the Spanish colonies of a powerful and all-scrutinizing Crown and Church, with a concern for the slave population as subjects and souls as well as labor. In the British colonies the practical absence of such a force, plus the early development of plantation agriculture, left few barriers to the systematic dehumanization of the Negro slave. There were no sanctions for insisting, as the Church could and did in Latin America, upon the inviolability of the slave's marriage bonds or the immortality of his soul. Add to this the Spaniards' distaste for manual work of any kind, which in effect opened a vast array of skilled crafts and trades to men of color, the absence of large plantations in the earlier period of Spanish rule, and the far greater ease of escape in all the Latin countries—and the vast difference in the character of these slave systems becomes, in at least some rough way, historically understandable.

From all these diverse explanations—and from still others which have caused me to see that some of my own earlier ones were not sufficiently refined—I think one major generalization may certainly be derived. The conditions of slavery everywhere in Latin America were such as to allow the slave an indispensable margin of social and psychological "space" in which he might function and develop as an adult human personality. The social and legal arrangements of British America and the United States all conspired to deny such "space" to the North American slave. The result, in contrast to Latin America, was a different order of social being.

In any event, most of the observations I have made in the course of this paper may be illustrated by a specific comparative case study of slavery in Spanish Cuba and British Virginia. Herbert Klein has recently completed just such a study, and I cannot resist concluding with a summary of Professor Klein's principal findings.[7]

The Spanish Crown, with the support of the Church, assumed and retained from the outset a firm grip on every aspect of Cuban life. The economic power of the first conquistadors, and later the Cuban creoles, was limited and held in check by the political power of the Crown's peninsular appointees, who determined taxes, land distribution, Indian affairs, and the treatment of slaves. In Virginia, the English Crown virtually abandoned any direct control to the trading companies in the seventeenth century. Its only concern was the profits of the tobacco trade. In the absence of any comprehensive program of its own for the colony, it tended to accept local usage in virtually all matters of daily concern. Most royal officials were native-born, and prominent local planters controlled the county courts, the House of Burgesses, and the church vestries. It was solely in accord with their needs and their demands that slavery, with its laws, customs, and procedures, was developed in the province of Virginia.

The growth of plantations in Cuba placed much strain on the law codes which protected the Negro slave, but the Roman Church exerted every effort to ensure that the codes remained operative and took an active part in imposing its will on the planter community. The marriage rate for slaves between 1752 and 1755 was the same as that for free whites; there were as many baptisms of slaves as free persons in the year 1827; and manumission was systematically encouraged. Religious brotherhoods and processions, especially in the cities, absorbed the energies of the entire slave community. The Church controlled the schools up to the university and insisted that all Catholics had the right to learn to read and write. It had the personnel, moreover, to make its will felt. There were 1,063 priests in Cuba in 1778, one for every 168 persons. The Anglican Church in Virginia, controlled by the local vestries, having no American bishop, and with only 104 ministers in 1774—one for every 4,298 persons —was quite without the power or prestige to coerce the planters in anything. The Church of England itself did not develop a strong concern for the welfare of slaves until after the American Revolution. The Virginia codes in the nineteenth century prohibited the educating of slaves, placed sharp restrictions on all church meetings, and put limits on a slave's peddling or hiring himself out. A progressive attack, moreover, was made against the rights of free Negroes.

The Cuban economy created a large number of skilled and semiskilled occupations for Negroes and freedmen. Being heavily concentrated in the major cities, they had a maximum opportunity to learn trades or to establish themselves as independent workers. Even at the highest point of the sugar plantations, less than half of Cuba's slaves, or 27 percent of the entire Negro population, worked on them. By 1855, 20,000 slaves—42 percent of the adult work force—were employed in urban manufacturing. In Virginia the position of the

---

[7] Herbert S. Klein, *Slavery in the Americas: A Comparative Study of Cuba and Virginia* (Chicago: University of Chicago Press, 1967). See also pp. 99–115 of this volume.

Negro was circumscribed by a supply of skilled white workers and indentured servants which was ample for the needs of the economy. Negroes were seldom allowed to supervise other Negroes, and the early establishment of plantations limited their opportunity to learn even the most rudimentary skills. Gang labor was the norm from the first, whereas such labor in Cuba, even for a minority, did not become common until nearly two centuries after the colony was founded.

The rate of manumission in Cuba, encouraged as it was by the Church from earliest times, reached about 2,000 a year by the mid-nineteenth century. By 1774, 41 percent of the colored population were freedmen. In Virginia, the free colored made up only 4 percent of the total Negro population in 1790, and 11 percent by 1860. The Negro populations of Cuba and Virginia in 1860 were almost identical, being about 550,000 each. Of these, 58,042 in Virginia were freedmen; the freedmen in Cuba numbered 213,167.

Once free, the Cuban Negro found a range of opportunities open to him. Negroes served as royal clerks and militia officers, and some mulattoes even entered the University and made careers in medicine and law. The most that any free Negro of Virginia could hope to become was a boatman or a barber.

It is such a heritage as this that President Johnson referred to when he said, "Much of the Negro community is buried under a blanket of history and circumstances."

3 SUGGESTIONS FOR FURTHER READING

Bancroft, Frederic, *Slave-Trading in the Old South**. Baltimore: J. H. Furst, 1931.
  ▪ A view of the internal slave trade that developed in the United States.

Botkin, Benjamin A., ed., *Lay My Burden Down: A Folk History of Slavery**. Chicago: University of Chicago Press, 1945. ▪ The reminiscences of former slaves, belatedly gathered in the 1920's and 1930's.

Boxer, C. R., *The Dutch Seaborne Empire: 1600–1800.* New York: Alfred A. Knopf, 1965. ▪ A survey that traces the extent of Dutch involvement in the development of the plantation system in the New World.

————, *The Golden Age of Brazil, 1695–1750: Growing Pains of a Colonial Society**. Berkeley: University of California Press, 1969. ▪ A study of colonial mining society in Brazil.

————, *Race Relations in the Portuguese Colonial Empire, 1415–1825.* New York: Oxford University Press, 1963. ▪ A study that provides evidence of racial prejudice in Latin America and shows that the Latin American slave system had its share of brutality.

Burns, Alan, *History of the British West Indies.* London: George Allen and Unwin, 1954; 2nd ed., New York: Barnes & Noble, 1965. ▪ A general survey that includes a discussion of the slave institutions of the American tropics.

Conrad, Alfred H., and Meyer, J. R., *The Economics of Slavery and Other Studies in Economic History.* Chicago: Aldine, 1964. ▪ A careful consideration of the economic aspects of slavery in the United States.

---

*Available in paperback edition

Davis, David Brion, *The Problem of Slavery in Western Culture**. Ithaca, N.Y.: Cornell University Press, 1966. ▪ A study that concentrates on the various attitudes of whites toward blacks and on the process by which legal structures to support the slave system were developed.

Davis, Edwin A., and Hogan, William R., eds., *The Barber of Natchez*. Baton Rouge: Louisiana State University Press, 1954. ▪ The diary of William Johnson, a free Negro, which presents an interesting and intimate view of black life in the South in late slavery.

Deerr, Noel, *The History of Sugar*, 2 vols. London: Chapman and Hall, 1949, 1950. ▪ A general history of sugar planting which traces the growth of sugar plantation slavery.

Douglass, Frederick, *My Bondage and My Freedom**. New York: Arno Press, 1968. Originally published in 1855. ▪ One of the best autobiographies of former slaves, giving first-hand information about the lives, behavior, and personalities of American Negroes in slavery.

Drake, Thomas E., *Quakers and Slavery in America*. New Haven, Conn.: Yale University Press, 1950. ▪ An exploration of early antislavery ideas.

Drew, Benjamin, *North-Side View of Slavery—The Refugee: or the Narratives of Fugitive Slaves in Canada*. New York: Johnson Reprint, 1969. Originally published in 1856. ▪ The only contemporary collection of interviews of former slaves.

Elkins, Stanley M., *Slavery: A Problem in American Institutional and Intellectual Life**. Chicago: University of Chicago Press, 1959. ▪ Elkins' much discussed study of the impact of slavery on blacks in the South. The emphasis is on docility, and the book has raised a storm of modern-day protest.

Fisk University Social Science Institute, *The Unwritten History of Slavery*. Nashville: Fisk University Press, 1945. ▪ A selection of slave narratives collected in the 1920's and 1930's.

Frazier, E. Franklin, *The Negro Family in the United States**. Chicago: University of Chicago Press, 1939. ▪ The major work on the black family system, containing some hard-to-find information on the slave family.

Genovese, Eugene D., *The Political Economy of Slavery: Studies in the Economy and Society of the Slave South**. New York: Pantheon, 1965. ▪ A discussion of the economics of slavery that contrasts with the views of Conrad and Meyer. Basically a continuation and a refinement of the thought of Ulrich Phillips.

————, "Rebelliousness and Docility in the Negro Slave: A Critique of the Elkins Thesis," *Civil War History* 13 (1967): 293–314. ▪ A challenge to Elkins' views on the effects of slavery on the personality of American blacks.

————, *The World the Slaveholders Made*. New York: Pantheon, 1969. ▪ A recent statement of the point of view presented by Ulrich Phillips in *American Negro Slavery*.

Gibson, Charles, *Spain in America**. New York: Harper, 1966. ▪ A description of the Spanish empire in the New World.

Goveia, Elsa V., *Slave Society in the British Leeward Islands at the End of the Eighteenth Century.* New Haven, Conn.: Yale University Press, 1965. ▪ One of the best available studies of slave society in the American tropics.

Harris, Marvin, *Patterns of Race in the Americas**. New York: Walker, 1964. ▪ A brilliant economic interpretation of the differing racial patterns in North and South America.

Hersey, John, *White Lotus**. New York: Alfred A. Knopf, 1965. ▪ A superb novel, sensitive to every nuance of understanding about slave life in the Old South collected by historians up to the time of writing. White Lotus, the central figure, is a girl taken as a slave from a tribalized America by a dominant oriental civilization after some future catastrophe.

Jordan, Winthrop D., *White Over Black: American Attitudes Toward the Negro, 1550–1812**. Chapel Hill: University of North Carolina Press, 1968. ▪ A treatment of the beginnings of slavery in the New World and an analysis of the white community's changing attitudes toward blacks.

Klein, Herbert S., *Slavery in the Americas: A Comparative Study of Cuba and Virginia.* Chicago: University of Chicago Press, 1967. ▪ A particular study that provides a comparison of the development of slavery in North and South America.

Levine, Lawrence W., "Slave Songs and Slave Consciousness: An Exploration in Neglected Sources," in *Anonymous Americans**, ed. Tamara Hareven. Englewood Cliffs, N.J.: Prentice-Hall, 1971. ▪ An evaluation of the Negro oral tradition as a source of information about slavery.

Lockhart, James, *Spanish Peru, 1532–1560: A Colonial Society.* Madison: University of Wisconsin Press, 1968. ▪ An intensive study of a particular area in the New World during the colonial period.

Phillips, Ulrich B., *American Negro Slavery**. New York: Appleton, 1918. ▪ A work that contains a great deal of valuable information, though it has come under fire in recent years for the seemingly racist attitudes of the author.

———, *Life and Labor in the Old South**. Boston: Atlantic-Little, Brown, 1929. ▪ Also a source of much valuable information.

Pitman, Frank W., *The Development of the British West Indies, 1700–1763.* New Haven, Conn.: Yale University Press, 1917. ▪ A particular study of considerable interest.

Roberts, George W., *The Population of Jamaica.* Cambridge, Eng.: At the University Press, 1957. ▪ A revealing demographic study.

Sellers, James B., *Slavery in Alabama.* Tuscaloosa: University of Alabama Press, 1950. ▪ An excellent study of slavery in a particular area of the South.

Stampp, Kenneth M., *The Peculiar Institution: Slavery in the Ante-Bellum South**. New York: Alfred A. Knopf, 1956. ▪ The most recent and most comprehensive study of slavery in the American South, based on intensive research in original materials.

Starobin, Robert S., *Industrial Slavery in the Old South*. New York: Oxford University Press, 1970. ▪ A recent study by one of Stampp's students. Here, too, the information is firmly rooted in exhaustive research in the manuscript sources.

Sydnor, Charles S., *Slavery in Mississippi**. New York: American Historical Association, 1933. ▪ A good study of slavery in a specific area of the American South.

Wade, Richard C., *Slavery in the Cities: The South, 1820–1860**. New York: Oxford University Press, 1964. ▪ A consideration of urban slavery, the least oppressive variety of slavery in the United States.

Wagley, Charles, *An Introduction to Brazil**. New York: Columbia University Press, 1963. ▪ A volume that contains a great deal of information about the institution of slavery and racial prejudice in Brazil.

Weinstein, Allen, and Gatell, Frank Otto, eds., *American Negro Slavery: A Modern Reader**. New York: Oxford University Press, 1968. ▪ A useful collection of essays and excerpts from recent studies of slavery.

Woodman, Harold D., ed., *Slavery and the Southern Economy: Sources and Readings**. New York: Harcourt, 1966. ▪ An excellent group of essays exploring the economics of slavery.

Woodson, Carter G., *The History of the Negro Church*. Washington, D.C.: Associated Publishers, 1921. ▪ A basic general study, with a good deal of information on religion among American slaves.

4

Ante-Bellum
Black Activism

Slave Resistance in the United States

HERBERT APTHEKER

Herbert Aptheker is a visiting lecturer in history and director of the black studies program at Bryn Mawr College; he is also national director of the American Institute for Marxist Studies. For many years he has been a writer and lecturer on Negro history. Among his books are *American Negro Slave Revolts* (Columbia University Press, 1943) and *Nat Turner's Slave Rebellion* (Humanities Press, 1966). He is presently editing the correspondence of W. E. B. Du Bois, to be published by J. B. Lippincott. In the following essay, Mr. Aptheker deals with the question of slave resistance in the United States. Tracing the patterns of resistance from the most mundane to the most dramatic, he argues that the slaves never ceased to oppose the system in a wide variety of ways, and that they emerged from slavery, not broken by their past struggles, but strengthened for those that lay ahead.

The African-derived peoples who experienced slavery in the United States for over two centuries faced three related challenges: one to survive, another to affirm their full humanity, and a third to achieve all the necessary and proper perquisites of such a status.

All peoples have been enslaved at one time or another in their history, and such catastrophe projected the problem of their endurance; not all peoples have successfully managed this, so that—as in the case, for example, of the original inhabitants of what is today Haiti—enslavement resulted in extermination. Where this was the case, the record is not devoid of accounts of resistance, of course, but the resistance was in fact futile. Effective resistance normally results in life rather than death, and not infrequently the former may be the more difficult choice; in any case, where genocide succeeds, resistance terminates.

Affirming Humanity

While a people must survive to resist and while the very fact of survival connotes resistance, it is also true that the urge to survive may suggest the wisdom of acquiescence: trees that can bend with the storm endure; however, excessive bending may produce stunting and deformation. In the case of the Afro-American people in slavery, survival was accomplished, and the record shows that this survival was accomplished not at the cost of deformation, but rather with the result of a tempering and honing. Further and higher struggles would be forthcoming and would shake the foundations of power and challenge the quality of the social order.

Slaves in the United States were faced first with the insistence that they were not human. It was only as this idea began to yield to reality that they faced the idea that, while they were of the human species, they were a significantly and permanently damaged example of that species; that is, that African-derived peoples were immutably and decidedly biologically inferior in moral and intellectual capacities, especially as compared with whites (and, to somewhat lesser degrees, as compared with other colored peoples).

This shift in white thinking constitutes part of the record of resistance; it is, after all, a matter of some consequence whether one is held to be a beast or a defective human being, though the latter may often mean, in fact, a human being with certain bestial qualities! The shift came because of capacities which black people persisted in manifesting; these were physical, sexual, artistic, psychological, and intellectual. Taken together they belong in any effort to comprehend the American slaves' resistance to enslavement.

The need to survive and to affirm humanity is significant in comprehending the particular meaning and role of religion and music for the slaves. There is penetrating illumination in a remark made by James Weldon Johnson in his introduction to the 1925 edition of *The Book of American Negro Spirituals:*

> Far from his native land and customs, despised by those among whom he lived, experiencing the pang of separation of loved ones on the auction block, knowing the hard task master, feeling the lash, the Negro seized Christianity, the religion of compensations in the life to come for the ills suffered in the present existence, the religion which implied the hope that in the next world there would be a reversal of conditions, of rich man and poor man, of proud and meek, of master and slave.[1]

Johnson went on to suggest that "how much this firm faith had to do with the Negro's physical and spiritual survival of two and a half centuries of slavery cannot be known."[2] One may add that there is another component to Christianity; it is not only a religion holding out the hope of a better life in the hereafter but also one that—in much of its text, at any rate—urges the achievement of justice on earth and in the present life. If God parted the seas to help the Israelites enslaved in Egypt to escape and then drowned the pursuing Egyptian army, surely He was rendering a judgment for now and here as well as for the

---

[1] James Weldon Johnson, *The Book of American Negro Spirituals* (New York: Viking Press, 1925), p. 20.

[2] Ibid., p. 21.

future and hereafter. That Nat Turner replied to his court-appointed inter-rogator—who was seeking from the rebel an admission of having been mis-taken and *guilty*—with the words "Was not Christ crucified?" surely shows that for many slaves religion served not only as a source of solace but also as a goad to action and resistance; thus, in more than one sense, it helped them to survive.

The songs hammered out on the anvil of slavery—the spirituals—were simultaneously evidences of the most profound discontent and yearning and of the will to survive; they, too, testify to slave resistance. As Frederick Douglass wrote of spirituals in *My Bondage and My Freedom*, "they were tones, loud, long and deep, breathing the prayer and complaint of souls boiling over with the bitterest anguish. Every tone was a testimony against slavery, and a prayer to God for deliverance from chains."[3]

All manifestations of human capacities and feelings were forms of resis-tance. Demonstrations of tenderness and rage, of love and hate, of scorn and pity, of pride and shame, of humor and artistry, were expressions of resistance to dehumanization and therefore to enslavement. When slave children insisted on staying with or going to their parents (as Frederick Douglass did), or when fugitives "loitered about" their wives or husbands (as a thousand advertise-ments for runaway slaves complained), or when slave parents did all they could to maintain some semblance of family life and reality (as did the parents of Nat Turner), this again was a form of folk resistance to slavery.

Active Resistance

Beyond this basic level, the record of slavery in America is full of dramatic examples of resistance on the part of black people.[4] When slaves by the thou-sands managed in one way or another to accumulate the wherewithal to pur-chase their own freedom and then that of their mothers or wives or children, this was resistance. When slaves volunteered, as hundreds did, for service in the Continental army during the American Revolution and then, having fought well, gained their freedom, that was a form of resistance. When slaves broke tools, destroyed harnesses and fences, were "unable" to learn this or that tech-nique, cut off their fingers, took their own lives (or the lives of their children), these were forms of resistance—not always and not in every case, of course, but generally, when considered as repeated social phenomena.

---

[3] Frederick Douglass, *My Bondage and My Freedom* (New York, 1855).

[4] Documentation for the material on slave resistance presented in this essay can be found in two of my previous works: *American Negro Slave Revolts* (New York: Columbia University Press, 1943); and "Slave Guerrilla Warfare," pp. 11–30 in *To Be Free: Studies in Afro-American History* (New York: International Publishers, 1948). References are numerous in both works, and the first contains a thirty-page bibliography. The revised edition of *American Negro Slave Revolts* (New York: International Publishers, 1963) also contains bibliographical references to works that appeared in the two decades following its original publication.

When slaves, in tens of thousands of cases, attacked overseers and masters (and at times their families) with clubs and knives and bare hands, that was resistance. When, in preparing food, they added poison to the pot, and when this became so common that it was referred to by the Southern press as "the Negro crime," that was resistance. When the "carelessness" of slaves with fire led planters in the James River valley area of Virginia to equip their homes with newfangled structures called fire escapes and led insurance companies to charge more for premiums on fire protection in the South than in the North, that was resistance.

It was very difficult for a slave to get a gun, of course; the law prohibited his having any weapon at all. But the slaves prepared the food and tended the fires; thus it was relatively simple for them to "accidentally" put the wrong ingredients into the soup or ignite the curtains rather than the kindling. Frequent indeed, despite heavy censorship, were notices like the following, from a Mississippi daily's report on the "frequent burning of [cotton] gin houses" in the area: "Either there is a great deal of very culpable carelessness, or a spirit of incendiarism is ripe through the country."[5] Also very common are reports of individual or group assault on whites, such as the *Yazoo Democrat's* 1860 account of the sudden death of the brother of Congressman Lawrence Keitt— "murdered in bed by some of his negroes, who almost severed his head from his body."[6]

Complaints on the part of the master class that the slaves were "uppity," which recur in the literature of the pre–Civil War South, reflect resistance. Complaints about their "laziness"—a word which applies only to those obliged to labor, for the rich are idle but never lazy—literally fill contemporary sources; "laziness" in time came to be considered an attribute not of slaves but of black people—that is to say, of those people who did most of the work! Labor under slavery was a constant war or contest between master and slave, with the former seeking maximum productivity from the slave and the latter producing the minimum consistent with his own survival. This, too, reflected resistance.

Slaves—that is, black people—were not only "lazy" according to the racist mythology of the masters; they were also thievish. Slaves regularly helped themselves to the "belongings" of the masters; they took food, cotton, money, produce of all sorts. They took whatever was removable if their chances of avoiding discovery were good. The masters called this stealing, but the slaves insisted that stealing—for them—meant taking something from one of their own. Helping themselves to something in the possession of the master was taking, not stealing. If their children were hungry and there was milk or meat in the master's icebox, they took it if they could. In any case, as the slaves said, they themselves belonged to the master, so that whatever they had, the master

---

[5] *Natchez Daily Courier,* 29 November 1859.

[6] *Yazoo Democrat,* 10 March 1860.

had; whether the food was in the slave's belly or in the master's icebox, it all belonged to the master.

Slaves—that is, black people—were not only lazy and thievish and careless and inefficient and incapable of learning how to manipulate machines and destructive of animals and tools; they were also thoroughly unreliable. That is to say, they were "here today and gone tomorrow"—shiftless and irresponsible and given to running away, the latter frequently at the busiest times, too.

Flight and "Flightiness"

In perhaps the single most dramatic chapter in the history of the United States, tens of thousands of slaves succeeded in making good their flight from slavery. (One may find as many as 5,400 advertisements for fugitive slaves in a single year in Southern newspapers.) How many tried and failed will never be known, but the latter total surely was many times greater than the former.

Normally these flights were individual efforts by a man or woman, but not infrequently two or three slaves, sometimes with children, fled together. From time to time, especially in the last ten or fifteen years of the slave system, a considerable number of slaves fled together or, in the disgusting language of the slaveholders' press, "stampeded."

Flight was an act of extraordinary resistance for the slave, and the fact that so many thousands accomplished it or even attempted it is a prime indication of the irresistible will for freedom that never left the Afro-American people. One must bear in mind that flight was hazardous and difficult. Where to go? When and how? With what means? A thousand questions intervened between the concept and the actual effort. Should a pass be forged? If so, by whom? Would it be best to move boldly down some main highway—or would it be better to take great care, to move only at night and to avoid all roads? Would money be needed? How much? How to get it? What clothing? Shoes? Whom can you trust? When are you safe? For whom will you work?—a million questions.

Even the most routine escape from slavery was a tale of high drama. Imagine Frederick Douglass—himself an escaped slave from Maryland—breakfasting in Rochester, New York. There is a knock at the door, and admitted is a black man or woman—from Norfolk or Charleston or Hinds County, Mississippi. The newcomer has walked—probably only at night—most of the way. Hunted and advertised for, he has trusted very few and eaten very rarely. Now, here he is—one thousand, fifteen hundred, two thousand miles from his journey's beginning.

Flight, even when individual, was often a collective act, for normally all remaining slaves might expect to be punished when one slave had fled. The others, it was assumed, had known of the plan beforehand and knew now which way the absconder was heading. They had very likely helped the fugitive with extra clothes or food, and so on. So, in fact, the flight of one was frequently the act of many.

Sometimes when the flight was collective its purpose was to force betterment of plantation conditions, such as more generous rations or even a change in overseers. In such cases, slaves would hide in nearby swamps or wooded areas and would arrange for negotiations with their owners. Their representative would be either one from their midst or one of the "hands" who had not fled. Such action verged very close to a strike; and, in fact, strikes, including work stoppages by slaves demanding money in payment for their labor, were not unknown during slavery. In these cases—and reports of them recur during the 1850's—the slaves were lifting themselves by their own bootstraps, as it were, from chattel slavery to the relative delights of wage labor.

While the slaveowners usually ascribed the frequent flights of slaves to the innate "flightiness" of blacks, another explanation was offered quite seriously by a well-known pre–Civil War physician, Dr. Samuel G. Cartwright. According to this eminent Southerner, the fleeing was a manifestation of a disease—"drapetomania"—to which black people (and cats) seemed especially and peculiarly prone. The strange disease had a unique remedy—removing the toenails of the sick one would usually produce a cure, if only temporarily.

Slave Guerrilla Warfare

Flight also brings to mind another significant form of resistance practiced by slaves in the United States. Many runaways turned to a kind of guerrilla life, living in the swamps, forests, mountains, and other wild areas of the South, where they terrorized the planters and defied recapture. While most dictionaries define "maroons" as fugitive slaves or their descendants who inhabited outlying areas in the West Indies, maroons existed within the present limits of the United States, in every Southern state and throughout the history of slavery. They seem to have been most numerous and active in Virginia, North Carolina, Florida, and Alabama. The maroon settlements served as havens to which other fugitives gravitated, and some seem to have been fairly permanent establishments, with slaves living out full lives within their boundaries. Because the maroons made frequent attacks on neighboring plantations for supplies, local patrols, state militia, and even United States army units were mounted against them from time to time.

Three quotations from contemporary sources, reflecting conditions during different periods and in different states, give some sense of the nature and dimensions of this phenomenon. The first dates from December 1816, when Governor David R. Williams of South Carolina explained, in a message to the state legislature, his employment of a major section of the militia earlier that year in the neighborhood of Ashepoo:

> A few runaway negroes, concealing themselves in the swamps and marshes contiguous to Combahee and Ashepoo rivers, not having been interrupted in

their petty plundering for a long time, formed the nucleus, round which all the ill-disposed and audacious near them gathered, until at length their robberies became too serious to be suffered with impunity. Attempts were then made to disperse them, which either from insufficiency of numbers or bad arrangement, served by their failure only to encourage a wanton destruction of property. Their new forces now becoming alarming, not less from its numbers than from its arms and ammunition with which it was supplied. The peculiar situation of the whole of that portion of our coast, rendered access to them difficult, while the numerous creeks and water courses through the marshes around the islands, furnished them easy opportunities to plunder, not only the planters in open day, but the inland coasting trade also without leaving a trace of their movements by which they could be pursued. . . . I therefore ordered Major-General Youngblood to take the necessary measures for suppressing them, and authorized him to incur the necessary expenses of such an expedition. This was immediately executed. By judicious employment of the militia under his command, he either captured or destroyed the whole body.[7]

In 1823, under the heading "A Serious Subject," the *Norfolk Herald* declared that the citizens of the southern part of Norfolk County

have for some time been kept in a state of mind peculiarly harassing and painful, from the too apparent fact that their lives are at the mercy of a band of lurking assassins, against whose fell designs neither the power of the law, or vigilance, or personal strength and intrepidity, can avail. These desperadoes are runaway negroes (commonly called outlyers). . . . Their first object is to obtain a gun and ammunition, as well as to procure game for subsistence as to defend themselves from attack, or accomplish objects of vengeance.[8]

Still later, in 1864, the *Richmond Examiner* reported on maroons in North Carolina. It was, said this newspaper,

difficult to find words of description . . . of the wild and terrible consequences of the negro raids in this obscure . . . theatre of the war. . . . In two counties of Currituck and Camden, there are said to be from five to six hundred negroes, who are not in the regular military organization of the Yankees, but who, outlawed and disowned by their masters, lead the lives of banditti, roving the country with fire and committing all sorts of horrible crimes upon the inhabitants.

This present theatre of guerrilla warfare has, at this time, a most important interest for our authorities. It is described as a rich country . . . and one of the most important sources of meat supply that is now accessible to our armies.[9]

---

[7] Governor David R. Williams, quoted in Harvey T. Cook, *The Life and Legacy of David Rogerson Williams* (New York, 1916), p. 130.

[8] *Norfolk Herald,* 12 May 1823.

[9] *Richmond Examiner,* 14 January 1864.

As these three passages demonstrate, the black guerrilla groups inspired a great deal of fear among slaveholders, both before and during the Civil War.

From Arson to Rebellion

The employment of poison, then, sometimes involved several slaves and numerous victims; arson not infrequently escalated from setting fire to one cotton gin or one house to setting ablaze many buildings or even entire communities; flight sometimes involved several slaves, and fugitives occasionally resisted recapture in pitched battle; individual fugitives, as we have seen, at times grew into maroon bands, and these at times grew into forces that struck against neighboring plantations. It is difficult, if not impossible, to draw distinctions between all such efforts and actual insurrection.

Nevertheless, in contemporary sources, certain characteristics of the insurrection distinguish it from other violent outbursts. Ordinarily, insurrection involved a number of slaves with a particular leader or leadership group. It was clearly labeled by contemporaries as a rebellion or revolt or uprising or insurrection. And it ended in a trial or some more irregular "hearing" or "investigation," in which participants were convicted for insurrection and, in many cases, condemned to execution. Normally, also, there were clear-cut contemporary evidences affirming the antislavery purposes of the insurrectionists.

As evidence of resistance, conspiracy to rebel is perhaps as plain as an actual uprising, and where conspirators were convicted, the punishment was equally awful and decisive. Naturally, with the system of control under slavery —of which more will be said at the close of this essay—and with the system of rewards set up to encourage the betrayal of any developing plots, a great many conspiracies were uncovered and suppressed before they got out of the planning stages. As in historical struggles for relief from oppression everywhere and always, the number of armed uprisings that actually took place was only a fraction of those that the ruling classes were able to avert.

In both cases—with both conspiracy and actual rebellion—it is important to bear in mind that here one is dealing with the ultimate manifestation of resistance. This was the crime of crimes for a slave; there could be no forgiveness for entering into such a pact, and he who did so was entering into a matter of life and death. Indeed, the odds against successful revolt being what they were in the United States, it seems clear that when slaves conspired to rebel or rose in rebellion, they were not only saying that they detested slavery and were willing to give their lives for freedom, but they were also saying that they could no longer live as they had in the past—that they preferred quite literally to die on their feet rather than continue to live on their knees.

When, therefore, in rural, Southern, pre–Civil War America, one could get a score of slaves or fifty or two hundred within some county to agree to rebel and then to rise up, one had what could be compared with the visible portion of an iceberg in terms of its full dimensions. Or, to vary the simile, the actual participants in an uprising were like the lava pouring from the mouth of an active volcano, a mere hint of the tremendous bubbling mass below. With slavery, there was no Labor Relations Board, no mimeograph machine, no street-corner leafleting, no picketing. Instead, to protest actively meant to put your life on the line, and to take up arms or to contemplate taking up arms was to engage in the ultimate revolutionary challenge.

The great fact in the history of slavery in the United States is that on hundreds of different occasions — on a minimum of two hundred and fifty such occasions — slaves did decide to rise up. They came together and affirmed their hatred of slavery; they planned together how to strike a blow for freedom; and on scores of occasions they actually did deliver such blows. This was true in rural and urban areas, in every slave state, for every generation of slavery.

It was true in the slave coffles moving overland from market to market; it was true dozens of times aboard the ships engaged in the domestic and the transatlantic slave trade. These phenomena still await the exhaustive study which they merit, but even now enough is known to show without any doubt that the reality of slave conspiracy and slave revolt was never far from "the peculiar institution."

Of course, at the root of all rebellions and conspiracies lay the slave system itself; where there is slavery there is bound to be protest and resistance to it. The Afro-American people resisted the chains, the beatings, the indignity, the humiliation, the torment of women, the selling of children, the endless labor, the awful present and the excruciating future, the iniquity, the injustice, the hell that was slavery.

In addition, there were particular precipitants to massive slave unrest. Periods of economic depression intensified the sufferings of the slaves. Significant changes in population proportions, so that the proportion of slaves to nonslaves rose, were related to unrest. Periods of excitement — intense elections, nearby rebellions (as in Latin America), libertarian stirrings (such as antislavery movements in the United States or elsewhere) — or almost any unusual event (such as the appointment in colonial times of a new crown governor) triggered manifestations of discontent, for the slaves regularly assumed that events of national importance had some relation to their condition. Because of such precipitants, and because people get tired and discouraged, and because when a conspiracy was revealed or an uprising crushed, despair or fear or shock or all three may have forced the slaves to take time for recuperation and refreshment, the uprisings tended to come in waves. Thus four definite high points in the history of mass unrest among United States slaves are discernible: 1710–1721, 1790–1802, 1821–1832, and 1850–1860.

Fear of slave unrest was profound in the slave South, and this helped induce a kind of hysteria that quickly appeared in the face of any evidences of discontent. Such hysteria in turn induced exaggeration in contemporary accounts of slave resistance, and this makes the historian's task in assessing this phenomenon difficult. A greater difficulty, however, results from the policy of censorship followed by the slaveowning class, a policy of not reporting evidences of slave unrest. As James Madison wrote to William Bradford in Virginia in 1774 upon hearing of a slave conspiracy, "It is prudent such attempts should be concealed as well as suppressed."[10] Indeed, there is abundant and explicit evidence that such concealment was practiced.

In any case, exaggeration can normally be uncovered by the historian; thus, if in 1831 newspapers report that slaves have burned Wilmington, North Carolina, to the ground and it later appears that the city still stands, then the fact of exaggeration is established. But where one is faced with a clear *policy* of concealment, it is manifestly impossible to know whether one's labors have been able to penetrate beyond that policy. It is rather altogether likely that the most prolonged and assiduous search for evidences of significant slave unrest will not reveal all. Yet enough is presently known to smash racist notions— whether unadorned, as in the case of Ulrich Phillips, or given a sophisticated veneer, as in the case of Gunnar Myrdal and Stanley Elkins—to the effect that the chauvinist stereotype of Sambo accurately depicted the Afro-American people either in the days of slavery or since.

Indubitable sources show, for example, that hundreds of slaves were involved in the well-known conspiracies to rebel led by Gabriel Prosser in Virginia in 1800, by Denmark Vesey in South Carolina in 1822, and by Nat Turner in Virginia in 1831. Under Turner, slaves actually rose up and slaughtered many whites.

Many further specific examples of slave resistance can be drawn from available sources. For instance, Virginia, in 1672, enacted a law providing no punishment for any who might kill harassing slaves, "Forasmuch as it hath been manifested to this grand assembly that many negores [*sic*] have lately beene, and now are out in open rebellion in sundry parts of this country. . . ."

Early in 1708 slaves on Long Island, New York, rebelled and killed seven whites; four slaves (of whom one was an Indian and one a woman) were tried and executed, the men being hanged and the woman burned. In New York City in 1712, slaves in rebellion killed nine whites and seriously wounded six others before being suppressed. Twenty-one of the slaves were executed: "Some were burnt others hanged, one broke alive on the wheele, and one hung a live [*sic*] in chains in the town. . . ."

In 1739 slaves in rebellion in South Carolina managed to kill perhaps twenty-five whites, while about seventy blacks died as the outbreak was put down and in subsequent executions. In one engagement incident to this uprising, according to a contemporary report, the slaves, though they "behaved boldly," were defeated. Fourteen were killed; the rest fled, but pursuers "within ten days killed twenty more, and took about 40; who were immediately some

---

[10] James Madison to William Bradford, 26 November 1774, in W. T. Hutchinson and W. M. Rachal, eds., *The Papers of James Madison,* vol. 1 (Chicago: University of Chicago Press, 1962), pp. 129–30.

shot, some hanged, and some gibbeted alive." The next year, an aborted slave uprising in the same area led to the hanging of fifty slaves—ten a day, in order, said the contemporary press, "to intimidate the other negroes."

In 1795 in Louisiana (not yet part of the United States, of course), about twenty-five slaves were killed in a pitched battle and twenty-five more were hanged for rebellion. Several bodies were left dangling for weeks, the better to inspire "order."

Early in 1811, about four or five hundred slaves, originally armed only with cane knives, axes, and clubs but soon equipped with some captured guns, rose in rebellion in the parishes of St. Charles and St. John the Baptist in Louisiana. Several whites were killed. Armed planters, soon reinforced by the state militia and one or two companies of United States army infantry, battled with the slaves, killing as many as one hundred. About sixteen slaves were executed. Their heads were strung aloft and exposed for weeks along the roadside between the plantation where the revolt had originated and the city of New Orleans.

In the summer of 1829, about ninety slaves in Kentucky managed to rebel and to kill two white guards in the course of being transported for sale. A posse succeeded in suppressing this outbreak, and six of the leaders, including a pregnant woman, were sentenced to hang. The five men were quickly disposed of, but the woman remained in jail for several months until the birth of the child, whereupon, in May 1830, she was publicly hanged. In reporting on the hanging of the men, the *Richmond Enquirer* said that "they all maintained to the last, the utmost firmness and resignation to their fate. They severally addressed the assembled multitude, in which they attempted to justify the deed they had committed."[11] According to a Maryland publication, one of the condemned rebels, "the instant before he was launched from the cart, exclaimed 'Death—death at any time in preference to slavery.'"

In September and October 1840, plots and uprisings involving hundreds of slaves—as well as a few whites—rocked seven parishes in Louisiana. A number of rebels were captured, two of whom cheated the gallows by suicide; dozens of others were executed, some by lynching. The latter activity became so widespread that a regiment of soldiers was called out to stop the slaughter.

In July 1845, about seventy-five slaves rebelled in three counties in Maryland. They carried scythes, swords, and clubs, and two had guns. Attacking parties killed several of the slaves and captured others, of whom one was hanged and others jailed or banished to the Deep South.

In August 1848 a somewhat similar event, again involving about seventy-five slaves, occurred in Fayette County, Kentucky. Again, the slaves broke for freedom; this time, they seem to have set out for the Ohio River and free territory. Unusual was the fact that a young white man, Patrick Doyle—then a student at Centre College in Danville, Kentucky—marched with the slaves.

---

[11] *Richmond Enquirer,* 28 January 1830.

Two pitched battles were fought between the slaves and scores of pursuing white men; one of the latter was killed and another wounded in these encounters, while at least one slave was killed. Three of the rebel leaders were hanged, and Patrick Doyle was sentenced to twenty years in prison.

The decade prior to the outbreak of the Civil War was marked by massive slave unrest, manifested in hundreds of instances of slave-initiated arson as well as numerous plots and uprisings. If this is understood, the 1859 raid at Harpers Ferry by John Brown and his white and black comrades is placed in proper perspective, and its enormous impact upon the South and the nation is better comprehended.

Even during the Civil War, outbreaks among the slaves were not uncommon. One of the last, prior to Union victory and the crushing of the slaveowners' own rebellion, took place in Amite County, Mississippi, in September 1864. Here, some thirty armed slaves were involved, most of whom were killed when attacked by Confederate soldiers.

Special Features of Rebellions

Concerning the slave plots and outbreaks, several additional comments may be offered. Participation by free blacks was rather rare, as was participation by whites, but neither was by any means unknown. In addition to Patrick Doyle in Kentucky, four white workingmen were jailed for being implicated in the Vesey conspiracy, and a white schoolteacher named Joseph Wood was involved in an 1812 slave effort and was hanged for it. A white farmer named George Boxley was sentenced to die for his part in a slave conspiracy in Virginia in 1816, but with the help of his wife he managed to escape, and it seems that he was never recaptured. During the 1850's, reports of white implication in slave resistance efforts were common, but it is difficult to affirm how accurate these were in view of the intense political partisanship of that period.

There are evidences, from time to time—again, especially in the 1850's— that slaves were concerned not only with striking against slavery but also with making more general attacks upon existing patterns of property ownership. Thus, explicit references to confiscating the plantations and dividing them among the landless appear occasionally in the sources.

Rather striking are the references in contemporary sources—all media dominated by the slaveowners, of course—to the special militancy and passion displayed by slave women. Thus, for example, a black woman urging haste in plans for a rebellion in Virginia in 1812 was quoted this way: "She said they could not rise too soon for her, as she had rather be in hell than where she was." And another slave woman was quoted by an informer in Mississippi in 1835 as saying that "she wished to God it was all over and done with; that she was tired of waiting on white folks." When one bears in mind the excruciating oppression borne by the black woman slave—as woman, as worker, as a black person—this particularly intense passion is understandable.

The Machinery of Control

In considering the impressive body of evidence of slave unrest and militancy in the United States, one must remember that all signs of resistance were manifested despite the complex and ingenious machinery of control maintained by the slaveowning class and its various institutions. First, of course, the masters *owned* the slaves; and, second, the masters owned the land and all means of subsistence.

Further, the state reflected the power and the will of the slaveowners; hence the law explicitly affirmed that the slaves' duty was obedience and the masters' power was absolute. The South, both before and after the Civil War, was an armed camp; in the days of slavery all weapons were in the possession of the masters and the police apparatus controlled by them. The superstructure of Southern society thus reflected and reinforced the material base. The patrols, the city guards, the state militia, the federal forces, all were used for slave control and suppression. And traditional modes of persuasion—including religion, education, and literature—were all geared toward justifying and bulwarking the system of slavery. Modes of behavior, from the most trivial to the most significant, also reflected the ruling class's commitment to slavery.

The machinery of control did not merely consist in these powers of the master. It also consisted in explicit restrictions on the slaves: they were forbidden to read or write; to own anything; to go anywhere without written permission; and of course they had no civil or political rights of any kind.

But this system did not break them. The proof of that is in the actual records of slavery, in the record of the titanic struggles waged then by the slaves and now by their descendants. Despite all that exploitative and oppressive ruling classes may do—and, in the case of the Afro-American people, such classes have well-nigh exhausted their imaginations—resistance characterizes all human history. Indeed, the dynamic of human history *is* resistance. This is true of all peoples, given only the ability to survive, and it is certainly true of the black people living within the present limits of the United States.

Freedom's Black Vanguard

BENJAMIN QUARLES

Benjamin Quarles, professor of history at Morgan State College in Baltimore, is the author of *The Black Abolitionists* (Oxford University Press, 1969). His other books include *The Negro in the Civil War* (Atlantic-Little, Brown, 1968), *Frederick Douglass* (Atheneum, 1968), *The Negro in the Making of America* (Macmillan, 1964), and *The Negro in the American Revolution* (University of North Carolina Press, 1961). In the following essay, Mr. Quarles examines the organization and the antislavery efforts of free blacks in the North in the years preceding the Civil War and places these activities in the context of the social reforms of the mid-nineteenth century.

In America the thirty-year span before the Civil War was characterized by a widespread enthusiasm for reform, brought on in part by a general belief in progress and a strong sense of mission. Among the varied programs for human betterment, including campaigns for women's rights, temperance, and international peace, one soon took first rank — the crusade against slavery. The crusaders in this case, the abolitionists, held that the institution of slavery denied to a portion of mankind its birthright and imperiled the civil liberties of all men. Dividing the country along sectional lines and eventually bringing about a conflict at arms, the movement to abolish slavery was destined to shape American history as did no other reform.

Individual protests against slavery had been voiced from time to time throughout the colonial period, notably by the Quaker John Woolman. And when the American colonies broke with their mother country in 1775, the first antislavery society, located in Philadelphia, was founded. It was not until the early 1830's, however, that the abolitionist movement became a force to be reckoned with. For it was then that a new breed of abolitionists, striking a militant, uncompromising note, raised the cry of immediate emancipation, and emancipation with no compensation to the slaveowners.

For many observers, both then and now, the personification of this new abolitionism was William Lloyd Garrison of Boston. As the white founder and editor of *The Liberator,* a reformist weekly, and as the perennial president of the American Anti-Slavery Society after 1840, Garrison was indeed an imposing figure. Yet in his early years Garrison himself owed much to the Northern Negroes, in doctrine as well as in financial support. At the annual meeting of the American Anti-Slavery Society in 1853, one of the speakers asserted that the abolitionist movement owed its success to "Mr. Garrison's forgetting he was white" and hence looking upon the "great questions of Church and State as the Negro looks at them."[1] As was befitting to a twentieth-anniversary celebration, this appraisal was more rhetorical than it was analytical. Nonetheless, it points up a central fact of the times: underlying the emergence of Garrison as a reform leader and the emergence of the new abolitionists as a class was the rise of a newly distinctive element in reformist circles—black men and women.

The important role of the Negro in the crusades on his own behalf has generally been overlooked by historians. White Southerners vigorously attacked the abolition movement as a matter of course, but they had to ignore the blacks taking part in it. Many of them were runaway slaves, and to acknowledge their existence would have been to undercut the Southerners' own position that the docile and apathetic sons of Africa were well-adapted, loyal slaves. White abolitionists, too, knew something of the role played by black men and women. But, hostile though they were to slavery, these reformers could not bring themselves to regard the Negro as an equal or his role in the movement as a major one. Rather, they tended to view their black coworkers as little more than extras in their own performance, spear carriers in the background, without faces.

Surely black workers in the cause deserved a fuller recognition. The business of abolition was not for the faint of heart, and abolitionists of any color ran the risk of personal assault. But black reformers aroused a twofold animosity, combining as they did an unpopular cause with an unpopular color. Moreover, the black abolitionists could less readily retire from the movement than could their white coworkers, for they had fewer options in general and deeply personal issues were at stake for them, such as the freedom of a relative in bondage or the possibility that they themselves might be seized as runaways. In their efforts, the blacks of the North received little help from the free blacks in the slaveholding states, who were themselves under close surveillance. Apparently, the fear that the free blacks would spread the gospel of freedom in forbidden quarters was in part responsible for the restrictions placed upon them.

Negro abolitionists wholeheartedly embraced the two objects of the organized movement—liberty for the slave and help for the black who was already free. In effect, these proclaimed goals were but two sides of the same

---

[1] *Proceedings of the American Anti-Slavery Society at Its Second Decade, Held in the City of Philadelphia, December 3, 4 and 5, 1853* (New York, 1854), p. 119.

coin. To set the bondman at liberty was an obvious goal; but with it went the aim of uplifting the free black, thus providing concrete proof that Negroes were worthy of freedom and ready to bear its responsibilities. Though certainly many of the white abolitionists were keenly interested in helping the free blacks as well as the slaves, others saw no further than emancipation. For them, the work for the elevation of the darker brother was entirely secondary, for it was neither as interesting nor as dramatic as thundering against the slaveholder.

Black Self-Help

Elevating the free Negro was a task that the organized abolitionist movement was ill equipped to undertake. Always forced to count their pennies, the various societies had little enough to spend on the fight to free the slaves. And although nearly every society had a special committee concerned with the welfare of the free Negro, such committees had no funds. In 1836 the national antislavery society sent out four white agents to work among the colored people, advising and encouraging them, but after three months in the field the agents were notified that the society had no money to continue the project. The organization's inability to sustain this effort was typical of the times.

Criticism of the white abolitionists for their lack of concern over the plight of the free Negro was voiced by Martin R. Delany, a prominent black abolitionist, in 1852. "It should be borne in mind," he wrote, "that Anti-Slavery took its rise among *colored men* just at the time they were introducing their greatest projects for their own elevation, and that our Anti-Slavery brethren were converts of the colored men, in behalf of their elevation." But expectations of assistance from white reformers were "doomed to disappointment, sad, sad disappointment," added Delany, for the blacks found themselves "occupying the very same position in relation to our Anti-Slavery friends as we do in relation to the pro-slavery part of the community."[2]

Lacking substantial outside support, Northern blacks had to rely on inner strength to keep their reform work going. As a result of their day-to-day experiences, they never fully believed in the goodness of man, an idea common among white reformers. Still, like most Americans of their day, the black people were given to an optimistic outlook, a faith in progress.

Since the first all-black convention in the United States, held in 1830 at Philadelphia, blacks had been bent on a varied program of self-help. Something of its scope may be gleaned from two contemporary works by black abolitionists. In *The Condition, Elevation, Emigration, and Destiny of the Colored People of the United States, Politically Considered*, published in 1852, Martin Delany touches upon the achievement of the Negro American as soldier, businessman, artisan, farmer, writer, and educator. And in *Colored Patriots of*

---

[2] Martin Robison Delany, *The Condition, Elevation, Emigration, and Destiny of the Colored People of the United States, Politically Considered* (Philadelphia, 1852), p. 27.

the American Revolution, which was brought out three years later, William C. Nell of Boston gives thumbnail sketches of outstanding Negroes from twenty states. Far broader than its title would indicate, this work also presents a general overview of the status of the Negro at the time of its writing.

As both Delany and Nell demonstrate, black self-improvement took many forms, including the formation of societies for mutual aid and the calling of national and state colored conventions. As significant aspects of black abolitionism, certain of these activities are of interest to us here.

Mutual aid societies, designed to keep their members out of the poorhouse and the pauper's grave, were formed in many cities. The Sons of the African Society, one such group, was founded in Boston in 1798, but the movement did not grow rapidly until the advent of the new abolitionists. Philadelphia outstripped all other cities in its programs of this sort, having 106 mutual aid societies in 1848. Many cities had a branch of the Dorcas Society, a black women's organization primarily concerned with dispensing food, clothing, firewood, or small sums of money to the needy. In addition, some women's groups concentrated on child welfare; the black women of Brooklyn, for instance, raised $1,400 for the Colored Orphan Asylum at a fair held in March 1860.

Hand in hand with self-help went self-culture. Blacks, like other Americans of their day, formed lyceum societies, whose members met periodically to discuss issues of current interest—intellectual, social, and political. Such organizations among blacks were distinctive in one important way—without exception, they took a strong antislavery position. Indeed, the leaders of these societies, such as New York's David Ruggles and Philadelphia's Robert Purvis and Sarah M. Douglass, were all active abolitionists. In particular, the black intelligentsia saw its role in the movement as that of dispelling, through its own example, the myth perpetrated by slaveowners that Negroes were inferior to whites intellectually.

Thinking also of their children's intellectual development, reform-minded blacks were keenly concerned about securing better schooling for the young. In the mid-1830's white abolitionists in New Haven and Canterbury, Connecticut, and in Canaan, New Hampshire, sought to establish schools for Negroes, but they were forced to yield in the face of local hostility. Groups of blacks then set themselves to the task of increasing the number of all-colored schools, of which fewer than twenty already existed. With black abolitionists leading the movement in each instance, schools were successfully organized in Pittsburgh, Cleveland, and New York.

During the same period black reformers also sought the desegregation of the public schools. Boston blacks, headed by abolitionists Lewis Hayden, Robert Morris, John T. Hilton, and William C. Nell, first petitioned the city to end separate schools. When this approach failed, they persuaded black parents to boycott the all-Negro Smith Grammar School. Finally, in April 1855, as a result of pressure from abolitionists both black and white, the Massachusetts legislature ordered the city of Boston to desegregate its public schools. Victories elsewhere would be slower in coming.

The abolitionist movement had an even greater impact on the development of the convention movement among blacks, another expression of the will to act together to improve the common lot. Certainly, the "joiner" impulse was strong among blacks of this day, as it was among their white compatriots—a fact which prompted the French statesman Alexis de Tocqueville to observe in 1835 that "Americans of all ages, all conditions, and all dispositions, constantly form associations."[3] But a far more basic bond among the Negro organizers was their common desire to speak out forcefully against slavery.

The first national convention met in 1830. Conventions were then held annually for seven years and sporadically thereafter. The delegates to these conventions represented a large cross section of the black population, and there were many issues on which they could not come to agreement, such as the establishment of manual labor colleges which would exclude whites, or the emigration of blacks from the United States. But however widely they differed in other respects, they were unanimous in their continuous and bitter denunciation of slavery and the slaveholders. Time and again, orators at the convention meetings proclaimed the iniquity of the system of bondage below the Mason-Dixon, and the resolutions drafted and approved by the delegates sounded the same note. Many state-wide conventions were also held during this period, with Ohio taking a lead as the state in which the most meetings with the widest influence took place. Even here, delegates did not permit local issues to divert their attention from the arch foe, slavery.

Though it was strong in rhetoric, the colored convention movement was apt to be weak in follow-up. Hence it was never as great a force as it might have been, and its antislavery influence was greatly overshadowed by that of an organization with a more homogeneous base—the Negro church. Coming into existence in the early 1800's when blacks refused to sit in gallery-located "Negro pews" in the white churches, this had been a protest organization from its very beginnings. And it was the natural enemy of slavery. Even in the South the local black church was regarded as harboring abolitionist sympathies, and its preacher was often summoned to the courts to answer for a slave who had taken to his heels.

Enjoying considerably more freedom than the church in the South, the black church in the North raised a powerful voice against human bondage. "Resolved, that we regard the system of slavery to be repugnant to the dictates of humanity, subversive to the principles of justice, and at open war with the best interests of the country and the laws of God,"[4] ran a statement adopted by

---

[3] Alexis de Tocqueville, *Democracy in America,* ed. Henry Steele Commager, trans. Henry Reeve (New York: Oxford University Press, 1946), p. 85.

[4] *A Convention of Presbyterian and Congregational Ministers in the Shiloh Presbyterian Church* (New York, 1857), p. 24.

a convention of Presbyterian and Congregational ministers that met in New York in 1857. At the second Presbyterian and Congregational convention, held in 1858 in Philadelphia, E. Payson Rogers, a clergyman from Newark, New Jersey, described slavery as "a sin against God and a crime against humanity."[5] These statements echoed the feelings of a long line of black clergymen, dating back to Richard Allen at the turn of the century. And hundreds of similar resolutions had been passed by black church groups ever since they had been in existence.

The black church was particularly free to speak out against slavery because it was dependent wholly upon black support. Many Negro breadwinners were not avowed abolitionists only because they were dependent upon whites for their jobs and did not want to risk losing them. But the black church had no fear of economic reprisals. Hence black church buildings could be used for abolitionist meetings or for sheltering fugitive slaves.

Of course, there were exceptions to the rule that black clergymen were strongly opposed to slavery—and these included such a notable figure as Lemuel Haynes, a man of impressive learning who had built his reputation as a clergyman of white congregations and had been licensed to preach as far back as 1780. But by the 1830's, when the new abolitionists emerged, the popularity of men like Haynes had run its course. His successors—almost to the man—held radically different attitudes toward current issues, particularly that of slavery.

For one thing, it had become apparent that the most effective, as well as the most satisfying, means of attacking slavery was through direct confrontation with its defenders. And for this purpose, societies with the sole purpose of fighting against slavery were organized and attracted large memberships, black and white. Black clergymen from all denominations joined together in these abolitionist groups—including Samuel E. Cornish, a Presbyterian; Daniel A. Payne, an African Methodist; Christopher Rush, a Zion Methodist; Nathaniel Paul, a Baptist; Samuel Ringgold Ward, a Congregationalist; and Alexander Crummell, an Episcopalian.

From the beginning, blacks were active in the new antislavery organizations. Three Negroes were present at the historic founding of the American Anti-Slavery Society, which took place in Philadelphia in December 1833. James McCrummell, of Philadelphia, presided at one of the sessions of this society, and young Robert Purvis, also of Philadelphia, made a deep impression on the society members through his eloquence on various occasions. In addition, Negroes numbered among the founders of many of the auxiliaries of the American Anti-Slavery Society, including the state societies of New York and Pennsylvania. In 1840, the American and Foreign Anti-Slavery Society was

---

[5] *The Minutes and Sermons of the Second Presbyterian and Congregational Convention, Held in the Central Presbyterian Church, Lombard Street, Philadelphia, on the 28th Day of October, 1858* (New York, 1858), p. 11.

founded, and eight Negroes took part in these proceedings. Significantly, all eight were clergymen.

Negroes commonly sat on the executive boards of the two national societies, and several became branch presidents. Frederick Douglass served for a year as president of the New England Anti-Slavery Convention, and Charles Lenox Remond served for a longer period as president of the Essex (Massachusetts) Anti-Slavery Society. Neither of these leaders was required to give much time to the office, however. Robert Purvis served still longer as president of the Pennsylvania Anti-Slavery Society, and he was far more active than his colleagues in other states. When he refused a sixth consecutive term in office, the members of this society were visibly saddened.

Although the large antislavery societies were predominantly white, as a rule they welcomed Negro membership. Still, all-black societies were no novelty—in fact, the Massachusetts General Colored Association, formed in 1826, anticipated the emergence of the new abolitionists. By 1837 over a dozen black societies had come into existence, the majority of them auxiliaries to the parent American Anti-Slavery Society. Maintaining their membership in white societies, the leaders of the black societies regarded their organizations as supportive rather than as separatist.

Black young people, like their white contemporaries, formed juvenile antislavery societies, four of which emerged in 1838. The members of these groups pledged themselves to support the parent society financially, generally at the rate of one cent a week per member. Characteristically, at juvenile antislavery meetings, one or more of the society members would deliver a declamation against slavery.

During this period, a young black crusader against slavery might well have gotten some of his inspiration from his mother. For the abolitionist movement had its female contingent, and not all of it was white. The Female Anti-Slavery Society of Salem, Massachusetts, made up entirely of colored women, was organized on February 22, 1832. In the following year black women helped to organize the Boston Female Anti-Slavery Society and the Philadelphia Female Anti-Slavery Society. Four years later there were two Negro delegates to the First Anti-Slavery Convention of American Women, held in New York City. And at the second meeting of this group, a year later, two colored women were given office—Susan Paul became a vice president and Sarah M. Douglass became treasurer. When in 1870 the Philadelphia Female Anti-Slavery Society met to disband, the concluding motion was put, appropriately enough, by a black woman, Margaretta Forten, who had been one of the founders in 1833.

Perhaps the two best-known black women abolitionists were Sojourner Truth and Frances Ellen Watkins—two women who could hardly have been more different in appearance and style. Gaunt and angular, Sojourner Truth was a freed slave who remained illiterate all her life. At antislavery meetings she addressed her audience as "chilluns" and sang plaintive songs about slavery. By all accounts, her rude eloquence and her deep personal commitment to the cause made her an engrossing speaker, and she left her listeners with a deepened sense of the agony of slavery. Frances Ellen Watkins, on the other hand, was slender and graceful; a former schoolteacher, she had a demure, ladylike appearance and a literary bent. Indeed, her first volume of poetry, published in 1854 and carrying a preface by William Lloyd Garrison, included such memorable poems as "The Slave Mother" and "The Slave Auction." Miss Watkins spoke in a soft, musical voice, and she was in great demand as an antislavery lecturer. She too made a deep impression on her listeners, and at least one newspaper reporter went so far as to call her the best speaker he had ever heard.

The Black Underground

Of course, not everyone was capable of effective lecturing at antislavery meetings. But there was one phase of the abolitionist crusade in which people of all talents could participate—the operations of the underground railroad. This was a large-scale movement to assist runaway slaves, helping them first to escape and then to find work. Naturally, it was an undertaking that held special appeal for black people, and they played a key role in making it a success. Abolitionist leader James G. Birney, for one, acknowledged this fact in 1837 in speaking of the large number of slaves who were then fleeing through Ohio, en route to Canada. "Such matters are almost uniformly managed by the colored people," observed Birney. "I know nothing of them generally till they are past."[6]

Negroes were especially well suited for the most hazardous of the underground railroad operations, the job of the conductor who actually traveled to the South to seek out escape-minded slaves and give them directions for flight. Some whites served as conductors in this sense, but they ran greater risks of detection than black operators. Moreover, they often had a harder time than their black counterparts when it came to winning the trust of the slaves. The black conductors who were themselves former slaves sometimes had a further advantage in that they were able to operate in familiar territory.

A case in point was Harriet Tubman, an escapee from Maryland who became one of the most renowned of all the underground railroad operators. Because of her numerous trips into slave territory, a price was placed on her head. But she was as skillful as she was courageous, and she was never apprehended. Not surprisingly, in the summer of 1859, when John Brown was thinking of recruiting followers among the fugitives in Canada, only two people for the job came to mind—himself and Harriet Tubman.

---

[6] James G. Birney to Lewis Tappan, 27 February 1837, in *Letters of James Gillespie Birney, 1831–1857,* ed. Dwight L. Dumond, 2 vols. (New York: American Historical Association, 1938), 1:376.

Another group of slave conductors operated, not in slave territory, but in the free states, where they helped to speed fleeing slaves on their way. These conductors secreted many a fugitive in a baggage car or in a false-bottomed wagon for transportation further northward. In addition, they arranged for overnight accommodations for their charges. Invariably, the homes of black people were used for this purpose—partly because it was felt that reliance on a white host might prove unsettling to the newly escaped blacks. The vast majority of those who provided overnight accommodations for the fugitive slaves remained anonymous. Every large city, however, had a corps of well-known black abolitionists who offered their homes as shelter for the runaways. These included barber George DeBaptiste in Detroit, the well-to-do tailor John Jones in Chicago, the physician-clergyman James J. G. Bias in Philadelphia, clergyman Charles B. Ray in New York City, clergyman Jermain W. Loguen in Syracuse, Frederick Douglass in Rochester, restauranteur George Downing in Newport, and custodian Lewis Hayden in Boston.

City dwellers who sought to help the fugitive slaves often joined together in what they called vigilance committees. These were basically aid societies, designed to help the new arrivals in the North get started in new lives. As a rule, they helped the fugitives to find jobs and took care of them until they were able to support themselves. In these groups, too, blacks played a dominant role. Most of the vigilance societies were predominantly Negro, and those that were not made it a point to place Negroes in the key executive positions.

Of the interracial vigilance societies, the most effective was the General Vigilance Committee of Philadelphia. Much of the success of this group was due to its resourceful executive secretary, William Still, a free-born black whose parents had both been slaves. In addition to his active field work, Still somehow found time to conduct a voluminous correspondence and to keep a record of the most dramatic escapes he heard about in his work. Later much of this material found its way into Still's massive book, *The Underground Railroad*, published in 1872.

The most successful of the all-black societies was the New York Committee of Vigilance, founded in 1835 by David Ruggles. In its first year it gave assistance to 335 former slaves, often providing them with food and clothing solicited on their behalf. Ruggles' organization also contributed to the abolitionists' cause by keeping an eye on ships arriving in the New York harbors, lest they try to smuggle slaves into the country despite the legal ban on the international slave trade.

One of the hundreds of slaves personally assisted by Ruggles was the young Frederick Douglass. When, as a penniless fugitive from Baltimore, Douglass arrived in New York in September 1838, Ruggles lodged him in his own home for two weeks. In the meantime Ruggles arranged the details of his guest's wedding, for Douglass' intended bride had followed him from Baltimore. Ruggles never befriended anyone who did more for the cause.

Any former slave who appeared before an abolitionist audience was assured of a heart-warming reception. And if he turned out to be an eloquent speaker, he was certain to be in great demand in reformist circles, for he was able to serve as living refutation of the alleged inferiority of the Negro. Thus many former slaves came to tour the abolitionist circuit; and of these, Douglass was one of the most effective and best known.

Undoubtedly the most eloquent black speaker of his time, Douglass joined the abolitionist ranks in 1841, three years after he arrived in the North. Well-built and strikingly handsome, he had all the gifts necessary to an orator. In the mid-1840's he spent two years in the British Isles, and upon his return to the United States he was all but lionized. Over the next twenty-year period he was an abolitionist drawing card second only to Wendell Phillips, who, though also a brilliant speaker, lacked the symbolic appeal of a black skin and a slave origin.

Douglass' greatest rival among the black speakers of the day was William Wells Brown, a former slave from Lexington, Kentucky. During his bondage, Brown had had a variety of jobs, working as a domestic, a printer's apprentice, and a steamboat steward at one time or another. His bondage took him many places, but he spent the longest time in St. Louis, where for one six-month period he was hired out to Elijah P. Lovejoy, a white editor who was destined to become abolition's first martyr.[7] Brown made one unsuccessful attempt at escape. He succeeded in a second attempt, however, largely due to the help of a Quaker named Wells Brown, whose name he added to his own. Once in the North, Brown, who had a melodious voice and a compelling way of thundering out against slavery, became a popular speaker, drawing large audiences for the abolitionist rallies.

In 1849, Brown was accompanied on the antislavery circuit by a young couple who were also former slaves—William and Ellen Craft. Their escape from the South had been so spectacular that just by telling their story they were able to do much for the abolitionist cause. Dressed in male attire, light-skinned Ellen had posed as a planter traveling to the North for medical treatment in the company of his slave. For five days the couple journeyed through the seaboard slave states, throwing off their constant fear of detection only when they pulled out of Baltimore on a train bound for Philadelphia.

Many former slaves offered written as well as spoken testaments to the inhumanity of slavery, and these were used effectively as abolitionist propaganda. Both Frederick Douglass and William Wells Brown wrote autobiographies that included eloquent accounts of their days in bondage. Written in 1845 and 1847 respectively, these narratives were both presented in a clear and simple style that bore the stamp of truth. Brown was so determined to represent the events of his life honestly that he included episodes throwing himself in an unfavorable light, such as the tale of a deception he practiced

---

[7] In 1837, Lovejoy was murdered by a mob in Alton, Illinois, who objected to his abolitionist activities.

on an unsuspecting fellow slave in order to avoid a whipping himself. Douglass' narrative, too, was soundly buttressed with specific references to real persons and places.

The many narratives published by former slaves added a new dimension to the body of abolitionist literature. For here the former slaves spoke for themselves, acting for the first time as their own interpreters. Thus a bit of light was cast on the familiar question of what it was like to be a slave. From the pages of narratives written by men like Brown or Douglass, there emerges no "Sambo" figure, childlike and fawning. What does emerge is the figure of a man determined to be his own master whatever the obstacles to be overcome.

Black abolitionists left their stamp on another important segment of abolitionist literature as well—the journalism of the movement. Significantly, the appearance of Negro weeklies coincided exactly with the coming of the new abolitionists. The first black newspaper in the United States, which appeared in 1827 in New York, bore the appropriate title *Freedom's Journal.* This paper, as well as the sixteen other weeklies published by Negroes in the years preceding the Civil War, had a strong abolitionist orientation. Indeed, the Negro press presented a united front against slavery, and every one of the weeklies that sprang up proclaimed that it had come into existence for the major purpose of bringing about the downfall of slavery.

In attacking slavery, Negro-edited journals made use of a variety of literary forms, sometimes printing serialized slave narratives, sometimes filling their columns with sermons, orations, and essays. Even efforts at poetry, most of it in simple ballad form, passed by the editors' desks. *Frederick Douglass' Paper,* the most influential of the black journals, carried weekly reports from unpaid local correspondents describing the situation from their vantage points. Journals of lesser note had to be satisfied with publishing a random sampling of letters sent in by readers.

Abolitionist journals, whether white or black, apparently found it impossible to make ends meet. Most Negro periodicals were started on a shoestring and were thus wholly at the mercy of their subscribers. This was a frail base to stand on, for delinquent subscribers have traditionally been the plague of reformist sheets. Negro periodicals were no exception; but though they were short-lived, they had made a lasting impression. They had furnished black reformers with a vehicle of communication. Moreover, they had strengthened the forces of democracy, for their continued call for freedom and equality had given new resolution to their readers, white no less than black.

The Influence of Fugitive Slave Law

The increasingly militant antislavery sentiment in the North was tested, as it would be strengthened, by the stirring events of the 1850's. To begin with, Congress in 1850 passed a new Fugitive Slave Law designed to make it easier for a slavemaster to recapture runaway slaves. Because the law denied the fugitives the right to a jury trial and the right to testify in their own defense, it was seen in the North as a violation of American legal and constitutional guarantees. Hence it was met with a chorus of condemnation, and some abolitionists vowed to make it a dead letter. Numbered among these advocates of direct action were the great majority of black abolitionists.

Coming to the assistance of runaway slaves who had been taken into custody was nothing new to black people—in fact, before 1850 they had been largely responsible for many such rescues or attempted rescues. Hence it is not surprising that in Negro circles the Fugitive Slave Law of 1850 simply ennobled the work of rescuing runaways, making it a sacred duty. Now black and white abolitionists joined hands in a series of attempts to free fugitive slaves from their captors which did much to deepen the rift between the South and the North.

Boston was the scene of three of the most widely publicized clashes between the custodians of the slaves and their would-be rescuers. On a February noon in 1851, a waiter who was better known as Shadrach than by his rightful name, Fred Wilkins, was seized as a runaway slave and rushed to the courthouse. The news quickly spread to the nearby Negro neighborhood, whereupon a group of some fifty rescuers pressed into the courthouse, bore Shadrach into the street, and whisked him off to Canada.

The other two major Boston cases ended in failure, leaving the abolitionists bitter and angry. Two months after the Shadrach affair, a runaway from Georgia named Thomas Sims was seized. Legal efforts to free him were unsuccessful, and a plan to effect his escape forcibly was thwarted, for the courthouse authorities had taken maximum security precautions and Sims was guarded by a force of one hundred policemen. Tear-stricken but erect, Sims was marched to Long Wharf and his return to slavery. Though he had been lost to slavery, the tattered coat he left behind became a talisman for the abolitionists. "See how they rent the sleeve away," Theodore Parker thundered in April 1852 at the observance of the first anniversary of the rendition of Sims.

The Sims affair foreshadowed that of Anthony Burns, both in its outcome and in the emotional response it evoked. Captured in May 1854 as a fugitive slave, Burns was put in irons. An attempt to storm the courthouse and seize Burns was repelled; in the skirmish one of his guards was fatally shot. When Burns was marched from the courthouse to the revenue cutter that would carry him back to Virginia, the buildings in downtown Boston were draped in black as some fifty thousand spectators witnessed the procession.

Disheartening as these defeats must have been, in none of the Boston outbreaks was a would-be rescuer charged with breaking the law and given a jail sentence. Even this was not the case in Philadelphia. Here, in May 1860, five Negroes attempted to rescue Moses Horner as he was being driven in a carriage to the railroad station and a Baltimore-bound train. Not merely were

CAUTION!!
COLORED PEOPLE
OF BOSTON, ONE & ALL,
You are hereby respectfully CAUTIONED and advised, to avoid conversing with the
Watchmen and Police Officers of Boston,
For since the recent ORDER OF THE MAYOR & ALDERMEN, they are empowered to act as
KIDNAPPERS
AND
Slave Catchers,
And they have already been actually employed in KIDNAPPING, CATCHING, AND KEEPING SLAVES. Therefore, if you value your LIBERTY, and the *Welfare of the Fugitives* among you, *Shun* them in every possible manner, as so many *HOUNDS* on the track of the most unfortunate of your race.
Keep a Sharp Look Out for KIDNAPPERS, and have TOP EYE open.
APRIL 24, 1851.

Notice posted by the Vigilance Committee of Boston after the rendition of Thomas Sims to slavery in April 1851. Courtesy of the Picture Collection, New York Public Library.

they thwarted in their attempt, but the five men were charged with obstructing the law and rioting and were sentenced to thirty days in prison. Needless to say, the jailing of the Moses Horner Five evoked widespread sympathy. New York Negroes held a meeting at Shiloh Church in Troy, New York, on May 11 in honor of "the men who had so nobly stood up in their persons to secure the liberty of one of their own race."[8]

The two most celebrated cases, in New York and Ohio, had sequels more to the liking of the abolitionists. In Rochester a former slave called Jerry (also known as William Henry) was seized at the police station, where his rescuers

---

[8] *New York Tribune,* 12 May 1860.

overpowered the guards by sheer numbers. For five days Jerry remained carefully hidden in this country; then he escaped to Ontario. Canada was also the refuge for John Price, the principal in the Oberlin-Wellington rescue case. Price had been seized as a runaway and taken to Wellington, where, with his captors, he was awaiting a southbound train. Some fifty Oberlin townspeople and students, hearing the news, hastened to Wellington and freed John Price before the train arrived. In the Oberlin-Wellington rescue, as in the others, blacks played an important role.

Reformist circles were stirred by the many slave rescues, but they were still more deeply affected by the case of a Missouri slave, Dred Scott, who sought freedom not through flight but through the courts. Scott had been taken by his master into the Wisconsin Territory, which was declared free soil in the Missouri Compromise of 1820, and he was contending that as a result he automatically acquired free status. In a decision that dismayed Northerners and blacks everywhere, the Supreme Court ruled in 1857 that a slave, as property, could be taken anywhere in the territories by his owner and still remain a slave. Further, dealing blacks an especially crushing blow, the Court ruled that Negroes were in no case United States citizens and therefore could not bring suits before federal courts.

Alarmed and angered as never before, Negroes in the North held a series of protest meetings which reached a high point in a gathering at Boston's historic Faneuil Hall on March 5, 1858. The speakers at this meeting, all active abolitionists, included black William C. Nell and John S. Rock and white William Lloyd Garrison, Wendell Phillips, and Theodore Parker. Songs for the occasion had been written by Frances Ellen Watkins and Charlotte Forten, a teacher in the Salem public schools, who was also on hand for the activities.

The meeting was deliberately set for March 5, the date of the Boston Massacre that had taken place nearly ninety years earlier. Further, the sponsors of this particular Dred Scott protest event had dubbed it Crispus Attucks Day in honor of Crispus Attucks, a mulatto, who was the first person to die in the massacre. This first Crispus Attucks Day was so successful that its sponsors were prompted to announce it would become an annual affair.

Attucks was a symbol of the spirit of the American Revolution. Hence the evoking of his name signified that the abolitionist movement, especially its black component, had taken a more militant stance, that it was looking less and less to gradualism and halfway measures and more and more to direct confrontation and, if necessary, violence. Protest by force of arms, hitherto generally repudiated by white and black abolitionists, now came in for real consideration.

The John Brown Crisis

The most explosive expression of the growing militancy of the abolitionist movement was John Brown's raid on the federal arsenal at Harpers Ferry in

October 1859. This event shook blacks like no other in their country's history, for its leader was a man they loved and admired. If ever there was a white man with whom they could identify, it was John Brown. Indeed, John S. Rock saw him as the reincarnation of the black man who fell at the Boston Massacre, exclaiming in March 1860 that "the John Brown of the second revolution is but the Crispus Attucks of the first."[9]

In black circles Brown's credentials were of long standing. As early as 1834 he had expressed a wish to adopt a colored boy. Money earmarked for parlor furnishings for his home in Springfield, Massachusetts, went to fugitive slaves. In 1849 Brown moved to North Elba in the Adirondacks in order to assist a group of Negroes who had settled there. At North Elba Brown's black hired hands took their meals with his family. When in the spring of 1858 one of Brown's Negro followers was refused breakfast at the Massasoit House in Chicago, Brown stalked out angrily, refusing to eat there himself and heatedly remonstrating to the proprietor.

It was natural for Brown to include Negroes in his Harpers Ferry venture. In May 1858, at Chatham, Ontario, he held a meeting with thirty-four Negroes, including Osborn Perry Anderson, who was destined to be the sole black survivor of Harpers Ferry. Four other Negroes—Shields Green, Dangerfield Newby, John A. Copeland, Jr., and Lewis S. Leary—were among the small band of nineteen men who marched into the darkened streets of Harpers Ferry on the night of October 16, 1859, with the aim of seizing the government arsenal and, ultimately, liberating the slaves.

The raid was quickly put down, and ten of Brown's band were killed, among them Newby and Leary. Seven more were captured, including Copeland, Green, and Brown himself. And five escaped, including Anderson and a white Brownite, Albert Hazlett, who managed to make their way out of the armory base and steal a boat to take them across the Potomac to Maryland. The captured men were found guilty of treason and sentenced to death by hanging, and Brown's execution was set for December 2.

"We are very apt to sympathize with almost anybody who is going to be hung," observed George Sennott, who served as legal counsel for the captured men.[10] But sympathy for Brown and his followers was far more deep-rooted than Sennott's comment implied. Brown's impending death deeply moved tens of thousands of Northerners who would have been unwilling to call themselves abolitionists.

Black people were among John Brown's most loyal supporters, and many black churches held special services on his behalf. "If prayers will be of any benefit to old Brown his day of deliverance is close at hand," remarked an unsympathetic daily, the *New York Herald*.[11] But prayer was not the only

---

[9] *Liberator*, 6 March 1860.

[10] *New York Times*, 14 March 1860.

[11] *New York Herald*, 2 November 1859.

activity at the John Brown meetings of black churches. At some of the gatherings money was raised for the soon-to-be-widowed spouses of the Harpers Ferry captives. At others, the dominant note was hardly one of resignation. From the pulpit of the Bethesda Presbyterian Church in New York, J. Sella Martin proclaimed that one of the lessons of Harpers Ferry was that the black man was possessed of courage.[12]

At Shiloh Church in Troy, New York, during the last week of October 1859, the militant black Henry Highland Garnet preached that it was the duty of every man who loved freedom to declare that John Brown was right, "and anyone who could not say so boldly had much better say nothing at all." A week later, however, Garnet did find fault with the Harpers Ferry plan of operation. He pointed out that Brown, although he had been on the side of the angels, had thrown away $20,000 when $20 would have been of more service. "All that was needed," Garnet continued, "was a box of matches in the pocket of every slave, and then slavery would be set right."[13] Arson was an old story to the slaves, but as a possible abolitionist technique it was somewhat novel to Garnet's listeners.

Neither prayers nor protests could stay the execution of John Brown. The day of his death, "Martyr Day," as black abolitionists called it, was a day of solemn mourning for the colored people in the North. Black businesses were closed. Black churches, their congregations dressed in mourning, held services throughout the day. Black settlements in Canada held appropriate services; at Chatham, "from 4 a.m. to a late hour every minute seemed devoted to the sad event."[14]

Two weeks later four of Brown's followers, including Green and Copeland, followed him to the scaffold. "The last Monday, Tuesday, Wednesday and Thursday that I shall ever see on this earth have now passed by,"[15] wrote young Copeland on the morning of his hanging. In his last minutes, Copeland was at peace with himself; as he left the jail, he said, "If I am dying for freedom I could not die for a better cause." Shields Green, an unlettered former slave, was less articulate than the Oberlin-trained Copeland. But both men "mounted the scaffold with a firm step," as reported in the *New York Tribune.*[16]

The John Brown affair gave a new urgency to the sectional debate over slavery. Moreover, it brought to the abolitionist movement a new depth of commitment and a new disillusionment with the techniques of nonviolent protest. The ladylike and hitherto gentle Sarah P. Remond, for example, informed a London audience in January 1860 that Brown had gone to Harpers

---

[12] *New York Times,* 8 November 1859.

[13] *New York Times,* 2 November 1859.

[14] *Liberator,* 6 January 1860.

[15] John A. Copeland, Jr., to his family, 16 December 1859, in Robert S. Fletcher, "John Brown and Oberlin," *The Oberlin Alumni Magazine* (February 1932): 138–39.

[16] *New York Tribune,* 17 December 1859.

Ferry to lead the slaves from the land of oppression to the land of freedom, and that slavery itself was a treasonable insurrection, with the slaveholders comprising an armed band of insurrectionists rising up against the rights and liberties of their fellow men. Black orators increasingly evoked the names of Denmark Vesey and Nat Turner, the black leaders of previous slave conspiracies. And a group of blacks in Albany formed an organization called the Irrepressible Conflict Society for Human Rights.

As Brown's comrade in arms Osborn Perry Anderson wrote a few months after his leader's hanging, "there is an unbroken chain of sentiment and purpose from Moses to the Jews to John Brown of America."[17] And, indeed, Brown's death had given the Negroes of America a new sense of dedication to the abolitionist cause. In New York in May 1860, at the first meeting of the American Anti-Slavery Society to be held after Harpers Ferry, the attendance of Negroes was "many times larger than ever before," as a *New York Tribune* reporter put it. And "they manifested their interest to a remarkable degree when the plates went around."[18] As black Americans readily sensed, John Brown had dramatized the issue of slavery in such a way as to preclude further postponement of armed conflict on a massive scale. The time was nigh. Hence, as never before, the faithful were obliged to make ready.

---

[17] Osborn P. Anderson, *A Voice from Harper's Ferry* (Boston, 1861), p. 5.

[18] *New York Tribune,* 9 May 1860.

The Negro Convention Movement

WILLIAM H. PEASE and JANE H. PEASE

Jane Pease and William Pease are both members of the history department at the University of Maine in Orono. Together, they have written extensively on the antislavery movement and black history. They are coauthors of *Black Utopia: Negro Communal Experiments in America* (State Historical Society of Wisconsin, 1963) and coeditors of *The Antislavery Argument* (Bobbs-Merrill, 1965). In the following essay, Mr. and Mrs. Pease describe the evolution of the Negro convention movement in the North during the thirty years before Emancipation, portraying the convention meetings as a vehicle for black self-expression and a means of moving toward group identity as well as a devise for social and political reform.

On September 20, 1830, between two and three dozen blacks representing five free states and two slave states gathered in Bethel Church, Philadelphia, for a five-day meeting. There they proposed to study the problems, needs, and interests of free Negroes throughout the United States and to explore ways of improving their condition.

That they met when they did was not surprising. Conventions in support of such causes as temperance, peace, and religion were, like political conventions, a newly popular means of group action. More important, the second great wave of American antislavery activity was just beginning. Benjamin Lundy had been publishing his antislavery newspaper, the *Genius of Universal Emancipation,* for nine years; William Lloyd Garrison was about to launch his *Liberator.* Old local and state manumission societies, long actively attempting to mitigate the evils of slavery, would soon be reinforced by abolitionist societies whose goal was total emancipation. Likewise, free Negroes would increasingly seek to express their own feelings and to improve their position in American society.

In 1827 Samuel E. Cornish, editor of *Freedom's Journal,* the country's first black newspaper, proposed holding race conventions to better the condition of Northern freemen. Cornish's suggestion was taken up by other leaders, especially Bishop Richard Allen of the African Methodist Episcopal Church, and it bore fruit in the 1830's in a series of conventions called and attended by free people of color. These conventions provided both a distinctive outlet for black self-expression and a means of establishing black identity in a hostile white environment. White abolitionists participated extensively in these early conventions, just as blacks participated in the predominantly white anti-slavery societies of the same period. Increasingly, however, it seemed apparent that biracial efforts could not meet the special needs of free Negroes. "Under present circumstances," the president of the 1834 convention, William Hamilton, advised, "it is highly necessary [that] the free people of color should combine, and closely attend to their own particular interest."[1]

The Scope of the Movement

Over the years, free blacks in the United States formed many groups devoted to community well-being. In New York City in the 1830's, for example, the Phoenix Society established a library, sponsored public lectures, and encouraged both academic and vocational education. At the same time, the New York Committee of Vigilance, established in 1835, provided needed assistance to fugitive slaves and to free blacks already residing in the city. And in 1850 the newly formed American League of Colored Laborers encouraged black craftsmen to establish their own businesses.

The convention movement, however, was different from these associations. Conventions were not permanent organizations. They were rather gatherings of delegates who assembled at specific times and places to transact particular business and then adjourned. Whatever continuity the convention process had was provided by committees formed at one meeting for the purpose of arranging for the next. Frequently, however, even that continuity was lacking, and the links between conventions were either local meetings or organizations quite independent of them. The function of the conventions, as their structure implied, was not to grapple with the details of day-to-day issues, but rather to provide members of the black community with a sense of direction, to establish their priorities, and to coordinate their efforts. After the first convention in Philadelphia in 1830, meetings were held for at least seven consecutive years. These first conventions, held initially by the Free Persons of Colour and then by the American Moral Reform Society, an offshoot of the broader group, provided for regular and frequent assemblies of community representatives throughout the 1830's.

The early meetings were modest affairs, ranging in size from fifteen delegates in 1831 to seventy in 1837. In addition, the particular delegates to the conventions varied from year to year. Nonetheless a steady corps of leaders developed, for nearly a third of the total delegates attended at least

---

[1] *Liberator,* 14 June 1834.

three of the six gatherings between 1830 and 1835. Although an overwhelming majority of the delegates to the meetings were black, whites also joined in debates and other proceedings as conventions considered measures to counteract racial discrimination, to aid free Negroes in the North, and, ultimately, to promote their assimilation of white middle-class values and life styles.

By the end of the decade, however, white abolitionists had become so absorbed in disputes over the best means to end slavery that they had less and less time for the needs of the free blacks. In response, the convention movement developed a more cohesive and distinctively black program, which was political in orientation and increasingly militant in spirit. From the 1840 convention in Hartford, Connecticut, which established the American Board of Disfranchised Commissioners, to the 1847 and 1848 conventions in Troy, New York, and Cleveland, Ohio, virtually every meeting demanded full political equality. And at the Buffalo convention of 1843, as well as at the Troy convention four years later, a sizable minority of the delegates advocated slave uprisings. Thus the meetings of the 1840's were characterized by greater vigor than had been their relatively quiet predecessors.

The convention movement reached its peak in Rochester in 1853 and in Cleveland the following year. Delegates to the Rochester meeting, eager to provide a more permanent vehicle to achieve their goals, established a National Council which was to meet every six months and to call conventions when they were needed. Although the council survived for only two years, it represented a full commitment to continuous and distinctive communal action, a policy which was in direct contrast to the goal of individual assimilation of the 1830's. Finally, at the Cleveland convention in 1854, a third theme was sounded: that of complete separatism. Delegates to this meeting advocated massive emigration of blacks from America, feeling their chances for self-fulfillment would be greater elsewhere in the Western Hemisphere.

Thus the national convention movement ran its course in the thirty years prior to Emancipation.[2] To be sure, only a small number of blacks took part in the meetings. Yet the number of delegates to the conventions rose over the years. Whereas only fifteen attended the 1831 meeting in Philadelphia, sixty or seventy attended the Buffalo and Troy conventions in the middle 1840's. And by the time of the Rochester and Cleveland conventions in the 1850's, delegate strength had increased to nearly 150. Significantly, almost all the national conventions were held in New York, Pennsylvania, or Ohio. Further, nearly all the delegates came from these states, as did the most dynamic leaders: from New York, minister Henry Highland Garnet and editor Frederick

---

[2] During this period, conventions of major significance were held as follows:

1830	Philadelphia, Pa.	1848	Cleveland, Ohio
1840	Hartford, Conn.	1853	Rochester, N.Y.
1843	Buffalo, N.Y.	1854	Cleveland, Ohio
1847	Troy, N.Y.	1855	Philadelphia, Pa.

Douglass; from Pennsylvania, physician Martin R. Delany; and from Ohio, John Mercer Langston, a lawyer. Nor was this distribution surprising, for it was in these states that most of the free Negro population lived. New England's disproportionately small representation at the conventions reflected the fact that the black community there was closely linked with the Garrisonian abolitionists, who condemned exclusive race action.

Representative though the national meetings generally were, they could not meet all the demands made upon the convention movement. Although they provided a variety of alternatives, ranging from the early emphasis on general reform and individual assimilation to later enthusiasm for black communal action and finally to separation and black nationalism, still the national meetings were inappropriate vehicles for political action. The problem was simple. On the national level the vast majority of the black population was slave, and that fact left the free Northern population with little effective political leverage. Primarily to grapple with political considerations, then, sporadic state conventions were called in those states where free blacks were most numerous. Delegates to these conventions emphasized the techniques requisite to achieving equal suffrage and using it effectively. Throughout the North, accordingly, blacks organized and used petitions, lectures, and public meetings to propagandize for basic civil rights and unqualified suffrage. Likewise, they employed whatever techniques of democratic politics were available to them to oppose economic discrimination, school segregation, and bans against interracial marriage.

The first state convention, which met in New York in 1837, sought the repeal of a special property qualification for black voters. Subsequently, in Connecticut and Pennsylvania, conventions protested state constitutional exclusion of blacks from suffrage; and in Ohio, they urged repeal of the highly discriminatory Black Code.

Even more frequently, free Negroes of the North gathered in countless local conventions. Generally, these meetings served two purposes. First, they dealt ad hoc with local issues: how to organize temperance societies, how to improve educational opportunities in the community, how to further one or another benevolent activity. Second, they served as forums in which to express grass-roots sentiment on major issues of all kinds. Here blacks first denounced the American Colonization Society's proposal for involuntary repatriation to Africa, and here they first condemned the Fugitive Slave Law of 1850. Here, also, they developed crucial ward-level support for their political demands and generated broad support for state and national conventions.

At the local level the convention movement was essentially parochial. Yet from the obscure ranks of the participants in these meetings emerged new leaders who later rose to state or national prominence. Indeed, in their local bases of support lay much of the strength of men like James McCune Smith and Ulysses Vidal of New York, Martin R. Delany and John Vashon of Pittsburgh, J. W. C. Pennington and Amos G. Beman of Hartford, Jermain W. Loguen of Syracuse, William Whipper of Columbia, Pennsylvania, and Uriah Boston of Poughkeepsie, New York. In addition, their day-to-day leadership experience on the local level gave these men useful contact with the white community. Though the drama of the movement played itself out at the state and national level, its practical action was largely at the local level.

Broadly, it can be said that the convention movement, at national, state, and local levels, served as the voice of Northern blacks from Maine to Michigan from early in the 1830's until the Civil War. Its meetings helped to unite the communities represented and to coordinate their efforts to attain equal rights.

The Early Reformist Conventions

The path of action which the convention movement pursued in the 1830's was most clearly indicated by the activity of the American Moral Reform Society. Meeting always in Philadelphia, the society's annual conventions defined the assimilationist ideals and goals characteristic of the decade. The minutes of the 1837 convention reported that its purposes were to promote peace, temperance, education, economy, and universal liberty. To achieve these goals, it proposed to establish local auxiliaries, to sponsor a newspaper, to appeal to various churches for assistance, and to petition Congress on relevant issues. Generally, the conventions of this period encouraged blacks to learn trades, to save their money, to buy their own homes, and to invest in land. From the 1830's into the 1850's, national, state, and local meetings urged as many as could to leave the cities, where exploitation "tend[ed] to grind the faces of the poor," and to settle in the country, where, by cultivating their own land, they could achieve economic independence and full manhood.[3] They were also urged to work for institutions which would educate the children and elevate the adults—schools, libraries, debating societies.

Indeed, education was a central concern of the convention movement throughout its history. Better schooling would provide the key to successful competition with whites and would create both individual and community self-respect. Plans for establishing manual labor colleges, which would combine academic instruction, vocational training, and student self-help, were frequently endorsed. The 1831 national convention supported a plan for such a school in New Haven, Connecticut. When this project failed, a subsequent meeting encouraged the founding of an advanced manual labor school in Wilberforce, Upper Canada. Later, at the Troy and Rochester conventions of 1847 and 1853, other plans for manual labor schools were endorsed. Although none of these projects succeeded, the support that they found at the various

---

[3] "Report of the Committee on the Social Condition of the Colored Race, at a meeting of colored clergymen, held in New York, March, 1851," *Liberator,* 4 April 1851, as copied from the *New York Evening Post,* n.d.

conventions attested to a major dissatisfaction with existing educational opportunities.

Equally characteristic of the meetings of the 1830's was their firm opposition to the American Colonization Society's program of emigration to Liberia. Almost as soon as the society was organized in 1817, a meeting of Philadelphia blacks had protested it. Thereafter, with persistent regularity, national, state, and local meetings from Washington to Pittsburgh, from Boston to Baltimore, resolved against the society's thrust, which, as they saw it, strengthened slavery by exiling free black dissidents and intensified prejudice by arguing that free Negroes could not coexist with whites. Their goal, conversely, was not deportation to Africa, but equality in America.

Nor was convention protest limited to African colonization. To move anywhere outside the United States was to give up black Americans' "claim to this being the land of their nativity" and to surrender "every sense of manhood."[4] Some convention delegates, to be sure, contended that migration to Canada or to unsettled territory in the western United States would not mean exile and humiliation, but rather a chance for the venturesome to "improv[e] their condition" and escape from "the *plough-share* of prejudice."[5] Most, however, rejected even that alternative. Theirs was the dream of assimilation. "On *our* conduct and exertions," wrote Samuel E. Cornish in 1837, "much, very much depends." Blacks, he added a little later, must be models of "honesty, punctuality, propriety of conduct, and modesty and dignity of deportment."[6] These were the imperatives of acceptance. The convention movement of the 1830's strove to fulfill that dream.

The Political Orientation of the 1840's

Thus the conventions of the 1830's focused on social problems and attitudinal change. They did not grapple extensively with the problem of legal discrimination, for to have done so would have been to enter the political arena, where blacks lacked the power to enforce the changes they sought. But the very failure to act politically during these years impeded both social reform and individual progress, for the mental, moral, and physical improvement which the conventions endorsed was blocked by restrictive state and local laws. To this problem the 1840's conventions addressed themselves.

---

[4] *Liberator,* 22 September 1832. *Frederick Douglass' Paper,* 1 April 1853.

[5] *Constitution of the American Society of the Free Persons of Colour, For Improving their Condition in the United States; For Purchasing Lands; and For the Establishment of a Settlement in Upper Canada, Also the Proceedings of the Convention, With their Address to the Free Persons of Colour in the United States* (Philadelphia: J. W. Allen, 1831), p. 9. *Minutes and Proceedings of the Third Annual Convention for the Free People of Colour . . .* (New York: Published by Order of the Convention, 1833), p. 28.

[6] *Colored American,* 4 March 1837, 6 May 1837.

Early in the decade the black community underwent a change of leadership. Early leaders, who had set the convention movement into motion and had served as a focus for community identity, were no longer in a commanding position. Bishop Richard Allen had died in 1831; James Forten, Sr., was now too old to respond to the enthusiasm of a new generation; and Samuel E. Cornish had lost touch with youthful impatience. But as the 1840's began, young men like Frederick Douglass, Henry Highland Garnet, Samuel Ringgold Ward, Jermain W. Loguen, and James McCune Smith, though scarcely national leaders yet, emerged as guides to future action. It was they and others like them who provided the vitality and imagination which made the new decade more militant and demanding than the one which had preceded it.

These new leaders challenged the assumption that cooperation with whites was the best route to black achievement. The Moral Reform Society of the 1830's had been racially mixed, and in its statement of principles, the "Declaration of Sentiments," it had explicitly stated that black freedom and reform could not be separated from the liberation and moral improvement of the entire American public. The major spokesman for the Reform Society, William Whipper, continued to assert that separatist action would only be used to undermine integrationist goals and to justify racial discrimination. Exclusive black action, the society contended in 1840, was "contrary to [its] principles . . . and the genius of republicanism."[7]

The younger leaders, however, disagreed. Dissatisfied with the meager accomplishments of the convention movement during the 1830's, they argued for all-black conventions and organizations—but not, they cautioned, as a way to opt out of American society. On the contrary, they held that such associations would be better able to ensure a meaningful black presence within that society. Exclusive action, the *Colored American* suggested in an 1840 editorial, would demonstrate that blacks were both willing and able to achieve and to carry out all the duties of citizenship. Rather than increase racial prejudice, this tactic would lessen it; by raising the estimation of blacks within the white community, it would pave the way for universal suffrage. It was important, the editorial admonished, not to play "second fiddle" to whites. "Where our object is confined to our own purposes and for our own advantage," the editorial concluded, "there 'the clearest necessity demands exclusive action. . . .'"[8]

In response to the increasing separatist sentiment, the *National Anti-Slavery Standard,* official organ of Garrisonian antislavery, warned against exclusive action, charging that it would "tear down" the gains free Negroes had already made. Charles B. Ray, editor of the *Colored American,* counterattacked with the charge that the *Standard* displayed a dictatorial and authoritarian attitude toward the matter. And David Ruggles, radical leader of the

---

[7] *Liberator,* 9 October 1840.

[8] *Colored American,* 27 June 1840.

New York City Vigilance Committee, rejected the *Standard's* warning altogether. "We shall never arrive to that equality which you so ardently desire," he lectured in the fall of 1840, "until we know our condition and feel ourselves as a disfranchised and enslaved people."[9]

This new determination to act independently was reinforced by several external events. The state of Maryland had recently enacted legislation favoring African emigration, and this posed the threat to voteless free blacks of an eventual forced migration. Moreover, the antislavery movement, the vaunted defender of the free blacks, was in disarray, and the prejudice of some of its white members was already obvious. In May 1840, delegates were summoned to a national convention at Hartford to apply their combined *"energies, intelligence and sympathies"* to the problem of political impotence.[10] When the convention assembled in September with David Ruggles at its head, it created the American Reform Board of Disfranchised Commissioners, which was to act as an agent for the entire community in its fight for the ballot.

At the state level similar moves were afoot. As early as 1837, blacks in New Bedford, Massachusetts, pressed candidates for political office to take a stand on the question of slavery; in the same year, Cornish headed a New York franchise petition campaign, and Garnet, still a student, participated in the Young Men's Convention on Suffrage in New York City. The next year in Pennsylvania a group of political activists published an "Appeal of Forty Thousand Citizens Threatened with Disfranchisement, to the People of Pennsylvania," which unsuccessfully protested a new constitution depriving blacks in that state of voting privileges they had exercised since 1790.

Thus the direction that would be taken by state conventions throughout the 1840's was clearly foreshadowed when delegates assembled in Albany in August 1840. This convention, led by Charles B. Ray, Charles Reason, Theodore Wright, and Garnet, launched a vigorous suffrage campaign in New York State, condemning particularly the $250 property qualification which was required only of Negroes. Drawing as many as 140 participants to its sessions, the convention adopted an "Address to the Public" charging that New York blacks were barred from political power, were denied educational opportunity, and were held back from economic advancement as a result of racial discrimination. Despite these obstacles, the address continued, Negroes had endured and had even risen in the world. Having thus proved their competence, they viewed their demands for basic political and economic rights as more than reasonable: "We *do* regard the right of our birthdom, [and] our service in behalf of the country . . ," the delegates concluded, "as favorable considerations . . . to banish all thought of proscription

---

[9] *National Anti-Slavery Standard,* 18 June 1840. *Colored American,* 18 July 1840. *Standard,* 1 October 1840.

[10] *Liberator,* 19 June 1840.

and injustice . . . and [to bring about] a hearty and practical acknowledgement of the claims and rights of a disfranchised people."[11]

Similar conventions were held throughout the decade. In Harrisburg in 1848, angry Pennsylvania blacks mourned the tenth anniversary of their disfranchisement and once more sought to have the word "white" stricken from the state constitution's list of voter qualifications. A month later, a similar group in Columbus, Ohio, protested that state's oppressive Black Code, which denied them political rights granted new immigrants. In such diverse places as Salem, New Jersey; Warren, Ohio; and Poughkeepsie, New York—as well as in urban centers like New York City, Troy, and Hartford—conventions and meetings kept up the pressure into the 1850's.

The political campaign was not without its difficulties, however. Throughout the 1840's, conventions provided the setting for ideological and factional disputes. What kind of action should they take? Should they endorse antislavery third parties or, instead, seek a voice within the major parties? Which of their leaders presented the best program? Indeed, the emergence of new and dynamic leaders accentuated the increasing diversity of views about all the central issues of the convention movement: the abolition of slavery; political rights; and opportunities for mental, moral, and physical improvement. In turn, this diversity contributed to a struggle for preeminence among the leaders. Yet despite these difficulties, it was clear that the convention movement had acquired a new drive, a new direction, a new vitality. What remained to be seen was how far the new momentum would carry it amid the crises and turbulence of the 1850's.

Militancy and Separatism

When the national convention met in Cleveland in 1848, harmony and good will prevailed. The delegates united to pass thirty-four resolutions on a wide variety of subjects and so reconciled the major positions of the principal factions. The unity which marked the occasion led Frederick Douglass to think the time was ripe to establish a National League of Colored People. Scarcely two years later, the passage of the Fugitive Slave Law in 1850 further intensified black solidarity as local meetings from Portland to Philadelphia, from Boston to Chicago, unequivocally condemned the new legislation.

The harmony and unity were, however, deceptive; for the convention movement of the 1850's was no more marked by oneness of purpose than by tranquillity. In frequency and number of meetings, the movement reached its peak early in the decade. Yet it was soon wracked by new divisions. At the same time that communal organization to achieve integration reached its height in the formation of a National Council, an equally aggressive separatist

---

[11] *Colored American,* 19 December 1840.

movement emerged. Nor was the conflict confined to ideologies, for the personal and organizational rivalries of past decades were harvested in the years preceding the Civil War. On the one hand, the intense activity of the early 1850's generated hope; on the other, the divisions it created led to despair. But although confusion and differences marked the period, so too did a dynamic momentum which the matured militancy and the deepening crisis of the decade produced.

Militancy was by no means a new phenomenon. In 1842 Boston Negroes had, in referring to "the last will and testament of the patriots of '76," indicated their own willingness to use force if necessary to achieve black freedom.[12] A year later the Buffalo convention made the point still more clearly. Its president, Samuel H. Davis, set the aggressive tone in his opening address. Liberty, he said, was more important than patriotism or the friendship of fellow citizens. To attain it, blacks should "rise up" and "assert" their rights.[13] The real dynamite, however, came later in an "Address to the Slaves" which Garnet wrote and presented on behalf of the business committee. Simply and pointedly it advised slaves to revolt against their masters. White Americans, it read, had fought against British tyranny for their freedom; slaves, in exactly the same position, had the same rights. To submit voluntarily to the tyranny of slavery was "SINFUL IN THE EXTREME."

> NEITHER GOD, NOR ANGELS, OR JUST MEN, COMMAND YOU TO SUFFER FOR A SINGLE MOMENT. THEREFORE IT IS YOUR SOLEMN AND IMPERATIVE DUTY TO USE EVERY MEANS, BOTH MORAL, INTELLECTUAL, AND PHYSICAL, THAT PROMISES SUCCESS. . . . You had far better all die—*die immediately,* than live slaves, and entail wretchedness upon your posterity. . . .
>
> Brethren, arise, arise! Strike for your lives and liberties. Now is the day and the hour. Let every slave throughout the land do this, and the days of slavery are numbered. You cannot be more oppressed than you have been—you cannot suffer greater cruelties than you have already. *Rather die freemen than live to be slaves.* Remember that you are FOUR MILLIONS.[14]

It was an exciting document, and in the first flush of enthusiasm the convention accepted it. But second thoughts led to reconsideration as the delegates debated long and hard whether to endorse and print the address. For an hour and a half, Garnet defended its merit. Douglass led the opposition. After several heated sessions, and by a single vote, the convention finally rejected making the address part of the convention record. But the issue did not die there.

---

12 *Liberator,* 23 December 1842.

13 *Minutes of the National Convention of Colored Citizens: Held at Buffalo, On the 15th, 16th, 17th, 18th and 19th of August, 1843. For the Purpose of Considering their Moral and Political Condition as American Citizens* (New York: Piercy & Reed, 1843), pp. 5–7.

14 Henry Highland Garnet, "An Address to the Slaves of the United States of America," in *A Memorial Discourse . . . Delivered in the Hall of the House of Representatives, Washington City, D.C. on Sabbath, February 12, 1865. With an Introduction by James McCune Smith* (Philadelphia: Joseph M. Wilson, 1865), pp. 44–51.

Four years later, at the Troy convention, Garnet delivered the same address as a speech. It "produced," read the minutes, "much sensation." Well it might have, for the Troy gathering also adopted a resolution which looked to the "propriety of instructing their sons in the art of war."[15] Then, lest the point be lost, the Cleveland convention of the following year debated, though it did not adopt, a resolution to establish a black militia. The delegates at this 1848 meeting compared their cause to that of the European revolutionaries who were striving for their freedom that same year. Now was the time, the call for the convention had said, for "oppressed freemen of America" to cast off their yokes.[16]

Thus emerged a militancy born of slavery, prejudice, and discrimination, and the frustration which their persistence produced in the freemen of the North. In New York in 1851, young blacks were urged "to organize military companies"; and in 1855 author and lecturer William Wells Brown exhorted free Negroes, "who ought to be united to a man, in opposition to the American Union," to align themselves with the antislavery radicals in seeking to dissolve the Union.[17] This new intensity, however, seemed only to make the divisions within the movement more acute. On the one hand, Douglass and his associates argued for more vigorous communal action to compel white America to give black America the same liberties and opportunities it enjoyed. On the other hand, Martin R. Delany advised his followers to turn their backs on America and seek their destiny in emigration.

The Rochester national convention of 1853 gave new definition to the integrationist position championed by Douglass. Delegates to this meeting rejected an assimilation in which the black man would blend indistinguishably into the white mass, achieving theoretical equality but losing his identity. Rather, the convention envisioned a distinctive black community which would develop its own institutions to serve its own special needs but which would at the same time play an integral part in the society, politics, and economy of America. In this position, the convention clearly anticipated what immigrant minorities later called cultural pluralism.

This vision of community had its roots in the all-black conventions of the 1840's, yet the members of these earlier conventions had been slow to embrace the idea of other distinctively black institutions. At the 1847 Troy convention, for example, delegates expressly called for the abolition, "as soon as possible," of "all *exclusive* colored institutions." In 1851 James McCune Smith, a successful New York City physician, argued that integration was inevitable in America

---

[15] *North Star,* 3 December 1847. *Proceedings of the National Convention of Colored People, and their Friends, held in Troy, N.Y., on the 6th, 7th, 8th and 9th, October, 1847* (Troy: J. C. Kneeland, 1847), pp. 16–17.

[16] *North Star,* 11 August 1848.

[17] *Liberator,* 4 April 1851, as copied from the *New York Evening Post,* n.d. *Liberator,* 18 May 1855.

because the country was like "a large and energetic stomach" whose "powers of assimilation [were] tremendous." Though Douglass might have rejected the metaphor, he agreed with its message. "All this talk about preserving races . . . ," he commented, "looks ridiculous."[18] In the end, however, the Troy convention backed the establishment of a Negro college, and both Smith and Douglass supported plans for a black manual labor school.

When the delegates assembled in Rochester in July 1853, therefore, they acted to clarify the course of integration by communal action. Representatives of nearly every faction deliberated its proposals for education, race organization, and a black press. In each case, they explicitly favored distinctive race action and institutions. To coordinate them, they voted to create a central agency, the National Council. Fulfilling Douglass' dream of a permanent national organization, the council would undertake educational programs, sponsor economic cooperatives, establish a press, and strive to enlarge employment opportunities. Though the projects themselves were not new, the spirit behind them was. In place of diverse plans for individual assimilation was a coherent model for unified action, designed to treat the community as a whole. The Rochester plan spelled out a new hope for equalizing status and promoting respect between blacks and whites. For the first time, James McCune Smith thought, free Negroes had banded together in an effective and progressive organization to work for their liberty and to improve their condition. "Personal independence, and class advancement" were to go hand in hand.[19]

For a time, considerable efforts were made to put the Rochester plan into effect. Auxiliary state councils were formed and held meetings in Massachusetts, New York, and Illinois, and the National Council itself met on three occasions. Within two years, however, the initial zest for organization began to fade, and the councils disappeared. In 1855, when a national convention assembled in Philadelphia, it was a tired affair. The address it adopted was dull and unimaginative, repeating the worn platitudes of the antislavery crusade, and its resolutions were a lifeless replica of the resolves of twenty years earlier.

Perhaps no race organization could have been strong enough to withstand the tensions of the 1850's. Neither President nor Congress could control the crises. The old parties disintegrated in the face of them. Conflict and ineptitude marked the struggle in Kansas; confrontation and decline, the abolitionist battle against the Fugitive Slave Law. Not surprisingly, the convention movement flagged too. Though some of its supporters remained optimistic and continued to hold state and local conventions, there were no national meetings from 1855 until the wartime National Equal Suffrage conventions. Indicative of the spirit of the time was the Cleveland convention in 1854. The last important national meeting before the war, it advocated voluntary emigration as the

---

[18] *North Star,* 3 December 1847, 10 April 1851. *Frederick Douglass' Paper,* 5 February 1852.

[19] *Frederick Douglass' Paper,* 22 July 1853.

sole solution for the American Negro. Dr. Martin R. Delany led in evolving this plan for mass migration—first to Canada or the Caribbean, later to Africa.

Not everyone, of course, followed Delany; nor did the Cleveland convention escape criticism. Douglass, faithful to the spirit of the Rochester convention, called the Cleveland departure "narrow and illiberal." A group in Ohio claimed that three-quarters of all the blacks in that state were and always had been opposed to any form of emigration. In Massachusetts the State Council of Colored Persons "regret[ted] the prominence . . . given to a general emigration scheme."[20]

Nevertheless, enthusiasm for emigration had gained ground. Spurred on by the Fugitive Slave Act of 1850, many blacks searched for a viable life outside the United States. Within a year an estimated 3,000 to 5,000 had fled north into Canada. Lewis Putnam had, in 1851, won the public support of New York's Governor Hunt for his United African Republic Emigration Society. Even before 1850, Garnet had concluded that emigration was a "legitimate means to wealth and power" for American blacks and had chosen Africa as the place most suited to their achieving economic development and commercial prosperity. "Liberia," he had predicted on one occasion, "will become the Empire State of Africa."[21]

The Cleveland convention, therefore, was not a sudden departure. Yet Delany, who organized the meeting, made sure he would dominate the proceedings. Over 60 percent of the delegates were friends and supporters from the Pittsburgh area, whom he had brought with him to Cleveland. No avowed anti-emigrationists were even admitted to the sessions. But packed or not, the convention focused attention on the new departure wherein ends and means coincided in a policy of complete race separatism. The official convention address asserted that only emigration would develop the cohesive and viable nationalism basic to black salvation and provide an "interested motive and a union of sentiment." "The truth is," the address continued, "we are not identical with the Anglo-Saxon or any other race of the Caucasian or pure white type of the human family, and the sooner we know and acknowledge this truth, the better for ourselves and posterity."[22] Then, like the Rochester convention, the Cleveland group acted to establish a permanent organization, a National Board of Commissioners, charged with maintaining correspondence with foreign countries, reporting on conditions at home and abroad, and sending out a foreign mission to investigate potential areas for settlement.

In direct challenge to the conventions that had preceded it, the Cleveland

---

[20] *Frederick Douglass' Paper,* 26 August 1853, 28 October 1853. *Liberator,* 24 February 1854.

[21] Howard Bell, "The Negro Emigration Movement, 1849–1854: A Phase of Negro Nationalism," *Phylon* 20 (Summer 1959): 133–34. Henry Highland Garnet to Samuel R. Ward, 10 February 1849, in *North Star,* 2 March 1849.

[22] *Proceedings of the National Emigration Convention of Colored People Held at Cleveland, Ohio on . . . 24th, 25th and 26th of August, 1854* (Pittsburgh: A. A. Anderson, 1854), pp. 22, 40.

convention boasted that it had "transacted business equal to the duration of a season, and of vastly more importance than any other similar body of colored people ever before assembled in the United States."[23] If the claim was exaggerated, it did not overestimate the timeliness of the convention's position in contrast with the Rochester platform. While the Rochester-initiated National Council faltered and failed, the emigrationists gathered strength. In 1858, four years after the Cleveland convention, they founded the African Civilization Society, and shortly thereafter they funded an exploratory expedition to the Niger Valley.

As the African Civilization Society took form, it split into two factions. One wing, based in Canada, was all black; dominated by Delany, it supported mass emigration. The other wing, American-based, was led by Garnet and differed from the Canadian group in supporting only selective emigration and in admitting whites to its ranks. From his northern outpost, Delany first sent missions to the Caribbean and South America and then in 1859 led a Niger River exploration group which negotiated for land in the Yoruba country on Africa's west coast. At the same time, in the states, Garnet sought prospective emigrants and financial backers.

Despite the efforts of the emigrationists, their impact in the states was minimal. Northerners generally preferred staying in the United States or emigrating to Canada to going so far from home, and Southerners had little choice in the matter. Neither Delany's pessimism about the American future nor Garnet's enthusiasm for African economic opportunity inspired the support needed to establish a separate nation "of which the colored Americans could be proud."[24] Yet in projecting the dream, Garnet and Delany offered a harassed people the hope and safety valve which whites found in the image, if not the reality, of the western frontier. The African Civilization movement meant opportunity, not escape; fulfillment, not despair; national identity, not surrender; aggressiveness, not submission; freedom, not slavery. Thus it continued the spirit which had motivated the Negro convention movement.

Accomplishments and Failures

The outbreak of the Civil War in 1861 did not end the convention movement. Meetings in support of suffrage, equal rights, and labor organization were held both during and after the war. Facing new problems of emancipation, these later assemblies brought to them thirty years of experience. The convention movement provided them a framework for action, basic training in organization, and a process for developing leadership.

More than that, despite their tendency to divisiveness and feuding, the conventions had agreed upon and forwarded positive goals: individual mental,

---

[23] Ibid., p. 15.
[24] Henry Highland Garnet, quoted in the *New York Daily Tribune,* 11 August 1858.

moral, and physical improvement; equal political, social, and economic rights; united community action; group and individual identity; and a sense of militant urgency and separatism which veered in the 1850's toward black nationalism. The Rochester and Cleveland conventions in 1853 and 1854 both highlighted these aims and illuminated the three strands which ran through the entire movement: individual assimilation, communal integrative action, and separatism. The first reached its peak in the American Moral Reform Society conventions of the 1830's; the second in the self-consciously distinctive conventions in the 1840's and the National Council of the 1850's; the third in the emigrationist enthusiasm of the 1850's and the African Civilization Society.

Though the strands overlap and are not entirely contradictory, they do demonstrate the conventions' major weakness—their failure to achieve mass support for any one program or technique. The movement suffered from divided leadership; it was fragmented by conflicting programs; it was weakened by perennial confusion over means and ends. In addition, it suffered constant defeat. Political, social, and economic equality—the heart of its program—remained virtually as remote in 1860 as they had been in 1830.

If the conventions failed to accomplish their goals, they did evolve techniques which helped the black community to achieve an organized and self-conscious identity, to produce a variety of able leaders, and to develop the three major strands of reform and protest thought which have continued to the present. Successful in some things, the thirty-year struggle for equal rights was also an experience in futility and defeat. The Negro convention movement was a blending of hope and despair.

4 SUGGESTIONS FOR FURTHER READING

Aptheker, Herbert, *American Negro Slave Revolts**. New York: Columbia University Press, 1943. ▪ An exhaustive and controversial secondary work on slave rebelliousness, sometimes considered the basic.

———, ed., *A Documentary History of the Negro People in the United States,* vol. 1, *From Colonial Times Through the Civil War**. New York: Citadel Press, 1951. ▪ A collection that contains excerpts from the proceedings of a number of Negro conventions as well as documents pertaining to slave resistance.

———, *Nat Turner's Slave Rebellion**. New York: Humanities Press, 1966. ▪ The basic work on the 1831 rebellion in Virginia. Includes the full text of Nat Turner's original confessions and the several appendices to that document.

———, *To Be Free: Studies in Afro-American History**. New York: International Publishers, 1948. ▪ See especially "Slave Guerrilla Warfare," pp. 11–30, for a discussion of the more violent aspects of slave resistance.

Bell, Howard H., "The American Moral Reform Society, 1836–1841," *Journal of Negro Education* 27 (1958): 34–40. ▪ A discussion of a major offshoot of the conventions of the 1830's.

———, "The National Negro Convention, 1848," *Ohio Historical Quarterly* 67 (1958): 357–68. ▪ An examination of the alignment with Free Soil politics.

———, "The Negro Emigration Movement, 1849–1854: A Phase of Negro Nationalism," *Phylon* 20 (Summer 1959): 132–42. ▪ A study of one of the directions taken by the convention movement in the 1850's.

———, ed., *A Survey of the Negro Convention Movement, 1830–1861*. Reprint ed., New York: Arno Press, 1970. ▪ The principal study of the organized efforts of Northern blacks to improve their lot by self-help and by combating racial prejudice.

---

*Available in paperback edition

Buckmaster, Henrietta, *Let My People Go**. New York: Harper, 1941. ▪ A clearly written, fast-paced work that recaptures the excitement and suspense of the underground railroad movement.

Carroll, Joseph C., *Slave Insurrections in the United States, 1800–1865.* Westport, Conn.: Negro Universities Press, 1938. ▪ A study of open slave resistance.

Delany, Martin Robison, *The Condition, Elevation, Emigration, and Destiny of the Colored People of the United States, Politically Considered.* New York: Arno Press, 1969. Originally published in 1852. ▪ A major statement by one of the foremost emigrationists and a prominent convention leader.

Douglass, Frederick, *My Bondage and My Freedom**. New York: Arno Press, 1968. Originally published in 1855. ▪ Douglass' moving autobiography, in which he describes his involvement in the antislavery movement and his tour of the British Isles. The book furnishes a valuable case study of a black reformer.

————, *The Life and Writings of Frederick Douglass**, ed. Philip S. Foner, 4 vols. New York: International Publishers, 1951–1955. ▪ A collection of the most important writings and speeches of a major black abolitionist and convention leader.

Farrison, William E., *William Wells Brown: Author and Reformer.* Chicago: University of Chicago Press, 1969. ▪ A meticulously researched study of the varied activities of an author-abolitionist who was well known in reformist circles in both England and America.

Franklin, John Hope, *The Free Negro in North Carolina, 1790–1860.* Chapel Hill: University of North Carolina Press, 1943. ▪ An excellent study of a specific area that offers insight into the lot of free Southern blacks before the Civil War.

Gara, Larry, *The Liberty Line: The Legend of the Underground Railroad**. Lexington: University of Kentucky Press, 1961. ▪ An analysis of a number of myths about the workings of the underground railroad, in which Gara points out that free Negroes, not white abolitionists, did most of the work.

Garnet, Henry Highland, *An Address to the Slaves of the United States of America.* New York: Arno Press, 1969. Originally published in 1865. ▪ A leading statement of black militancy by one of the leaders of the convention movement, originally presented as an address to a convention in 1843.

Halasz, Nicholas, *The Rattling Chains: Slave Unrest and Revolt in the Ante-Bellum South.* New York: David McKay, 1966. ▪ A study of the patterns of slave resistance.

James, C. L. R., *Black Jacobins: Toussaint L'Ouverture and the San Domingo Revolution**. New York: Dial Press, 1938. ▪ The story of a successful revolt among Caribbean slaves that may have profoundly affected slavery in nineteenth-century America.

Johnston, James H., *Race Relations in Virginia and Miscegenation in the South, 1776–1860.* Amherst: University of Massachusetts Press, 1970. ▪ A study that focuses on miscegenation, laws, attitudes, and practices bearing on race relations in a specific Southern state.

Kelley, Donald B., "Harper's Ferry: Prelude to Crisis in Mississippi," *Journal of Mississippi History* 27 (November 1965): 351–72. ▪ An excellent article on John Brown's famous raid on the federal arsenal.

Kilson, Marion D. de B., "Towards Freedom: An Analysis of Slave Revolts in the United States," *Phylon* 25 (1964): 175–87. ▪ A thorough analysis of all the known slave revolts.

Lofton, John, *Insurrection in South Carolina: The Turbulent World of Denmark Vesey.* Yellow Springs, Ohio: Antioch College Press, 1964. ▪ A good treatment of a specific slave conspiracy.

Negro Conventions, *Proceedings.* Reprint ed., New York: Arno Press, 1970. ▪ The proceedings of the major Negro conventions—an invaluable first-hand source for understanding the entire movement.

Pease, Jane H., and Pease, William H., eds., *The Antislavery Argument**. Indianapolis: Bobbs-Merrill, 1965. ▪ An exploration of ante-bellum abolitionist activity.

———, "Black Power—The Debate in 1840," *Phylon* 29 (1968): 19–26. ▪ A study of black militancy in the convention movement.

Pease, William H., and Pease, Jane H., *Black Utopia: Negro Communal Experiments in America.* Madison: University of Wisconsin Press, 1963. ▪ A description of ante-bellum efforts to establish all-black communities for the purpose of promoting self-help and self-improvement and demonstrating the black man's readiness for full citizenship.

Quarles, Benjamin, *The Black Abolitionists**. New York: Oxford University Press, 1969. ▪ The leading study of the entire scope of organized black activity in the ante-bellum period. In particular, this volume points out the varied and unique role of free blacks in the movement against slavery.

Starobin, Robert S., *Industrial Slavery in the Old South.* New York: Oxford University Press, 1970. ▪ See especially Starobin's discussion of slave resistance, pp. 75–115.

Staudenraus, Philip J., *The African Colonization Movement, 1816–1865.* New York: Columbia University Press, 1961. ▪ A survey of attempts by both blacks and whites to remove blacks from America.

Still, William, *The Underground Railroad.* New York: Arno Press, 1968. Originally published in 1872. ▪ A contemporary description of the railroad's activities by a black participant.

Strother, Horatio T., *The Underground Railroad in Connecticut.* Middletown, Conn.: Wesleyan University Press, 1966. ▪ A carefully documented study of the runaways who reached Connecticut—the land and sea routes they took, the risks they ran, and the adjustments they made to their new environment.

Styron, William, *The Confessions of Nat Turner**. New York: Random House, 1967. ▪ An attempt at historical fiction that is significantly less well informed than it should be.

Woodson, Carter G., *The Education of the Negro Prior to 1861*. Washington, D.C.: Associated Publishers, 1919. ▪ A pioneer but still useful study of efforts by blacks to get an education, whether secondary or higher education, state-supported or church-related, vocational or general.

————, ed., *The Mind of the Negro as Reflected by Letters Written During the Crisis, 1800–1860*. Washington, D.C.: Associated Publishers, 1926. ▪ A volume in which the ante-bellum black speaks for himself, primarily in long, revealing letters to friends, sympathizers, and reformist organizations.

5

Emancipation and Racism

Black Self-Assertion
Before and After Emancipation

JOEL R. WILLIAMSON

Joel Williamson, professor of history at the University of North Carolina in Chapel Hill, is the author of *After Slavery: The Negro in South Carolina, 1861–1877* (University of North Carolina Press, 1965) and the editor of *The Origins of Segregation* (D. C. Heath, 1968). He is currently completing a study of race relations in the South between 1865 and 1915. In the essay that follows, Mr. Williamson challenges the validity of the Sambo stereotype as a description of the Negro slave personality. He holds that though Sambos did exist, they were the exceptions and not the rule. Stressing the progressive confusion of colors in the South, the great variety of the slave experience, and the persistent manifestations of assertiveness among both slaves and freedmen, Mr. Williamson sees Emancipation as a vital turning point in blacks' ability to realize preconceived and already accepted ideals.

A Confusion of Colors and Cultures

Far from exhibiting the conditioned servility of black people, Reconstruction in the South illustrated that blacks identified with the ideals offered by the dominant white culture and, further, that they were aggressive against white prejudice in the pursuit of that identity. If life in slavery had been uniformly severe, as severe as life in the concentration camps of Hitlerite Germany, and if the psychological message of his fixed inferiority and the impossibility of his ever achieving whiteness could have been transmitted more perfectly to the slave, then the black man's psyche might have been broken and he might have become the childlike "Sambo" white people wanted him to be. But the slave system in the South was a distinctly different institution in a very different culture. It varied from killing severity to a rather libertarian paternalism, with the result that people who served under the system had various experiences and emerged from it with various personalities. Some few black people did, indeed, internalize the Sambo role and continued to be Sambos in Reconstruction and throughout their lives. However, the great masses of blacks were not Sambos, either in Reconstruction or before.

In teaching blacks to be better slaves, Southern society often taught blacks to be—in the cultural sense—better whites, and that process began generations before universal emancipation came to the South. In its modern phase it began in the mid-fifteenth century when a European culture rising to dominance commenced to transport enslaved Africans from south of the Sahara north to Iberia. The process accelerated after about 1510 when the Spanish diverted that trade westward to the New World as a means of replacing the labor of the vanishing Indian. In three and a half centuries, probably five million Africans were so transported. That migration was one of the grand movements of the world's peoples—comparable to the movement of the Russians into Siberia, or the flow of the Scots-Irish into America, or the return of the Jews to Israel. It was a movement which has worked to shape our lives and to set the course of human history.

Black people came to British America relatively late in the total time of the Afro-American migration. In 1619, a Dutch ship brought the first twenty "neegars" into Jamestown. Until the late 1600's the black population in the South remained comparatively small. For instance, in Virginia in 1649 only 2 percent (about 300 people) of the population was black. As late as 1681 there were only some 3,000 blacks in Virginia in a total population of from 70,000 to 80,000. However, after the establishment of the Royal African Company in 1670—primarily for the purpose of engaging in the slave trade—a group of the king's friends had a large financial interest in pressing Africans into the American colonies, and they proceeded to do so. During these same decades, English planters in the Barbadian islands in the West Indies began to transfer their operations to the mainland in low-country Carolina. With the West Indian planters came large numbers of blacks already integrated into a well-developed slave system. In the early decades of the eighteenth century, the number of slave immigrants rose to a peak of about 30,000 yearly. Most of these early Americans were funneled into the tobacco plantations of the Chesapeake world and the rice plantations along the Carolina coast. Thus, more than a century after the first Englishman settled on the continent, the face of the new American darkened with a rush. It is perhaps worthy of some consideration that the Revolutionary generation in the South—that of Washington and Jefferson—was the first to be born in the midst of human blackness. Slavery and the quality of blackness came early to the South, but blackness in high quantity was a flower of later growth.

The uprooted blacks who were fed into the Atlantic slave trade were truly the wretched of the earth, dispossessed in almost every way. Selectively stolen for their youth and strength by alien blacks, marched to the sea in coffles and thrust into the trauma of the infamous "middle passage," deliberately separated from their linguistic brothers to lessen the danger of mutiny, scattered along the Atlantic seaboard, scattered again among the plantations around their places of landing, and carefully replanted in the midst of slaves who were already "seasoned" to the American way, it was small wonder that the one of three Africans who survived the journey saved little of Africa beyond his dark skin. It is easily understandable, too, that each succeeding generation was a mutation in the direction of Americanization. No man can live again his father's life, and much of Africa died with the African who died in America. The possibility of recreating a perfect Africa in America was vastly lost to the first black born into American slavery, and each succeeding birth marked a further travel away from the cultural shores of Africa.

Slavery worked viciously to squeeze Africa out of the black man, and Southern society worked vigorously to press English and American culture into the void. Obviously, the economics of slavery made it necessary that blacks be educated into plantation living. In addition, the drive for a sense of social security within the white community increasingly made it necessary that black people be raised to a feeling of contented belongingness in the order of things in America. Southern whites had either to tame the tiger or be eaten by it. If the tiger was not tamed, it might be a useful pretense—perhaps a living necessity—to imagine that he was so. Consequently, in the last three decades of the "travail of slavery," whites invaded black lives as never before, behaving as if they felt a compulsion to remake blacks in the image of whites, to make blacks Christians as whites were Christians, to make them civilized as whites were civilized, and of course ultimately to make blacks harmless to whites. But even as whites moved to embrace the black man more closely, they acted to hold him apart. More strenuously than ever, perhaps, white people strove to define the Negro as distinctly different—and distinctly subordinate. In the last days of slavery, the perfect black man in white eyes would have been white-like but clearly not white. Translated into cultural terms, he would always be a child in the great white way but never a man.

It appears that the ante-bellum Southern regime was signally successful in making blacks white-like. Well before the emergence of the concept of America as the melting pot of Europe (a concept which strikingly excluded from the mixture blacks, reds, and yellows), the South had been a melting pot of Africa, reducing a variety of black peoples to one sable mass. In the colonial South there had been Ibos, Coromantees, Foulahs, and a dozen other African groups, each with a distinctive and widely recognized appearance and style. Indeed, success in the slave trade depended in part upon a knowledge of the supposed marks and traits of each African people, for buyers' notions about the character of various tribes did much to fix the price of the slave. Then, in the decades before Emancipation, there were only blacks, and those blacks were being aggressively pressed into an American mold. The process went on in the plantations, but it also proceeded—and probably proceeded more effectively—among slaves on the farms, among slaves trained as domestics and in the trades, among free blacks skilled and unskilled, black and mulatto, and, perhaps most of all, among all Negroes in villages, towns, and cities. If a black person in the South in 1850 knew about Africa at all, probably the only kinship he could have understood was the simple fact that his skin was darkish like that of Africa's children.

One group of people which was classified as "black" in the ante-bellum South had little difficulty in identifying itself with whites precisely because it was white. That is, there were tens of thousands of mulattoes who were legally black but who were actually more than half white. It was manifestly easy for mulattoes, many of them free, to see themselves as the ministers, businessmen, and even slaveholding planters which in fact they sometimes were. The free Negro communities in Charleston and New Orleans were famously white-like, not only in the appearance of their citizens but in their behavior and institutions.

Furthermore, the kinship between individual mulattoes, slave and free, and certain Southern whites was probably much more intimate and lasting than historians have taught—and, perhaps, than they have wanted to believe. The popular idea that mulattoes were the offspring of fly-by-night affairs between poor whites and black slave women, usually caught unawares but not unwilling on the back side of the cotton patch, is much more a Southern white upper-class myth than a reality of the slave period. Mulatto slaves were often enough the children, not of some neighboring Snopes, nor of an itinerant Irish or German ditchdigger, nor of a cruel alien overseer, but of some slaveholding neighbor, and still again often enough of some member of the very family by which they were owned. The records are sufficiently full of traces of mulatto maids who had not only one child by a man of the planter class but two or three or four or more, all fathered by the same white man. One of the great and neglected facts of interracial life in the South is that in almost every community some planter had a mulatto family that lived in the very shape, shadow, and shame of his white family.

Children lightly dark learned to value their whiteness, and they were ambitious to know precisely who their white fathers were, a knowledge they commonly came to possess. In striking contrast to the mulatto's certain knowledge of his ancestry was the publicly professed ignorance of whites about the origins of the mulatto population. However, the historical evidence shows quite clearly that whites generally knew who had fathered each mulatto in the community. It is easy to imagine why white people would behave in this way. Mulattoes were a sore upon the social sight of white Southerners; each was a living indictment of the failure of the strictly biracial society envisioned by the white Southern ideal, a walking, talking, and mocking symbol of a white man's lapse in morality, a fall from Grace, a not-so-strange fruit of an all too familiar evil. White Southerners in late slavery were deeply and—by their own standards—appropriately distressed by the rising confusion of colors in their midst. Indeed, if tints, shades, and hues could do violence—and in that society they could—Southern whites were terrified by what seemed to be a riot of colors in their very midst.

Witness, for instance, the reaction of Ella Thomas, a young matron on a Georgia plantation, one Sunday morning in January 1858. The nearly white slave maid Susany proudly brought in her daughter Lulah for the mistress to see and admire. "A remarkably pretty child she is and as white as any white child," Ella wrote in her diary when the maid had left. She then fell into a monologue on the subject, a happening apparently not unusual among plantation women in that decade. Susany, she complained, was "having children constantly without a husband," and the fathers all too clearly were not black. "Ah after all," sighed the Southern lady, "there is the great point for an abolitionist to argue upon." Susany reminded Ella of Amanda, another mulatto servant who was reared in one of the best white families "knowing but little more of negroes than I do." Still another female servant she knew was educated in *"mistaken kindness"* and then sold for debts, possibly to men "but one degree removed from the brute creation." Her mind drawn to the subject, Ella's thoughts spilled out onto the pages of her diary, willingly it seems, like welcomed tears: "I know that this is a view of the subject that it is thought best for women to ignore but where we see so many cases of mulattoes commanding higher prices, advertised as 'fancy girls,' o is it not enough to make us shudder for the standard of morality in our Southern homes." She related the story of a local slaveholder's son who carried a mulatto slave to the North with him and passed her off as his wife. The home community condemned him for living with the woman, and when he actually attempted to marry her, his father tried to have him declared a lunatic. Mrs. Thomas could not understand why the father was so much less horrified at the prospect of having a descendant in slavery than he was of having a mulatto child bear his name. But it did happen, she knew, that owners sometimes had issue themselves by their slaves and sold their very own children away:

> I once heard Susan (Ma's nurse) speaking of her respected father in a most contemptuous manner. Laughingly I said to her, why Susan, was not he your Father? What if he was, she said, I don't care anything for him and he don't for me. If he had he would have bought me when I was sold. Instead of that he was the auctioneer when I was sold for 75 dollars. She was sold for debt, separated from her mother and has lived in the yard ever since she was three years old. What a moral. It speaks for itself and these "white children of slavery" as Miss Bremer calls them lower the tone of the South. They are not to blame—oh no! They know no incentive for doing well and often if they wished they could not. The happiness of homes are [sic] destroyed but what is to be done. There is an inborn earnestness in woman's nature to teach her to do right, but this is a mystery I find I can not solve. Southern women are I believe all at heart abolitionists but then I expect I have made a very broad ascertion [sic] but I *will stand* to the opinion that the institution of Slavery degrades the white man more than the Negro and oh exerts a most deleterious effect

upon our children. But this is the dark side of the picture, written with a Mrs. Stowe's feeling, but when I look upon so many young creatures growing up belonging to Pa's estate as well as others, I wonder upon whom shall the accountability of the future depend.[1]

If the mulatto population had a high potential for flowing into the personality forms offered by white molds, other Negroes in the South had the same potential in a degree only slightly diminished. In the cities significant numbers of free Negroes had both the freedom and the means to emulate closely ideal examples taken from the white community. Soon after the war, a Northern writer observed that some Charleston Negroes were "unusually intelligent" and "assumed the dress, manners, and speech of the whites to perfection."[2] Whites might take pride in and gain some sense of security from the emulation of the best class of free Negroes, but they were distinctly less happy with urban agglomerations of less affluent free Negroes, slaves who somehow hired out their time on their own and paid their masters fixed rentals for themselves, domestics and artisans who were not so thoroughly beaten down by hard labor as were slaves in the country, and slaves who had somehow fallen out of the system—runaways and physical and mental defectives whose labor was not profitable and who had been allowed to "disappear." In a pioneering study titled *Slavery in the Cities, 1820–1860,* Professor Richard E. Wade concludes that whites were very much frightened by the freedom possessed by urban blacks—especially the freedom to steal and to engage in the vices of drinking, gambling, and prostitution in the nightly retreats of the low life of the cities. It was precisely because blacks were becoming too white in their behavior that segregation began in the South, he contends.

On the farms of the South, where a family of slaves might live with a family of whites, the tutoring of blacks in the white way was close and fairly complete. It was a truism in South Carolina that up-country, farm-bred Negroes were more white-like than their low-country, plantation-bred brothers. A Northern correspondent in 1866 reported that "in the upper country, especially in the mountain districts, they rise in intelligence and in social condition, and approach more nearly to the whites with whom they are thrown into contact."[3]

Obviously, as the proportion of blacks to whites increased, the exposure of black people to white culture diminished. In 1860, in two entire states—South Carolina and Mississippi—blacks outnumbered whites, and in many of the black-belt areas ratios rose to ten to one and higher. In the coastal region of South Carolina, and particularly in the area of the Sea Islands, the ratio of black to white was very high, and the process of acculturation was probably

---

[1] Diary of Ella Gertrude (Clanton) Thomas, 2 January 1858, Duke University Library, Durham, N.C.

[2] *New York Times,* 20 May 1866, p. 1.

[3] *New York Times,* 9 November 1866, p. 1.

least advanced. One estimate has it that during the brief period between 1804 and 1808, the year federal legislation put an end to the importation of slaves from abroad, 40,000 additional blacks were brought into South Carolina. Probably a large number of the new arrivals were fed into the plantations south of Charleston which had turned to the marvelously profitable cultivation of Sea Island cotton. Even at the time of Emancipation there were several Negroes living on the Sea Islands who had come from Africa. Some bore tattoo markings on their faces, one remembered the crossing to Charleston, and another recalled worshiping in Africa. On Limerick, a rice plantation on the Cooper River, a slave named Nero drew beef rather than the usual pork as his weekly meat ration because, it was said in the plantation journal, he was a "Mohammedan."[4]

When one has said that the process of acculturating blacks proceeded relatively rapidly and relatively far, and when one has observed too that vestiges of the African heritage persisted, the problem remains of defining the life style of blacks in the ante-bellum South. It is not enough to describe Afro-American culture solely from the viewpoints of either white America or black Africa. Black culture, no doubt, was not perfectly knowable to a white American of the time, nor would it have been fully comprehensible to a visiting black African. The sad truth is that we know too little about the manner in which Africa, Europe, and America, and blackness, whiteness, and slavery combined in that time and place to make up total lives for individual blacks.

Still it is possible to construct a schema which describes the broad outlines of black existence in the ante-bellum South. In the least as well as the most concentrated areas of black population, there was a slave culture. And slave culture was part of a broader thing which might be called black culture, a style that embraced all Negroes, free as well as slave, Northern as well as Southern. Most of what constituted black culture was a survival response to the world the white man made; most blacks had to shape their lives largely within the round of possibilities generated by whites. Sometimes the movement toward a distinctive culture was negative, a protest against the denial of whiteness to blacks. For instance, blacks were rebellious in greater or lesser degrees, much as whites would have been rebellious in the same situation. Rebelliousness, manifested in numerous ways, became an integral part of black culture and gave it a quality which the dominant white culture did not have. Most often the movement was positive, an assertion of whiteness—as with the attempts of free blacks to acquire education in the white way. Another element in black culture sprang from the physical environment. Like the European, the Afro-American was an alien in the New World, and no doubt this new frontier—the soil he came to know so well, the plants, and the animals—affected him in ways which had little to do with being black.

---

[4] Plantation books of William J. Ball, vol. 3 (microfilm), Southern Historical Collection, University of North Carolina, Chapel Hill.

While black culture in America was not African in a large measure, a part of it was undeniably African, and probably much of it was African transmuted by the New World experience. The problem of defining the African origins of black culture in America is every bit as difficult as the problem of defining the European origins of white culture in America. Indeed, it is more difficult because African survivals were deflected by the special experience of slavery, which persisted in the mass into 1865, and because Afro-Americans are, simply, black, and black in the white world meant bad. There is a peculiar insensitivity in the argument that blacks have to "make it" in America just as other immigrant groups have done. The real historical problem of the African heritage of the black American is not whether that primal legacy survived slavery, nor even in what quantity it survived. It is, rather, how those multiple African cultures transplanted to the American environment worked to help shape the ever changing face of the whole society.

The problem of defining black culture is further complicated by the fact that as whites, in the last days of slavery, came to embrace blacks more closely than ever before in the cultural sense, they not only acted upon them but reacted to them. White people in the last generation of slavery probably had an intensified effect upon blacks, and inevitably blacks had an intensified effect upon whites. Southern whites of that time (and of this) were actually blacker than they were pleased to see. White people learned things from black people even as they thought themselves exclusively the teachers. Southern Methodism, for example, which was fundamentally different from Northern Methodism by 1860, may have gained its distinct character in a minor part because of the existence of slavery and in a major part because for three decades it had made a concerted effort to reach the black masses—and the black masses in turn had reached it. Certainly whites learned something from blacks in language and religion, in music and manners, and in cuisine and conjuring. But the process was much more intricate than a simple exchange. Whites taught blacks Christianity, for instance, but blacks lost something and added something— spirituality, perhaps—in the translation, which they then fed back to the whites, who also lost something and added something, and so on without end.

The result was that white culture became progressively blacker and black culture became progressively whiter. It was not so much a matter of white over black—though whites certainly would have seen it that way—as it was a matter of white *and* black. A parallel pattern was all too apparent in the physical world, where whites were becoming black and blacks were becoming white. In brief, the South was experiencing a growing confusion of cultures and colors.

From Resistance in Slavery to Assertion in Freedom

Historians have long puzzled over a supposed lack of rebelliousness among slaves in the South. If in fact blacks on the plantations were submissive and servile, and slaves in the cities, in the trades, and on the small farms did have a comparatively good life which defused their rebellious tendencies, there is no problem to ponder. But I believe that there was constant resistance by blacks, slave and free, against an establishment for racial inequality, and that only the ever ready vigilance and militancy of Southern whites kept that resistance from assuming the proportions of bloody, if limited, wars.

In colonial America insurrections did occur in which blacks and whites killed one another in appalling numbers. One Saturday night in 1739 in South Carolina about twenty rice-plantation slaves on the Stono River broke into a warehouse, armed themselves, and set out for St. Augustine, then in Spanish hands. There is every indication that the slaves knew the Spanish governor of Florida had offered freedom and land to those who reached that sanctuary. During Sunday morning, the rebels burned several houses and killed ten whites. With drums sounding a military beat and cries of "Liberty!" some sixty blacks then headed for Florida. All during the day they marched, some drunk with freedom, others drunk with rum liberated from plantation stores along the way. Finally, about four o'clock in the afternoon, hastily gathered, hard-riding militia managed to confront the rebels. The blacks fought desperately before being overrun by the more numerous and mounted militia. Altogether, a score of whites and twice as many blacks were killed. It was a recognition of the very real dangers of Spanish proximity and black rebelliousness which led British authorities to deny slaves to the new settlers in the buffer state of Georgia.

The history of Southern slavery is studded with white panics over slave insurrections, and beneath that seething surface there were more real threats than we can ever know or imagine. Much of this might have been the creature of white imaginations, but after August 1831, Southern whites could never be certain again that the fear was very far from the fact. In that summer, near the Dismal Swamp in southeastern Virginia, Nat Turner led a rebellion which took the lives of some fifty-seven whites and countless blacks and robbed both whites and blacks of whatever sense of security they may have managed to build.

Until the Civil War there was not another Nat Turner in the South, but rebellions there were aplenty. One cannot travel far into the letters and diaries of that time without encountering reports of the slave who killed the master or mistress or the overseer. Seldom was it a quick death or a clean one; most often it was by hacking with a knife, a hoe, or an ax, by firing the big house at night, or slowly by poison. Slaves did not always submit easily to physical punishment, and some turned in a reckless fury to punish the punishers and ended by killing them.

Offering violence to whites was only one way to rebel, and a highly danger-ous way. There were hundreds of lesser means of resistance. One might run away—often not to the North but to the woods or swamps nearby, and often precisely when one's labor was most needed. Malingering became a way of slave life, until the most thoughtful whites came to believe that it was an inherent Negro trait. George Washington, that very observant planter, reputedly timed his slaves at work and calculated their productivity at a fraction of that of white laborers. The three-fifths figure in the Constitution, providing that five slaves should be considered the equivalent of three free men in determining the states' representation in Congress and the levying of direct taxes, probably represented a carefully considered estimate of the wealth a black person could produce relative to what could be expected of a white person. In a society which valued property representation and in a land of vast resources where wealth was very much a function of population, that fraction was a highly important one. The persuasiveness with which black people played a role of lesser capacity for productivity is documented not only in the three-fifths provision of the Constitution, but also in what might be called the white practice of black medicine. Indeed, by the 1850's white medical myths had produced virtually a third branch of medicine somewhere between that of white people on one side and that of animals on the other.

Sabotage was another device of rebellion. A hoe stealthily broken against a stone in the field not only destroyed the master's property but frequently took a hand out of the field to replace the tool. Stones in the cotton bag might raise credit for the amount of fiber picked, and when dumped into the cotton gin they might produce damage equivalent to the market value of a small slaveling. Fire was the supreme weapon of the slaves, and the one most feared by whites. Ultimately, it was not possible to guard against the midnight arsonist, and the fire itself often destroyed all evidence against the criminal. Whites learned to index serious black restlessness by the burning of outhouses and barns. But the great white terror was the ease with which the manor house itself could be quietly and secretly fired in the night, becoming a funeral pyre for the master family thus caught in sleep. Probably it was no casual simile which the slaveholder and planter Thomas Jefferson made when he declared of the Missouri crisis in 1820: "But this momentous question, like a fire bell in the night, awakened me and filled me with terror. I considered it at once as the death knell of the Union."[5] With Southerners locked in life to slavery, Jefferson too easily evoked the awful image they all shared of red fire in a black night, the roar of the inferno, the searing heat, the cries of terror and despair, and death by burning. Poisoning, too, was a secret and potentially lethal tool of rebellion. And so on down the scale, to manifestations which were physically harmless but could be psychically devastating—a cook's committing an unmentionable in the master's soup, an averted face, a frown, a mumbled grumble, and sullen silence, all pregnant with meaning.

As the war came on, the rebelliousness of slaves sometimes broke into

---

[5] Thomas Jefferson to John Holmes, 22 April 1820, in Adrienne Koch and William Peden, eds., *The Life and Selected Writings of Thomas Jefferson* (New York: Random House, 1944), p. 13.

shocking visibility. Witness the story reported in the diary of a young Charleston woman under the date of July 16, 1861:

> Aunt C. B. dined with us and gave us an account of the illness of cousin Nora's infant, occasioned by the most diabolical wickedness of the nurse, an old negro woman owned by cousin N. who has minded all her children and one whom they have always considered a good and faithful servant. What was the cause of the act, we cannot imagine. The baby was born soon after the Battle of Fort Sumter, and while cousin James was away on duty; during the first fortnight, the nurse scarcely held it, the ladies of the village almost taking her place. It was a fine healthy child till it was three weeks old, when it went off suddenly into convulsions, without any apparent cause, and has been desperately ill ever since and suffering agony almost constantly, then again, lying for hours as if dead, then waking with agonizing screams. The physician said he could do nothing, he had never seen or heard of such a case. Everybody thought it was similar to that of Uncle John's Carrie and hoped that it would die, as was daily expected. Seven weeks of nursing and anxiety passed, when it was discovered that the child had been made to swallow *eleven large pins,* some of which were working their way out of the child's body at the side, while nature relieved it of the others. During this time the nurse was the only servant who had anything to do with the baby. . . . Suspicion was aroused. Cousin James sent his whole family to Mr. McFadden's and all his servants to jail to await their trials, except his house-servant, whom he left in charge of his house, and two guards placed there also. Cousin James himself is obliged to leave for Virginia tomorrow with his Regiment, but Mr. McFadden, Dr. Haynesworth and the other gentlemen of the neighborhood have taken the case in hand, and are determined to find out everything and if the child dies, the woman will be hung, as she probably will be anyway.[6]

Slave rebellions there were in the ante-bellum South, and they were frequent. But it would be imperceptive of us to fix an image in our minds of every black man burning out his life with hatred for all white people. Slavery was a various thing. Slaveholders were sometimes ruthlessly exploitative; sometimes they were warmly paternalistic; sometimes the same man was both. Slaves sometimes hated their masters and carried that hate over to all whites; slaves sometimes were fond of their masters and suspicious of other whites. The unhappy fact that often enough white planters lived long with certain female slaves and sired second families in the homes of the first suggests something more human and more intricate than a perfectly regular biracial system. While one might look cynically at such interracial liaisons and regard them all as still another form of exploitation, some white men manifested a deep and lasting concern for their mistresses and mulatto children.

For instance, in 1856 an extremely well-to-do Alabama planter died, freeing

---

[6] Diary of Emma E. Holmes, 16 July 1861 (microfilm), Southern Historical Collection, University of North Carolina, Chapel Hill.

by his will forty of his slaves and leaving them an estate valued at more than $200,000—including other slaves who were not freed. Two years previously, a relative of the deceased, probably his father, had left an estate of some $500,000 to his two mulatto children, a settlement other heirs contested successfully. Correspondence over the next two decades attests to the faithfulness of the executor in carrying out his friend's last will in regard to these forty people. He took great care to resettle the heirs on free soil in Zenia, Ohio, and Leavenworth, Kansas. Apparently, he sent some of the younger members of the group to Wilberforce University, a vigorously antislavery school in Ohio. Further, he managed the estate so well—in part by buying and selling slaves —that it grew in value. Almost certainly this peculiar phenomenon is explained by the fact that the master family and a plantation "clan" had become inextricably mixed. In this case, the wealth and the wills of the two slaveholders were unusual enough to leave clear traces of that happening. In fact, there is a rising tide of evidence to suggest that while some whites were hateful toward their mulatto children, others were considerate of them.

Just as some whites in slavery took good care of blacks, some blacks after Emancipation took good care of their late masters. During the hard months after the war, a Negro seeking relief for a white family from a Freedmen's Bureau officer explained: "I used to belong to one branch of that family, and so I takes an interest in 'em."[7] Just as there seemed to be no lines—economic, denominational, or educational—dividing whites who were sympathetic to blacks from those who were not, so too there seemed to be no lines dividing blacks who were sympathetic to whites from those who were not. Domestic slaves, for instance, were no more loyal to their late masters than field hands. Indeed, the faithful old family retainer was often literally that—too old (or too infirm or too young) to run away from his late owners. It appears that very often it was field laborers who cared, in the style of the Good Samaritan, for their late masters. "I called one morning and found him dead and the dogs in bed with him," one up-country South Carolinian reported in 1873 concerning a neighboring planter. "Strange to say there was no white person ever called to see him. The negroes were the only persons who gave him any attention at all."[8] But then, as one might imagine, black care for white people in distress was not a function of slave place but rather of simple humanity.

The records offer abundant opportunity for judging the nature of slavery by the experience of blacks as they spilled into freedom. Late slavery and Reconstruction was peculiarly an age of record keeping, note taking, and letter writing. It is evident that black people in slavery suffered a certain confusion of identity and an ambivalence in their feelings toward whites. The great mass

---

[7] De Forest, John William, *A Union Officer in the Reconstruction,* ed. James H. Croushore and David M. Potter (New Haven, Conn.: Yale University Press, 1948), p. 65.

[8] R. N. Hemphill to W. R. Hemphill, [summer] 1873, W. R., J. C., and R. R. Hemphill Papers, Duke University Library, Durham, N.C.

of blacks saw themselves in the image of white men, but the access of black people to whiteness was less than perfect. Often the white shore was but dimly seen, even though, as a black leader in Reconstruction South Carolina declared, it had been the Negro's "business all his life to find out the ways of the white man—to watch him, what he means."[9] To some extent, then, black people in the slave period seem to have identified in their ideals with white people, and that identification was a reflection of the exposure of blacks to white culture. Free mulattoes could and probably did see themselves as nearly white, culturally as well as biologically. But even though Negroes identified with white society, white people persistently rejected the Negro. And that rejection was itself confused. On the one side whites wanted blacks to be and to behave in the white image. On the other side they could not brook blacks appearing to be perfectly white—either biologically or culturally. The awful paradox of the last thirty years of slavery was that the black man was at the same time pulled into the white man's culture and kept stiffly at arm's length. If blacks were, indeed, less than full persons, the system should have worked beautifully. But if underneath his black skin and in his mind he was a man like any other, it was a system to breed frustration, ambivalence toward whiteness and himself, a measure of insanity, and, ultimately, violence. The result was that blacks, if we can believe the written words of contemporaries, valued whiteness at the same time that they hated everything—including slavery and the remnants of slavery—which kept them from whiteness.

Far from hating all whites, freedmen soon developed a high respect and often a love for one group of whites—the Northern teachers in the Reconstruction South. Northern teaching in the South was often more than pure academics and even more than religion, politics, and economics; it was a lesson in whiteness. As black people read Northerners in the South, Reconstruction was an invitation to whiteness. It said, "You too can be white like me." And it never seemed to think that black people could have any other goal. It is significant that during Reconstruction ambitious and intelligent young blacks emigrated from the North to the South, a flow of people which was to be reversed within two generations. The South was the land of promise, and particularly that part of the South which was most black. Ironically, in the land of greatest blackness, it was possible for the black man, ideally speaking, to find whiteness. In a curious way, in those last three decades when Southern slavery was most jealous in its control of the black man's psyche, it was giving blacks a head start in the primary school of whiteness. In Reconstruction, black men, it seems, wanted to see that the barriers were lowered and that full whiteness could be theirs. Thus late slavery and early Reconstruction operated in push-pull fashion to thrust black people into the white world and to deprive them of a separate black identity. In Reconstruction, confusion gave way to clarity, and ambivalence yielded for a time to assertion.

---

[9] *New York Times,* 9 August 1867, p. 2.

This is not to say that slavery left no mark of oppression, for indeed it did. In slavery some blacks were Samboized, and not all these were on the large plantations. Richard Gayle, for instance, was brought as a slave from Virginia to Barnwell County in South Carolina. There he worked at extra tasks for money and saved enough to buy his own freedom. By extraordinary industry and frugality he bought freedom for some members of his family only to see them die and bought it for others only shortly before they would have been emancipated anyway. By 1868 Gayle was making speeches for the Democrats, advising Negroes to join their true friends, the Southern whites. The whites were certain to win, he argued, because they had conquered the Indians and the forest, built great cities, and developed the telegraph, the railroad, and the steamboat. Indeed, Sambo did exist, but Sambos in Reconstruction were few and far between.

Viewed from the white man's perspective, slavery tended to decrease the black man's capacity for either virtue or vice. The slave who lived as the white man attempted to make him live could neither behave nor misbehave precisely as the white man did. For instance, the male slave could hardly be the perfect family man and father, but neither could he abuse his wife every day if he so chose, nor be a habitual drunkard. The oppression of slavery did mark its victims, and those marks, both good and bad, persisted in freedom. Northerners in the South during the war found blacks timid, evasive, suspicious, mendacious, malingering, and given to petty thievery. Well into Reconstruction, white observers thought that they saw a high degree of sexual promiscuity among Negroes. In 1867, a surprisingly well informed Northerner in the Sea Islands reported that hardly a girl on two nearby plantations attained the age of fifteen or sixteen without giving birth to a bastard and that eight women were then pregnant by men other than their husbands.

If slavery bred a culture in which such vices as stealing became a virtue, it also promoted traits which were generally thought to be virtues. Thomas Wentworth Higginson, the abolitionist colonel of the first black regiment raised in South Carolina, found his soldiers obedient, submissive, and easily organized. "I have heard of no man intoxicated, and there has been but one small quarrel," he wrote after a year of command. "I suppose that scarcely a white regiment in the army shows so little swearing."[10] In 1870 a British traveler observed that the Negro "continues, save on election nights or other periods of great excitement, to turn into bed at the early hour in the evenings prescribed to him by a sort of curfew law in the days of slavery."[11]

One of the most interesting fruits of freedom was the haste with which black people rushed to embrace both the virtues and the vices of the white

---

[10] Thomas Wentworth Higginson, *Army Life in a Black Regiment* (Boston: Lee and Shepard, 1890), p. 18.

[11] Robert Somers, *The Southern States since the War, 1870–1871* (New York: Macmillan, 1871), p. 39.

world. Just as slavery destroyed the African in the slave, the freedman hastened to destroy the slave in the Negro. He found that many of the traits nurtured in slavery were incompatible with his new status. "I ain't got colored-man principles," Corporal Landon Simmons of the First South Carolina Volunteers told his colonel, "i'se got white gemman principles."[12] As used by black people themselves, the term "nigger" scornfully indicated the ways of the blacks in slavery. A visitor in Charleston in the summer of 1874 overheard a Negro girl in the streets ridiculing the rendition of a tune by her male companion as "nigger like," and an aged Negro urging his mules along wisely declared that "niggers and mules is hard to drive."[13] By the end of Reconstruction a native observed that the best class of blacks in South Carolina emulated the best class of whites in their social behavior: "paying homage to the ladies, preventing the females from working, sending the children to school, living in fine houses, employing servants, supporting a good table, and keeping carriages and horses.[14]

Some blacks used their freedom to cultivate vices which, presumably, had been denied to them in slavery. Surely vicious practices were not alien to the slave, but the system had worked to eliminate them and without doubt had had some success. In freedom, vice, like virtue, flourished in a new style. Intoxication, profanity, and fighting were soon all too common in the lower orders of the black community. In 1875 an Episcopal priest spent an uncomfortable Saturday night in a room over a drinking establishment operated by one of his vestrymen in a small Southern village. "In the street in front of the grogshop are heard the voices of Negroes, boisterous laughter, wrangling, & awful profanity," the reverend gentleman lamented in his diary.[15] Slavery, certainly, would not have tolerated such an exhibition.

Land Redistribution as an Assertion of Racial Equality

The embracement of white cultural ideals and the rejection of even the appearance of servility was everywhere apparent in the behavior of black people in Reconstruction. It was evident in politics and in the struggle for civic and religious equality. But it was most striking, perhaps, in a nexus of relations which might be called economic and familial.

One of the often noted grand truths of Reconstruction is that the plantation system, which had so marked the South in the prewar years, almost ceased to

---

[12] Higginson, *Army Life,* p. 260.

[13] Iza D. Hardy, *Between Two Oceans; or Sketches of American Travel* (London: Chapman and Hall, 1884), p. 300.

[14] A South Carolinian [Belton O'Neall Townsend], "South Carolina Society," *The Atlantic Monthly* 39 (June 1877): 676.

[15] Diary of John Hamilton Cornish, 13 November 1875, Southern Historical Collection, University of North Carolina, Chapel Hill.

exist. That occurrence was not nearly so much an economic affair as it was a social and racial one. More precisely it was in accord, not with the economic intelligence of the landowners, but rather with the assertiveness of black people. It was the freedmen, not the owners, who caused the great plantations to be fragmented, and they did so in the pursuit of an agrarian ideal learned from the whites.

The very fact that all the plantations of the South did not cease to be worked as plantations after 1865 is evidence of the compatibility of the plantation system and free labor. Indeed, there were obvious physical and economic forces which pressed for the maintenance of the plantation system. In some crops, large-scale production was not a choice but a necessity. Rice cultivation, for instance, required a system of dikes, ditches, and gates for flooding and draining the fields, which could be worked only by a "gang" of about thirty hands or more. At the time of the Civil War efficient sugar production seemed to demand about one hundred workers cultivating an area of about seven hundred acres on plantations of about two thousand acres. Cotton and tobacco could be and were raised in units which ranged down to the one-man farm, but even in these great "democratic crops" a rather solid tradition ordained that plantations be of a minimal size and that they be worked by a minimal labor force. There were other factors which argued for a continuation of the plantation system: buying supplies and selling the product were most efficiently done in large-scale operations, much as in agriculture today. The sugar mill, the steam-powered gin and rice thresher, and horse-driven planting machines and reapers were well known in the South before the war. Cyrus McCormick, after all, invented the reaper in the 1830's while living not on the western plains but in his home county of Rockbridge, Virginia.

There was nothing in free labor per se which compelled planters to divide their lands into small farms and rent them out. Free labor could have worked the plantations as units as well as slave labor and did so often enough to show that it could be done. Early in Reconstruction many plantations continued to operate under systems in which the planter contracted with the whole labor force as a body, usually allowing the group a third of the product, which they then divided among themselves in predetermined ratios. What had changed, of course, was that four million blacks had been freed. These people now had a choice, and enough of them opted to break the plantation system to make it a general fact. There were many reasons they did so. One important reason was that they identified that system with the degradation of slavery, and another reason was that they identified the alternative—the family farm—with freedom.

One of the first manifestations of a free spirit among blacks was the desire of each to live on his own farm with his own family. Far from persisting docilely in the economic patterns they had known as slaves, blacks showed themselves eager to desert the plantation and its task and gang system of labor. For instance, probably more than half of the 550 great rice plantations ceased to function after Emancipation because black workers refused to continue in the way of their slave lives and simply deserted the land. Rice workers were perfectly well aware that the arduous, back-breaking labor, often in fields under water, was a deadly tax upon their health and longevity.

Withdrawal from the cotton plantations, of which there were some 74,000 on the eve of the war, followed a different form. Whereas much rice land was surrendered to nature, cotton land continued to be worked. Plantations generally were divided into small plots which were rented to individuals, and the new tenants used or abused them much as they chose. In the cotton areas the breakup of the plantation was itself an early form of segregation. In slavery the black worker lived in a slave village under the eyes of his ever present white masters. In freedom he left the village and separated himself from the white man by settling with his family on some rented plot. Sometimes the desire of the black man to remove himself from the associations of slavery and from the proximity of whites was dramatically displayed as the slave cabin was hitched to a team of animals and literally dragged away from the slave village and the master's house to some rented plot on the old plantation.

Ironically, while blacks evinced a stong desire to get away from their former owners, they also showed a desire to remain on or near their home plantation. I have the distinct impression that even as most freedmen left the slave villages, they spent their lives on farms carved out of plantations within a few miles of the place of their previous servitude. Probably most white landowners looked upon the breakup of the plantations with misgivings. They were afraid that black farmers would misuse their soil, and they would have preferred to continue to supervise the labor of the blacks as closely as they had in slavery. In this special sense, whites were the advocates of integration and continued close contact; but black people would not have it so.

During the early years of Reconstruction, black farmers favored the device of renting. Even working for cash wages by the task or by the day was considered less desirable than the renting of a farm for a year. David Golightly Harris, a cotton and cereal planter before the war, visited a neighboring village on January 4, 1866, and reported that the "negroes all seem disposed to rent land, and but few are willing to hire by the day, month or year."[16] Planters were often appalled by the passion for renting among blacks. "I am about renting some land on the aint [Aunt?] Juriy Hemphill place to Bek, Smith Sam & Peggy," a large cotton planter wrote to his brother. "They have hardly corn for Bread and will make nothing but are rent Crazy and must be gratified."[17]

Generally without capital, black farmers relied upon an infinite variety of complex systems to pay their rents. The basic arrangement was to promise

[16] Farm journal of David Golightly Harris, 4 January 1866 (microfilm), Southern Historical Collection, University of North Carolina, Chapel Hill.

[17] R. N. Hemphill to W. R. Hemphill, 15–16 November 1869, W. R., J. C., and R. R. Hemphill Papers, Duke University Library, Durham, N.C.

a share, usually one-third, of the prospective crop for the use of the land. Typically, the landowner provided all the necessary supplies—farm tools, seed, work animals and their feed—for another third of the produce. Acting as supplier apparently made it necessary for many planters to assume the banking and commercial functions which the "factors" in the towns and cities had performed for them before the war. The country store, which proliferated only after the war, was in most respects the plantation commissary transmuted into the postwar pattern of small farms. In the late 1860's another novel element was added to the Southern agricultural scene—the use of processed fertilizers in massive quantities. Financing the purchase of fertilizer added to the intricacy of the farm credit system, but the most significant result of its introduction was a vastly increased production. The lavish use of fertilizer and its remarkable effects render it almost impossible to judge whether blacks were more productive as farmers than they had been as slaves. One is tempted to guess that they worked less and produced more, probably due to the use of fertilizer. At all events, it is very clear that black people lived better on their farms than they had as slaves; they simply consumed more. Whereas plantation records attest to the simplicity of the food and clothing of the slave, country store records indicate that black farmers claimed a goodly share of the fruits of the American economy—from candies and canned peaches to tin cups and pearl stickpins.

Blacks in freedom also bought farms. Probably a much larger number of freedmen acquired their own farms in Reconstruction than has previously been supposed. The progressive reforms of Reconstruction state governments, such as the establishment of public school systems, required funds that were derived primarily from taxes upon real estate. Landowners faced the necessity of either making the lands productive or else paying the tax from other resources. The effect of the legislation was thus to depress land prices. Republicans in power in South Carolina made no secret of their design to use taxation to achieve land redistribution. Further, they actually set up a state commission to buy lands forced onto the market cheaply and then resell them on easy terms to settlers in family-sized plots—often about forty acres. By the census of 1890, the first to seek statistics on such matters, approximately 20 percent of the black farmers in South Carolina owned their own farms. In 1900 roughly 59 percent in Virginia and 48 percent in Kentucky did so. In South Carolina the proportion of black landowners remained quite stable through 1900 and 1910, suggesting that black farmers acquired their lands early and held them rather securely.

Why did the freedmen act to break up plantations in favor of small farms when the great majority of white landowners objected that it was uneconomic? The answer is, I think, that the blacks saw themselves striving to live the agrarian ideal the whites had so long and so eloquently espoused. Black people shared with their white neighbors a conviction that the good life, the only proper life, grew naturally from having your own farm and upon that farm your own family. Both blacks and whites assumed that industry and frugality opened the door to personal progress and security. Indeed, for many it was so. Blacks and whites further shared that classical ideal—one is tempted to say that Jeffersonian ideal—that somehow living close to the earth is living right, that morality, righteousness, and wisdom as surely spring from the soil as do the green plants which give us life.

In the last several years, historians have often argued that land redistribution was the vital omission which caused the failure of the first Reconstruction. The willingness to settle for such a facile explanation might be a measure of the bankruptcy felt by recent historians after a hundred years of writing have failed to explain why the attempt to remake the Southern world faltered so disastrously. The argument ignores the fact that land *was* redistributed in Reconstruction in a significant measure. Renting, after all, was a form of land redistribution, and in that day, as in this, renting was not necessarily less economical than buying. However, given the racial climate in which the black farmer had to work, it is easy to understand how owning his own farm might increase his sense of security and independence. It was another increment to black power, just as having served in the Union army, or owning a gun, or sitting in the witness box or on a jury, or voting, or holding office all combined to enable black people to maintain their freedom and to stretch out toward civil equality. Still, there was no magic in land ownership. It could not have guaranteed the civil integrity of the black man in Reconstruction any more than land ownership guaranteed the civil integrity of Populist farmers in the 1890's. Furthermore, and perhaps more relevantly, a perfectly equal share in the economy for blacks in Reconstruction would not have guarded them against prejudice and discrimination any more than affluence among blacks in our society does so today. The running sore of race in the South is not and probably never has been a matter of economic class. Would that it were so simple.

It may be that recent historians of the first Reconstruction, embarrassed by the distressing sight of the broken wreckage, physical and mental, of the dying second Reconstruction, and by a sense of responsibility for the failure to fulfill expectations which they themselves helped to raise, have transferred their frustrations to that first great movement to remake the South in a new image. It is easier after all to solve difficult problems in the sweetly reasonable realm of written history that it is to bridge the bottomless chasm between what is and what ought to be in the endlessly complicated and changing lives of living people. Fleeing from our own seemingly insolvable problems, a generation or two of historians who would like to believe in the Jeffersonian ideals—as many of us would—have fallen into a rather simple evocation of the formulas of the agrarian dream. The fact that we turn from such an infinitely complex social and psychological problem to such a simple economic solution attests again to our proclivity to fence in our lives with the horizons that traditional thinking has built into our minds.

The Black Family as an Assertion of Whiteness

In the first Reconstruction, then, black men insisted upon having farms, and they were hardly less insistent upon having families. In reality, if black families had not existed in slavery, it is possible that the farm would have created them. On the farm there were a variety of tasks ranging from simple to difficult, tasks requiring many small hands (such as picking out the cotton) and tasks requiring muscular strength and stamina such as only grown men could provide. On the home farms of the South there was a place and, indeed, a need for the man, the woman, and the children, little and large. The fragmented family, today a phenomenon both of white affluence and of black urban poverty, was a luxury the black yeomen in Reconstruction could ill afford. A black matriarchy probably did exist in cities, towns, and even villages; it was probably especially widespread in the family arrangements of females who served as domestics in white households. But black life was overwhelmingly rural, and there matriarchy did not prevail. Far from it: the indications are that black families in Reconstruction were father-led rather than mother-led. We have erred in modern times, it seems, in applying twentieth-century urban observations and a popular assumption about the nature of black family life in slavery to what happened in between.

The indications are strong and increasing that even in slavery black families had more substance than has previously been assumed, and one can presume that the family order presented by the freedmen was very much a continuation and refinement of arrangements begun in slavery. Before the surge of the plantation system into trans-Appalachia and into the Southwest early in the nineteenth century, slave populations on plantations in the East were probably fairly static. Afterwards, of course, there must have been large-scale population dislocations in which men, women, and children were sold away from their families into the South and West. Broken families were doubtless a result of slavery, but the question remains as to how numerous they were.

A measure of the degree to which the black family was fractured in the slave period can be found in the frequency with which the freedmen searched out fathers, mothers, sisters, and brothers from whom they had been separated, sometimes by half a continent and thirty years of bondage. The fervor of those searches attests to the strength of family ties in slavery. Whites often observed the phenomenon with contempt or amusement, considering it a simple affectation by Negroes, an empty-minded aping of white concerns. Blacks who had labored along a thousand miles to rejoin their families might have thought differently.

In freedom individual blacks seem to have learned their family roles from whites, Southern and Northern, and they played them well. In Reconstruction, Negro males, like white males, asserted themselves by insisting that wives spend more time in home management and less in field work, by demanding that mothers care for their children, and by exhibiting such common masculine exclusiveness as leaving the wives at home while they themselves attended fraternal and political gatherings. In legal and economic matters, black men assumed the power to speak for their wives and children. For instance, in January 1866 on one Carolina cotton plantation, Ned affixed the mark of his wife, Victoria, to a contract with the landowner, and their son, Zack, made his mark "with Ned's consent."[18] On the same contract, another laborer named Frank Tom made his own mark and those of Giles and Neil, his wife and his son.

White observers disagreed about the attitudes and behavior of black parents toward their children. Some suggested that Negroes felt no affection, others that they beat their children sadistically. But black parents were much like white parents and operated on the same parental premises. Cynthia, for example, had been a maid in slavery and after the war lived with her husband, her daughter Harriet, and her son Billy. When her late mistress suggested that Cynthia was not able to make Billy obey, Cynthia answered: "*Yes ma'am I can. I makes Harriet hold him and turn up his frock and if I don't make these old bones (holding out her hand) work on him, he'll tell you.*" Cynthia paused a moment and added, "For you know Miss Grace, de Bibble says, use the switch and don't spile de chile."[19]

If one asks where lay the primary loyalty of the slave and the freedman, the answer is with the family. And when one seeks the next level of loyalty, it seems to rest in the plantation clan. Scattered evidence suggests that plantations of any size supported several clans composed of several slave families and that the clans on any plantation might be related in some degree by blood ties. A Northern teacher on the Sea Islands during the war noted a strong affinity among the Negro refugees for "massa's niggers," meaning those from their home plantations. Refugees even tended to settle by "plantations"; that is, those from a given plantation gravitated together in the camps on the islands. The same clannishness continued in Reconstruction. About one-fourth of a tract of state land in Abbeville County, South Carolina, was settled by seven families of Williamses and six families of Moragues. On the Alexander Hamilton Boykin plantation in Kershaw County in 1875 (one of the few cotton operations which continued to function as a plantation throughout Reconstruction), five of the eleven laborers were Boldens belonging to two or three separate households.

A highly significant indicator of the self-image of the black man was his choice of names. It is a rare occasion when each member of a nation of adults has an opportunity to choose a name appropriate to his sense of identity. In

---

[18] Contract, 1 January 1866, Allan MacFarland Papers, Duke University Library, Durham, N.C.

[19] Diary of Grace B. Elmore, 30 November 1866, Southern Historical Collection, University of North Carolina, Chapel Hill.

slavery, of course, the great mass of black people had only one name, and that name was assigned by the master family. Those names suggested more about whites than blacks, and they ranged from the simplified British, such as Jim, through the biblical, such as Martha, to the classical, such as Caesar, Scipio, and Bacchus. On large plantations where two slaves of the same name might live, greater differentiation might be required, and often physically descriptive adjectives were added. Thus on one rice plantation a woman was known as "yellow Martha," no doubt signaling the fact that she was a mulatto. Distinctions were also made by identifying family connections among slaves. Thus on a plantation where there were two Sarahs, Jim's wife might come to be known as Jim's Sarah. Children of the same name were commonly distinguished by reference to a parent. Thus daughter Jane might become Liza's Jane. Perhaps over the years, and particularly after Liza died, slurred pronunciation might yield a Liza Jane. Also often a child was given the name of the parent with the prefix "Little" added. Liza Jane's first daughter might thus be called Little Liza Jane. Interestingly enough for the matriarchy thesis, fathers and sons often went through the same process. Thus there might be a Big John and a Little John and a John's Henry who might later become simply John Henry. Southern whites have a well-known proclivity for double names, and that practice might very well have arisen in unthinking emulation of the black family in slavery.

Much might be learned from a study of the names black people took for themselves in freedom—and the names which they ceased to use. Very generally name-selecting suggests the images of self to which black people aspired.

The basic pattern is evident in first names. In slavery there had been a fair number of Caesars and—from the African—Cuffees. These were cast off in favor of the common British names. Biblical names continued to be popular. Diminutives escalated to their proper forms. Thus Jim became James and Eddy became Edgar. On one plantation, a strong and leading worker who had been known as Captain's Margaret during slavery because she was married to Captain came in freedom to be called Captain Margaret, which was precisely what she was—a captain of industry in the fields. Quite a number of freedmen took as first names honorific titles such as King, Prince, and Duke; General, Colonel, Major, and Captain; and occasionally Senator, Governor, and Judge.

More about the black man's sense of self-identity is revealed in his choice of family names. The names of great cities were often selected—thus London, Paris, or Boston—as were the names of great leaders—thus Washington, Lincoln, or Grant. Randolphs, Lees, Middletons, Davises, and Hamptons abounded. To some extent acceptance of the names of the great slaveholding families was probably a matter of real affection for master families and a desire for association with the higher aspects of Southern culture. In some degree taking the master's name might have been a simple convenience, a quickly and widely recognized identity. But at another level it was an acknowledgment of kinship with the plantation clan—its members were all interrelated, and the simplest way to symbolize that kinship was for "massa's niggers" to take massa's name. Incidentally interesting is the fact that the names of some large slaveholding families were conspicuous in that they were so seldom selected—as with, say, Calhoun and Aiken. Finally, sometimes freedmen took their family names from neighboring slaveholders rather than from their late masters.

Often family names changed in the early years of freedom as if to dignify their bearers. During the war, a slave pilot who stole his own ship in Charleston and steamed out into Union waters under the guns of Confederate-held Fort Sumter was known as Robert (sometimes Bob) Small. His last name probably began as a description of his height. However, as he rose rapidly in Reconstruction politics to become a Congressman, he somehow became known as Robert Smalls, and the name lost meaning as a descriptive adjective. Some freedmen took surnames that signified their professions—as with Sam Tailor—and those names sometimes came to have new spellings—as Sam Taylor. Other blacks took surnames that signified locations—as Washington Sumptor, who used an antique spelling of Sumter, the name of the town in which he lived. Colorful last names were as popular among blacks as among whites. Greens, Browns, and Whites were plentiful. But among the tens of thousands of Negroes in the Reconstruction South whose names I have seen, I have encountered only one whose last name was Black. Even he was often called "Jimmy of the Battery" as well as "Jimmy Black," and, further, it is not certain that he accepted the latter name as it was given to him. A Northern teacher asked her small scholars why his "title" was Black. "Oh, him look so," they chirped. "Him one very black man."[20]

In sum, in their familial relations and in their choice of names, black people in Reconstruction exhibited a ready facility in assuming white identities already largely formed in their minds. The rapidity and the seeming ease with which they made the transitions suggest that the black mind had grasped the essence of those images in slavery and, within the limits of slavery, had already realized them. While the first impetus of freedom was upon them and Northerners were present in large numbers to urge them on, they rushed quickly to make the real the twin of the ideal.

The Drive for Civil Rights

"For a time during Reconstruction, a Negro elite of sorts did emerge in the South," Professor Stanley M. Elkins writes in his brilliantly provocative book *Slavery: A Problem in American Institutional and Intellectual Life.* That early leadership, he suggests, sprang from house servants, urban mechanics, slaves hired out under their own management, free Negroes, and from Northern-

---

[20] Elizabeth Hyde Botume, *First Days Among the Contrabands* (Boston: Lee and Shepard, 1893), p. 49.

bred blacks who came south. Professor Elkins' suggestions seem accurate enough, and indeed, Professor Carter G. Woodson, the famous Negro historian, maintained several decades ago that a serious "brain drain" of blacks from the North to the South had occurred during the war and afterward. The result was that Northern black communities suffered a peculiar laggardliness and that in the North it was only after Reconstruction that significant progress was made by blacks in securing full participation in civil life. But all this only supports the claim that black leaders after the war were largely drawn from the ranks of those who had been black leaders before the war. It is probably true that few political leaders in Reconstruction came out of the fields and into the legislative halls, and the fact that they did not do so only suggests a slave system in which natural talents were valued and utilized, if, indeed, not exploited. Further, to look exclusively at the political leadership among blacks in Reconstruction for evidence of assertiveness is to focus too narrowly. Hundreds of thousands of black people emerged from plantation gangs to become small landowners and tenant farmers. Millions came out of slavery to become highly conscious actors in father and mother roles. In the very first months after Emancipation virtually all blacks came out of the white churches to become ministers and leading laymen as well as full members in black congregations. They did not leave their old churches because of significant theological or ritualistic or organizational differences (which did not exist), nor from economic or sociological distinctions (which did exist). They left, as they often said, because the whites would only have them as subordinate members. Freedmen were assertive, too, of their right to vote, and this even before their voting was allowed. Black people, South and North, and very much through the "Colored men's conventions," had something to do with the passage of the first Reconstruction Act, which, in essence, gave Southern blacks the vote and opened wide the door of political possibilities. In the elections which followed, the evidence suggests that blacks persistently asserted themselves at the polls, often against the most violent manifestations of white exclusiveness.

While black voters in the Reconstruction South avoided the Democracy, Republican stalwarts regarded them as distressingly unpredictable. A Northerner attending a Republican caucus in one heavily black township in 1869 saw the pre-arranged slate of town officers turned down in a sudden show of independence and observed that the Negroes "nominated their men without regard to party dictation."[21] Far from suffering political dictation by whites, black voters suffered from the divisions engendered by their own independence. When state Republican parties in the South splintered, as they often did, black voters could be found on all sides. In pursuing the Negro vote, Democrats often dropped their traditional name and fused with Republican splinters under all sorts of labels because, as one fusionist declared, "We

---

[21] *New York Times,* 14 June 1869, p. 5.

can't get it under the name of Democracy, for the nigger has been taught to hate that as he does cold."[22] Fusionists invariably found the blacks as a group too politically astute to be fooled and too individualistic to be led. "I have been very busy for the past two months," lamented one unhappy Democrat-as-fusionist campaigning for re-election as a county clerk of court in 1870, "not only in my office, but electioneering among the infernal negroes, and after all my trouble, and all the humiliation which I have to undergo, and the concessions made I am defeated by over thirteen Hundred Majority." The disappointed candidate, a member of a family that had held many slaves before Emancipation, had taken pains to pay his "respects to the 'colored friends'" on what had been a family plantation "and got the promise of several votes, but I understand that they all marched to the Polls by sunrise and voted the full Radical ticket."[23]

Admittedly, in 1867 and 1868 there was some reluctance among blacks to seek high offices. In the summer of 1867 one national black leader, Martin R. Delany, who was himself never totally engaged in politics, urged his people to "be satisfied to take things like other men in their natural course and time, preparing themselves in every particular for municipal position, and they may expect to attain to some others in time."[24] That quality of restraint soon passed, and where black people had the votes there was a tendency among black leaders, just as among their white contemporaries, to grab the highest offices they could get. Particularly after the ratification in February 1870 of the Fifteenth Amendment, which provided that the right of every United States citizen to vote "shall not be denied or abridged by the United States or by any State on account of race, color, or previous condition of servitude," there was a vigorous push among Negro leaders for equality in all public places, including the highest offices. By August a leading national magazine concluded that "negro senators and representatives may be looked for regularly, and that the colored man has definitely decided that he will no longer 'take a back seat!'"[25] In the short span of the Reconstruction period, blacks did indeed gain significant public offices: two senatorships, more than a dozen seats in Congress, one acting governorship, one lieutenant governorship, a scattering of judgeships, and several hundred seats in state legislatures. In South Carolina in 1872 Negroes held 106 of the 156 seats in the legislature, four of the five congressional seats, and four of the eight statewide elective offices. In 1874 a Northern reporter related that the blacks of South Carolina were "already talking of assuming, themselves, the management of the political machinery

---

[22] A. P. Aldrich to A. L. Burt, [late spring or early summer?] 1871, Armisted L. Burt Papers, Duke University Library, Durham, N.C.

[23] David Hemphill to R. R. Hemphill, 27 October 1870, W. R., J. C., and R. R. Hemphill Papers, Duke University Library, Durham, N.C.

[24] *New York Times,* 21 August 1867, p. 4.

[25] *The Nation* 11 (11 August 1870): 82.

of the State."[26] The reason why black supremacy did not become the rule in South Carolina in the 1870's was that the whites, who were a minority, still had a majority of raw physical power, and shortly after they used that power to recapture control of the state.

The assertiveness one finds in politics, in church organizations, in economics, and in family relationships was evident everywhere among blacks in Reconstruction. In a thousand and one ways black people showed their intention of living as white people did. This was evident in their dress, in their manners, in their behavior upon the streets, in their development of associations among themselves, and in their attempts to educate their children. It was also manifested in their drive to secure full access to public accommodations. Segregation in the horse-drawn streetcars in Charleston, for instance, so irritated the black community that in 1867, soon after the passage of the first Reconstruction Act, a sit-in and a near riot, much in the mood of a century later, brought the intervention of the military and the opening up of the cars without regard to color. In the spring of 1870, apparently as a direct manifestation of the ratification of the Fifteenth Amendment in February, there was a wave of integrationist activity among blacks in the South, some of which was successful, some not. But black people generally, and black Congressmen specifically, helped pass the Civil Rights Act of 1875, which spelled out the right of equal access by blacks to all public facilities with one great exception: proposed and rejected was a provision for the opening of all public schools to all children of all colors. Without denigrating the contributions of Northern white liberals, it can be safely said that when black people in America have made progress toward a recognition of their equal humanity, it has usually been more because black people asserted themselves than because white people acted in their behalf. Black leadership, not white leadership, was the vital ingredient in the progress of the race in Reconstruction.

What one believes about the "Sambo thesis" in slavery and Reconstruction depends much upon one's view of the depth of human personality. If one believes that people's natures are relatively deeply rooted, that personality is fixed early in life (and perhaps even before birth), then it is strongly suggested by Reconstruction that black people who seemed servile in slavery were dissembling. They were playing a rather serious game in which a winner was a survivor, particularly in the super-psyched, terrified years after Denmark Vesey and Nat Turner. Sambo, then, to borrow an idea from James Baldwin, was more the creature of the white mind, and his existence told infinitely more about white people than it did about blacks. If, on the other side, one thinks that human personality and behavior are rather surface things, moving as the psychological flux of the situation changes, then it is possible that when blacks played Sambos they actually were Sambos and when they played freedmen they actually were free. It is possible to imagine that when the

---

[26] *New York Times,* 21 June 1874, p. 1.

"significant other," the person with power to reward or punish in an impressive way, was a master or an overseer, the black man was Sambo, and that in the slave cabin at night or in the clandestine religious meetings in the woods he was something quite different, and that in freedom, when he had been exposed to Northern teachers, he quickly and easily became still something else.

My own conclusion is that the great mass of blacks in slavery were rebellious in greater or lesser degrees; that the Sambo the whites saw was a mask created either by themselves or by blacks or, most probably, by both; and that, as a whole people, blacks found it relatively easy to move from rebelliousness and dissembling in slavery to assertiveness in Reconstruction.

Toward a Social Interpretation
of the Development
# of American Racism

GEORGE M. FREDRICKSON

George M. Fredrickson, associate professor of history at North-western University, is the author of *The Inner Civil War: Northern Intellectuals and the Crisis of the Union* (Harper, 1965) and the editor of the John Harvard Library edition of Hinton Rowan Helper's *Impending Crisis of the South: How to Meet It* (Belknap Press, Harvard University Press, 1968). He has recently completed a study of white thought on Afro-American character and destiny, to be published by Harper & Row in 1971. In the following essay, Mr. Fredrickson distinguishes between societal racism and its more explicit counterpart, ideological racism, and traces the historical development of both in America. According to Mr. Fredrickson, conscious and unconscious psychological factors have certainly contributed to the rise of racism in the United States, but the key role in this phenomenon can be attributed to purely social factors.

Before discussing the historical development of American racism, we must define the term, which has become a source of considerable confusion. In its limited, precise, and original sense, racism is "the doctrine that a man's behavior is determined by stable inherited characters deriving from separate racial stocks and usually considered to stand to one another in relations of superiority and inferiority."[1] Racism, according to this definition, is a matter of conscious belief and ideology and can be distinguished from prejudice, which is a matter of attitude or feeling, and discrimination, which is a description of behavior. In recent popular discussion, however, racism has tended to lose this original meaning and to become synonymous with patterns of action that serve to create or preserve unequal relationships between racial groups. This, for example, is the sense in which the expression "white racism" is now commonly used. One way to bridge the gap between the academic and the popular meanings of the term "racism" is to distinguish between the explicit and rationalized racism that can be discerned in nine-teenth- and early twentieth-century thought and ideology and the implicit or

---

[1] Michael Banton, *Race Relations* (London: Tavistock, 1967), p. 8.

societal racism that can be *inferred* from actual social relationships. If one racial group acts as if another were inherently inferior, this is racism in the second sense, despite the fact that such a group may not have developed or preserved a conscious and consistent rationale for its behavior. As will be plain from the historical survey to follow, implicit racism can exist without explicit racism; indeed, events in the twentieth century suggest that societal racism can continue to thrive long after ideological racism has been discredited in the educated circles of a dominant group. Nevertheless, explicit or ideological racism is of some historical importance and merits attention. By giving legitimacy to pre-existing patterns of racial subordination, it strengthens a system and enables it to counter serious ideological challenges, such as those which emanated from the democratic revolutions of the eighteenth century and from the rise of bourgeois democracy.

This dual definition of racism is broad, but not so broad as to make it impossible to distinguish between genuinely racist societies and other inegalitarian societies where there may be manifestations of racial prejudice and discrimination but which nevertheless cannot be described as racist in their basic character. Most members of one racial group in a certain kind of biracial or multiracial society may be in a de facto subordinate situation, even in slavery, and unfavorable stereotypes about this group may be part of the mythology of the dominant race. Yet such a society is not racist in the full sense of the word if the resulting status differences can readily be justified on nonracial grounds—as part of a generalized belief in social hierarchy, for example—and if the discrimination for reasons of color is not consistently and universally applied to individual members of what is, in a statistical sense, the socially inferior group. If some members of this group can, despite their physical characteristics, achieve high status because of such attributes as wealth, education, and aristocratic culture, there is evidence of the overriding importance of nonracial status criteria. In such a situation, race becomes only one factor in determining status, an attribute which can be outweighed or neutralized by other factors. Students of comparative race relations will readily recognize that the pattern just described is what many observers have found to be characteristic of the biracial or multiracial societies of Latin America. The Brazilian phrase "money whitens" sums up the values of a society for which race is far from irrelevant as a basis of social classification but which nevertheless does not draw a rigid color line or sanction behavior that could be justified *only* on the grounds that blacks or mulattoes are innately inferior to whites.

Unlike Brazil and other Latin American countries, the United States has been a genuinely racist society. On the whole it has treated blacks as if they were inherently inferior, and for at least a century of our history this pattern of rigid racial stratification was buttressed and strengthened by a widely accepted racist ideology. Although few would deny that explicit or ideological racism—the formal doctrine of inherent biological inferiority—became popular at a relatively late date in American history, there has been a tendency among recent historians to see implicit or societal racism as having sprung up very early, partly because of certain pre-existing European attitudes toward blacks which gave a special character to the natural antipathy of English settlers toward any people who were obviously strange and different. In this essay, I will examine this proposition critically with an eye to shedding some light on the following question: To what extent was America really born racist as a result of pre-existing attitudes and to what extent did it become so as a result of social, economic, and political developments which took place well after the colonists' initial contacts with Africans?

Attitudes Toward Blacks Before Colonization

It is clear that among Englishmen there was indeed a vague prejudice against blacks even before the first colonists set foot in North America. As a result of early contacts with Africa, Englishmen tended to associate blackness with savagery, heathenism, and general failure to conform to European standards of civilization and propriety. Contributing to this predisposition to look upon Negroes with disfavor were the conscious and unconscious connotations of the color black. The association of black with evil was of course deeply rooted in Western and Christian mythology; it was natural to think of Satan as the Prince of Darkness and of witchcraft as black magic. On the unconscious level, twentieth-century psychoanalysts have suggested, blackness or darkness can be associated with suppressed libidinous impulses. Carl Gustav Jung has even argued that the Negro became for European whites a symbol of the unconscious itself—of what he calls "the shadow"—the whole suppressed or rejected side of the human psyche. The rudiments of such a complex may have manifested themselves in Elizabethan England. A tendency to project upon blacks the kind of libidinous sexuality that whites tried to suppress in themselves would certainly have been helped along by a hazy and inaccurate knowledge of African sexual practices and by a smirking consideration of what was implied by the fact that Africans went around completely or virtually naked. In Shakespeare's *Othello,* Iago pursues his vicious campaign against the Moor by skillfully playing on associations of blackness with bestial sexuality, as well as on a sense of the unnaturalness of interracial union. He tells Desdemona's father, for example, that "an old black ram / Is tupping your white ewe" and that his daughter is "covered with a Barbary horse."

There is no question, then, that there was a predisposition among sixteenth- and seventeenth-century Englishmen to accept an unfavorable stereotype of the black character. But how significant is this as an explanation of the development of societal racism in the colonies? Recent sociological investigations suggest that there is no simple cause-and-effect relationship between stereotyped opinions about a given group and discriminatory actions or policies. It is quite possible for an individual to have a generalized notion about members of another race or nationality that bears almost no relation to how he actually behaves when confronted with them.[2] To provide a contemporary example, many Americans who lived through World War II developed an extremely unfavorable set of stereotyped opinions about Germans and Japanese, which, as long as the war lasted, were salient and action-oriented. These stereotypes did not dissipate immediately at the end of the war, but they almost immediately ceased to be a reliable index of behavior. Individual Germans and Japanese could now be encountered without great tension or embarrassment, and support could readily be aroused for ties with Germany and Japan that seemed to be of benefit to the United States. What had changed was that Americans had ceased to feel threatened by Germans and Japanese.

Obviously such a process can be reversed. Phillip Mason, the British authority on race relations who first discerned the racial implications of *Othello,* has contended that "fear may . . . act as a catalytic agent" in the creation of race feeling, "changing the nature of factors previously not actively malignant, such as the association of the metaphor of the ideas of white and black with good and evil."[3] It seems likely that the stereotypes about blacks and blackness held by some Englishmen on the eve of colonization were opinions casually held—beliefs that were "not actively malignant" and that would not, under all circumstances, have led directly to societal racism. Good evidence that this was indeed the case comes from a study of domestic servitude in Great Britain in the eighteenth century. Although servants from the continent were the object of widespread hostility, blacks were popular with the British lower classes and benefited from an "almost complete lack of racial bias."[4] The most obvious explanation for this state of affairs would seem to be that there was no sense of a threat from the blacks whereas the continental servants were associated with countries of origin which were international rivals of Great Britain.

Slavery and Racism in Seventeenth-Century America

The story of white-black relations in seventeenth-century America is the story of an evolution toward societal racism. This development was not simply

---

[2] See Earl Raab and Seymour Martin Lipset, "The Prejudiced Society," in Earl Raab, ed., *American Race Relations Today: Studies of the Problems Beyond Desegregation* (New York: Anchor Books, 1962), pp. 29–55.

[3] Phillip Mason, *An Essay on Racial Tension* (New York and London: Royal Institute of International Affairs, 1954), p. 80.

[4] J. Jean Hecht, *Continental and Colonial Servants in Eighteenth Century England* (Northampton, Mass.: Smith College Library, 1954), p. 56. Quoted in Banton, *Race Relations,* p. 369.

the consequence of a priori attitudes or stereotypes, for here as elsewhere a catalytic agent was required, and as usual the catalyst was fear, a fear that can be described in social terms.

In order to comprehend what occurred, it is necessary to confront the vexed question of the relationship between slavery and racism and to take account of the chicken-and-egg debate among historians over which came first in the southern colonies, slavery or racial prejudice. The basic facts, as near as they can be determined, would seem to be these: between 1619 and the 1640's, a small number of blacks were introduced into Virginia as "servants." Some, and perhaps most, of these early arrivals were freed after a limited term of service, somewhat in the manner of indentured servants (indigent white immigrants who were bound to service for a limited period in payment for their passage to the New World). By the 1640's, two trends had become evident: *some* blacks, but no whites, were in fact being held in servitude for life; and there is fragmentary evidence of discriminatory practices which seemed to set black servants off from whites of similar status—for example, Negro women, unlike white women, were apparently used for field work, and a Virginia statute of 1640 enjoined masters to provide arms for all their servants except Negroes. By the 1660's, the status of slavery for some blacks was recognized in law, and the first legislation was passed bearing on the subject of interracial marriage and sex relations.

It should be evident from this summary that it is extremely difficult to say which came first, whether slavery preceded rudimentary forms of racial dis-crimination in Virginia or vice versa. Winthrop Jordan has probably drawn the safest conclusion that can readily be deduced from such data by arguing that slavery and race prejudice "may have been equally cause and effect, continuously reacting upon each other, dynamically joining hands to hustle the Negro down the road to complete degradation."[5] But perhaps the entire debate, in which Jordan provides what is clearly the last word, is based on dubious premises. It has been assumed that the early development of black slavery among English colonists in Virginia requires special explanation because slavery in a strict sense no longer existed in Great Britain at the time of settlement. But a comparison with other early seventeenth-century British colonies suggests that the remarkable thing about Virginia was that all immigrants were *not* regarded as slaves from the beginning. It seems likely that the ten blacks who arrived in Barbados with the first shipload of white settlers in 1627 were enslaved. In any case, the governor and the council of the island proclaimed in 1636, when there were still only a relatively small number of blacks, that all Negroes would serve for life unless they had specific contracts of indenture. Similarly, the first blacks to arrive in the Massachusetts Bay Colony in 1638 seem to have been regarded as slaves, although at this

---

[5] Winthrop D. Jordan, *White Over Black: American Attitudes Toward the Negro, 1550–1812* (Chapel Hill: University of North Carolina Press, 1968), p. 80.

time, as we have seen, there was still some ambiguity about the status of blacks in Virginia.

How can we explain this tendency of other colonies to assume from the beginning that Negroes were slaves, despite the lack of positive law affirming such a condition? First of all, it must be recognized that although slavery was not sanctioned in the domestic law of Great Britain and did not in fact exist as a social condition, neither was it expressly prohibited. As late as 1547 a law had been passed in England enslaving vagabonds. It had proved unworkable and was repealed purely on economic grounds, because other forms of labor were cheaper. There is no reason to assume that if slavery, even white slavery, had appeared profitable in seventeenth-century England, it would not have been introduced. It actually took a series of judicial decisions in the changed ideological context of the eighteenth century to establish the fact that slavery was contrary to English common law. Before that time, there was no general bias against slavery as a condition; it was widely assumed that, by one means or another, most men must be compelled to work and that coercion was the mainspring of any economic system. Furthermore, international law in the seventeenth century regarded slavery as licit and as a proper condition for those who could be defined as captives of war. This was the "legal" basis of the participation of countries like Great Britain and the Netherlands in the international slave trade, which was justified as a legitimate commerce in those captured in African wars. It is no mystery then that when blacks arrived in most colonies, even those of countries that no longer had slavery at home, they were readily seen as enslavable because of their origin in the international trade. We do not, therefore, have to assume that whites were driven by intense racial prejudice in order to explain what happened. That blacks were physically vulnerable to enslavement, that there was no deep-seated bias against the institution, and that there was an actual or anticipated need for labor should be explanation enough for the development of black slavery in the colonies of European nations such as Britain, the Netherlands, and France, each of which, unlike Spain and Portugal, no longer practiced slavery at home.

Hence there would seem to be no obvious reason why the first blacks who arrived in Virginia were not automatically and universally regarded as slaves and held to lifetime servitude. They were products of the international slave trade and, unlike most white immigrants, had neither a "free" background nor contracts of indenture. Possible explanations for the fact that many were freed after a limited term of service might include simple ignorance of their international status or the lack as yet of any plans for general dependence on unfree black labor. In any case, it would appear that what really needs to be explained is not that some blacks, of those who arrived before 1640, were held to lifetime servitude, but that some acquired free status despite their background and the presence of selfish economic motives which might have been expected to tempt white masters to take advantage of their de facto vulnerability.

It would of course be absurd to argue that ethnic prejudice played no role in the gradual degradation of the blacks that took place in Virginia. Ethnocentrism—the tendency to discriminate against the stranger, the alien, the physically different—is a virtually universal phenomenon in group contacts, and it is not surprising that there were some early examples of this in Virginia. But Marvin Harris is probably close to the mark when he contends that "the Negroes were not enslaved because the British colonists specifically despised dark-skinned peoples and regarded them alone as properly suited to slavery: the Negroes came to be the object of virulent prejudices because they alone could be enslaved."[6] In seventeenth-century Virginia, the vulnerability of blacks, as well as international precedent, probably made them seem the logical candidates for enslavement, even before there was any large-scale dependence on their labor (Virginia did not in fact become a slave plantation society until the end of the century). And a case can still be made for the thesis that "virulent prejudices," as compared to milder forms of ethnocentrism and stereotyping, followed in the wake of enslavement and probably did not take full possession of the white mind until slavery had become fully established as the basis of the economic and social order. Earlier examples of what some historians have taken as indications of virulent prejudice are in fact ambiguous. Although Virginia passed a law in 1662 imposing a special fine for interracial fornication, it did not get around to banning interracial marriages until 1691. In Maryland, where slavery and discrimination developed along nearly the same lines as in Virginia, a law was passed in 1664 which Winthrop Jordan has described as having "banned interracial marriages."[7] Actually it only banned marriages between "Negro slaves" and "freeborne English women." It said nothing about marriages between whites and free blacks, and it was explicitly motivated by a desire to prevent the offspring of indentured servant women and male slaves from following the condition of the mother, as prescribed by law, and eventually becoming free.

Indeed most of the evidence of "full-throated indignation against miscegenation" before the 1690's can be explained in large part as a manifestation of the traditional desire to prevent intermarriage between people of different social stations, something which could be very inconvenient to masters of slaves and servants. The resulting legislation was also a clear indication that marriage with Negroes, even Negro slaves, was not deeply repugnant to "freeborne English women." If it had been, no law against it would have been necessary. Actually the tangled and complex history of Maryland's efforts to regulate interracial marriage from 1664 to 1715 provides some strong indications that a deep-seated repugnance to intermarriage on grounds of race alone was slow to develop. The act of 1664 sought to prevent the marriage of white women and Negro slaves because of the legal complications developing from

---

[6] Marvin Harris, *Patterns of Race in the Americas* (New York: Walker, 1964), p. 70.

[7] Jordan, *White Over Black,* p. 79.

such unions. But the law did not clearly state that such marriages could not take place; it merely prescribed that the women involved, and their children, should henceforth be slaves themselves. Far from preventing interracial liaisons, this law actually encouraged them, because it now became advantageous to masters to use their influence to bring about such unions. "Hence," reports a historian of the Negro in Maryland, "the terms of [white] servant women were bought up and the women themselves were married to slaves apparently with a view to invoking on them the penalties just recited."[8] Here then were Southern slaveowners who were willing for their own economic advantage to connive for the marriage of white women and black men and, what was more, for the reducing of "freeborne" whites to slavery in a way that was incompatible with the notion that slavery was based strictly on race. In 1681 another law was passed, designed not so much to prevent interracial marriages as to save white servant women from being reduced to slavery. This law merely exempted such women from the prescribed penalty for marrying a Negro slave when it could be demonstrated that the marriage had been contracted at the instigation of the master. But interracial marriages between white servant women and black slaves apparently continued to take place fairly frequently in Maryland until the early eighteenth century.

Another kind of evidence for the delayed development of societal racism in the Chesapeake colonies can be deduced from what we know about the status of free blacks. If free blacks and mulattoes are treated in a way that is not flagrantly discriminatory, then it is clear that actual status and not race per se is the basic determinant of social position. Such appears to have been generally the case in seventeenth-century America. As might be expected, the most unequivocal evidence of such a state of affairs can be found in northern colonies that were not evolving toward a slave-based economy. A recent study of the Negro in seventeenth-century Massachusetts indicates that free blacks were accorded the same basic rights as whites and were the victims of no significant, discernible social or economic discrimination. Even slaves enjoyed a semblance of equal rights before the law.[9] For Virginia, the picture is less clear because late in the century the status of free blacks was already undergoing a change which would eventuate in the quasi freedom or lower-caste status characteristic of free blacks in the eighteenth and nineteenth centuries. Although we cannot determine with any accuracy how many free blacks there were in Virginia in the late seventeenth century, it would appear that they comprised a larger portion of the total black population than they would at any subsequent time during the slave era. The origins of this class were diverse.

---

[8] James M. Wright, *The Free Negro in Maryland, 1634–1860,* Columbia University Studies in History, Economics, and Public Law, 97 (New York: Columbia University Press, 1921), p. 27.

[9] Robert C. Twombly and Robert H. Moore, "Black Puritans: The Negro in Seventeenth-Century Massachusetts," *William and Mary Quarterly* 24 (April 1967): 224–42.

Some became free after serving a definite term or were the descendants of beneficiaries of the early tendency to regard black servitude as similar to white indentured servitude. Others were "manumitted" after slavery had become a recognized institution (it is significant that private manumission was common until the 1690's, when the first efforts were made to discourage it). Still others, as in Maryland, were the mulatto children of white mothers, who were free at birth.

Before the eighteenth century, free blacks in Virginia apparently had little difficulty in acquiring property or exercising an equal right to vote; some even took legal action against whites or held minor public offices. In short, they seem, for most purposes at least, to have been full-fledged members of the community. A few became substantial landowners and had slaves of their own. Free blacks were even permitted to own white servants before 1670; indeed, the law passed in that year prohibiting the practice was perhaps the first significant piece of legislation that infringed on their rights. A historian of the free Negro in Virginia has concluded that during the seventeenth century free blacks had "social privileges about equal to those accorded to freed white servants. A few were prosperous owners of personal and real property, respected by white persons, dealt with by white men in business relations, and permitted to participate in elections. . . . At that time the theory that the Negro was fit for nothing but slavery or some servile capacity had not been so carefully elaborated nor so generally applied as it was in the eighteenth or nineteenth century."[10] In fact, there would seem to be grounds for arguing that Virginia before the 1690's was not a consistently racist society, despite the presence of black servitude; its racial pattern may have resembled the Latin American model as much as it did the rigidly hierarchical biracialism that later developed.

In the 1690's, however, the situation began to change dramatically. Intermarriage was outlawed, and the first restrictions were placed upon private manumission of slaves. In the eighteenth century, and particularly after an act passed in 1723, free blacks were formally deprived of many of their rights, including the right to vote. This transformation of the free Negro group from a participating element of the community into a pariah class obviously paralleled the transformation of Virginia into a slave plantation economy. Before the 1680's, white indentured servants had provided most of the colony's labor. After that time the shift to a slave-based economy took place very rapidly, largely as a result of the expansion of British slave-trade activity, which meant that slaves were offered in larger numbers and at better prices than previously. Although there was undoubtedly a prior trend toward the degradation of all blacks because of the enslavement of most of them, the final decision to relegate all free blacks to lower-caste status was probably stimu-

---

[10] John H. Russell, *The Free Negro in Virginia, 1619–1865,* Johns Hopkins Studies in Historical and Political Science, 31 (Baltimore: Johns Hopkins Press, 1913), p. 125.

lated principally by the growing fears and anxieties of what was now a slave-holding society. Certainly one of the main justifications presented for discrimination against free blacks and for the effort to prevent growth of this class by restricting manumission was the belief that Negroes who were not slaves would provide an unfortunate example for those in servitude and would use their freedom of action to encourage insurrections. As the slave population grew rapidly after 1700, such fears became more intense and led not only to further efforts to limit and control the free black population but also to the elaboration of the severe slave code that served to distinguish North American slavery from its Latin American counterpart.

Comparison with Latin America, however, suggests the need for a further explanation for the growth of societal racism in the slave-based colonies of British North America. In Brazil, for example, a slave plantation economy developed without the same emphasis on purely racial distinctions and without similar efforts to prevent manumission and to degrade free men of color. Marvin Harris has attempted to explain this difference by reference to demographic factors. Unlike Brazil, Virginia had from the beginning a relatively large nonslaveholding white population. This population was able to provide necessary services for the slaveholders that in Brazil could only be performed by free blacks and mulattoes. The nonslaveholding whites of the South were available for putting down insurrections, catching runaways, and patrolling plantation areas; for employment as overseers; and for auxiliary economic activities such as the raising and herding of livestock. In Brazil, according to Harris, such functions were generally performed by free men of color. There was, in short, no role for the free blacks of the colonial and ante-bellum South to play which would contribute in any way to the security and profitability of the plantation system.[11] Such an interpretation is very persuasive and obviously possesses considerable validity. But Harris' tendency to find the origins of racism almost exclusively in the conscious efforts of the master class to manipulate the nonslaveholders does not fully explain the depth and the apparent spontaneity of the racial feeling that developed.

Another way of explaining the different lines of development in Latin America and British North America might be derived from an understanding of the contrasting social structures within which plantation slavery was accommodated. When Spain and Portugal established their American colonies, they were still fundamentally feudal societies. Those who emigrated and became colonial slaveholders were imbued with the assumption that society was an elaborate but clearly defined hierarchy of mutually dependent corporate groups or estates. To their way of thinking, slaves were simply the lowest-ranking group in the hierarchy. If a man ceased to be a slave, it did not mean that he became equal to those at the top, only that he moved up to the next highest rank. The complex system of social differentiation that evolved in

[11] Harris, *Patterns of Race,* Chapter 7.

Latin America can be seen as an adaptation of medieval concepts of social order and hierarchy to a multiracial situation. In plantation societies, the system meant that those at the bottom were mostly or exclusively black, while those at the top were at least defined as white; in the middle ranks was a range of mixed-blood categories. But an individual could in fact belong to a social class which was predominantly of another physical type if he had the necessary social and cultural characteristics.

The British settlers in North America came from a society that was undergoing a transition from a traditional medieval social structure with a hierarchy of corporate groups to a capitalist society with an emphasis on competing individuals and a tendency to divide society into two principal classes, a hard-working and productive middle class—"the industrious sort of people"—and a mass of unworthy poor, the dregs of the emerging social system. One spokesman for the rising social and political values of early seventeenth-century England described the poor as "rogues, beggars, vagabonds," members of a "cursed generation" who should be punished and forced to work.[12] The precise attitudes of the earliest Virginia masters toward their white servants—who were often drawn from the lowest levels of British society—cannot be determined, but they probably partook to some extent of the increasingly virulent contempt of propertied Englishmen for the lower classes. If so, it would have been difficult for them to see black slaves as much lower on the scale of humanity. But it seems probable that the ability of white servants to gain their freedom in the New World and, because of the plenitude of land, to become freeholders rapidly tended to undercut the sense of a huge social chasm between whites, especially in the period before a plantation aristocracy emerged. This leveling process and the gradual decline in the importance of white servitude eventually made the blacks the only conspicuous local examples of a despised lower class that allegedly had to be coerced into working. The existence of universal male suffrage in Virginia before 1670, when property restrictions were imposed by the Crown, was perhaps indicative of the rough sense of equality that developed in the early period. By the end of the century, however, palpable class divisions were developing among free whites, not so much because of the impoverishment of the lower class, which remained by and large an independent yeomanry, but because of the ability of a small number of families to engross land and slaves and take some of the trappings of an aristocracy. But free whites who had once thought of themselves as equal to anyone in the colony were probably unwilling, to say the least, to accept the notion that they had a clearly defined inferior status.

If this was in fact the situation, we have what a sociologist might recognize as the ingredients of full-fledged societal racism. From the point of view of the "aristocracy" there was a functional need to incorporate nonslaveholding

---

[12] The Reverend William Perkins, quoted in Christopher Hill, *Society and Puritanism in Pre-Revolutionary England* (New York: Schocken Books, 1964), p. 283.

whites into the social order on some basis other than that of an acknowledged hierarchy of corporate groups with differing privileges, for such a social ideal was inapplicable to the relatively egalitarian American setting. From the vantage point of nonslaveholders there was a natural tendency to project upon the blacks their own suppressed sense of inferiority as a way of gaining or retaining a sense of status. If this admittedly somewhat hypothetical analysis is valid, it would help explain the ostentatious effort to relegate the highest black to a status below that of the lowest member of the dominant race; it would also account for the origins of the persistent Southern emphasis on race as the foundation of a kind of pseudo equality among whites. Here indeed might be found the basis of the powerful mythology that would later serve to guarantee a consensus in favor of slavery and racial subordination.

The Rise of Ideological Racism

Although societal racism — the treatment of blacks as if they were inherently inferior for reasons of race — dates from the late seventeenth and early eighteenth century, a rationalized racist ideology did not develop until the nineteenth century. This gap of more than a hundred years between practice and theory can be explained in various ways. First of all, full-fledged racist thought required a change in the conception of man and his relation to the natural world. It took the eighteenth-century Enlightenment to replace the traditional view of man as a child of God who stood above the rest of creation with an image of man as a physical being who was part of the natural world. The new emphasis on the physical side of human nature led to the first systematic efforts to classify the races and to provide scientific explanations of the differences between them. But the dominant eighteenth-century view was that racial characteristics were not innate but were rather the result of environmental factors, such as climate and social habits. The environmentalist theory of human differences, combined with the natural-rights philosophy, led during the era of the American Revolution to an intellectual assault on the institution of slavery, an assault which contributed to the triumph of gradual emancipation in the North and provoked some soul-searching in the South. But the new biological concept of man, with its emphasis on the importance of physical characteristics, could also be used to support the idea that blacks were inherently inferior, a different order of beings from whites and therefore not entitled to the same rights. The view that blacks were created permanently unequal was enunciated by a minority of theorists in the eighteenth century, including the Englishmen Lord Kames and Charles White and the negrophobic Jamaican physician Edward Long. But, despite the fact that Jefferson speculated in the 1780's about the possibility that blacks were inherently inferior in some respects to whites, no one in the United States actually defended institutionalized inequality on the basis of racial theory until well into the nineteenth century.

Societal racism did not require an ideology to sustain it so long as it was taken for granted. Until the revolutionary era no one had seriously challenged slavery and black subordination in the southern colonies. During and after the Revolution there was a challenge of sorts, but the most recent historical studies suggest that it was half-hearted and ineffectual. Even those, like Jefferson, who talked about the abolition of slavery as desirable or even necessary could do so only on the assumption that somehow the Southern black population would be removed after being freed, because it was unthinkable that large numbers of the two races could live together in the same territory in a state of mutual freedom. In the absence of a serious political and intellectual challenge to the implicit assumptions of Southern biracialism, slaveholders found that they could protect their interests merely by encouraging the belief that emancipation was impractical, or, if pushed, by standing firm on their "rights" as owners of slave property. After all, a basic natural right for which the Revolution had been fought was the right of property.

Obviously, however, the egalitarian philosophy that had been made part of the American creed by the language of the Declaration of Independence carried a long-range threat to slavery and racial caste, a threat which had only briefly surfaced during the revolutionary era before being temporarily put to rest by the provisions of the Constitution which recognized the existence of slavery and provided for its protection. In the 1830's, the application of the concept of equal rights to blacks was made with a new evangelical immediacy by the Northern abolitionists, who, unlike their colonizationist predecessors, not only argued that slavery was an evil but also demanded that blacks be freed immediately and granted full equality. This assault from William Lloyd Garrison and his followers on the foundations of societal racism forced proslavery Southerners and their Northern sympathizers to develop and promulgate a racist theory that accorded with their practice.

In a pamphlet entitled *The South Vindicated from the Treason and Fanaticism of the Northern Abolitionists* (1836), William Drayton of South Carolina presented a concise statement of the newly articulated proslavery doctrine: "Personal observation must convince every candid man, that the Negro is constitutionally indolent and prone to vice; that his mind is heavy, dull, and unambitious; and that the doom that has made the African in all ages and countries, a slave — is the natural consequence of the inferiority of his character."

As long as the traditional order, societal racism, was not challenged by a radical ideology calling for revolutionary change, it was not necessary to bring ideological consciousness to social assumptions. Before the abolitionists forcefully demanded consistency in the application of egalitarian ideals, it was even possible to subscribe in a general way to an egalitarian philosophy without confronting directly the contradiction between such a creed and the acceptance of slavery and racial discrimination. Once the abolitionists had thrown down the gauntlet, however, proslavery apologists had two choices. They could either reject egalitarianism entirely, as did George Fitzhugh and other theorists of Southern paternalism, or they could define blacks as members of another, subhuman species and keep the entire egalitarian, natural-rights philosophy as a white prerogative. It was the latter view that achieved the greatest popularity because of its obvious appeal to the nonslaveholding classes of the South and because it could win converts in the North as well. In 1860 William Yancey, the militant Alabama secessionist and fire-eater, told a Northern audience, "Your fathers and my fathers built this government on two ideas: The first is that the white is the citizen and the master race, and the white man is the equal of every other white man. The second idea is that the Negro is the inferior race."[13] The fact that Northerners had discriminated increasingly against their own free blacks during the prewar period of rising white democracy was probably the basis of Yancey's expectation that his doctrine would find favor above the Mason-Dixon line. Northern Democrats of that era even vied with Southern proslavery politicians to see who could give the greatest boost to the white ego by repeating *ad nauseam* that blacks were inherently and unalterably inferior to "the master race" and were therefore suited only for slavery.

Explicit racism, a public ideology based on the doctrinaire conception of the black man as a natural underling, developed, therefore, directly out of the need to defend slavery against nineteenth-century humanitarianism. The appeal of this doctrine in the North and the degree to which it eventually contaminated even some of the opponents of slavery are complex subjects which can only be touched on here. In a period when the sweeping egalitarianism associated with the age of Jackson was undermining most social and political distinctions, frightened Northern conservatives were led to emphasize racial distinctions as one remaining barrier that could be defended, and they were often aided and abetted by insecure lower-class whites who longed for some assurance of their own status, a sense that they were superior to someone, if only by virtue of the color of their skin. When, by the 1850's, an expansive Southern "slavocracy" was seen as a threat to the Northern way of life, the tentacles of racist thought and feeling had gained such a stranglehold that most Northern opponents of the extension of slavery carefully disassociated themselves from the abolitionists and their ideal of racial fraternity and argued that theirs was exclusively a white man's cause. The fact that Northerners could oppose slavery without a commitment to racial equality helps explain why the Civil War resulted in the emancipation of the Negro from slavery but not from caste discrimination and the ravages of racism.

Racist thought did not reach its crescendo until the end of the nineteenth century, when it latched on to Darwinism—a more convincing scientific support than the earlier theory that blacks had been created separately by God before Adam and Eve had begotten "the superior white species." But pseudo-scientific Darwinian racism did not differ from the pre–Civil War variety in its basic assumptions about the differences between blacks and whites. What

---

[13] William Yancey, quoted in the *Liberator,* 26 October 1860.

gave the reformulated doctrine its new virulence was its association with an aggressive Southern campaign for the legal segregation and disfranchisement of the blacks who three decades earlier had been freed from slavery.

In the modern era a campaign has been mounted against ideological racism, and it has had considerable success. Societal racism, however, has retained much of its strength, and its persistence has now plunged America into a new racial crisis.

In short, it can be said that the long story of the development of American racism, first as a way of life and then as a system of thought, suggests that purely social forces have played a key role. Subliminal and deeply rooted psychological factors were undoubtedly present, but they can hardly explain the extent to which racial feeling and ideology have been developing and changing, subject to situational variations in intensity and character. America, I would conclude, was not born racist; it became so gradually as the result of a series of crimes against black humanity that stemmed primarily from selfishness, greed, and the pursuit of privilege.

5 SUGGESTIONS FOR FURTHER READING

Banton, Michael, *Race Relations*. New York: Basic Books, 1968. ▪ An excellent introduction to the study of race relations which draws on material from many cultures and disciplines.

Bennett, Lerone, Jr., *Black Power, U.S.A.: The Human Side of Reconstruction, 1867–1877**. Chicago: Johnson Publishing, 1967. ▪ An impressive study, though possibly an overstatement of black assertiveness in Reconstruction.

Cruden, Robert, *The Negro in Reconstruction**. Englewood Cliffs, N.J.: Prentice-Hall, 1969. ▪ A succinct statement about the black experience during Reconstruction.

De Forest, John William, *A Union Officer in the Reconstruction*, ed. James H. Croushore and David M. Potter. New Haven, Conn.: Yale University Press, 1948. ▪ A first-hand account of the experience of blacks immediately following Emancipation, and a story whose relevance has persisted through changing times.

Degler, Carl, "Slavery and the Genesis of American Race Prejudice," *Comparative Studies in History and Society* 2 (October 1959): 49–66. ▪ An essay that argues strongly for the thesis that racial prejudice existed before the establishment of American slavery and was in itself an important cause of slavery.

Du Bois, W. E. B., *Black Reconstruction in America**. New York: Harcourt, 1935. ▪ A pioneering study that continues to rank among the best.

Franklin, John Hope, *Reconstruction After the Civil War**. Chicago: University of Chicago Press, 1961. ▪ A cogent and brief statement about black self-assertion after Emancipation.

Fredrickson, George M., *The Black Image in the White Mind: The Debate on Afro-American Character and Destiny, 1817–1914*. New York: Harper, 1971. ▪ A study of white racial thought and imagery as applied to American blacks in the nineteenth and early twentieth centuries.

---

*Available in paperback edition

Gossett, Thomas F., *Race: The History of an Idea in America**. Dallas: Southern Methodist University Press, 1963. ▪ A survey of the history of race theories in the United States. Constitutes a good introduction to systematic race thinking in its historical setting.

Handlin, Oscar, *Race and Nationality in American Life**. Boston: Atlantic-Little, Brown, 1957. ▪ A series of essays on American racial and ethnic attitudes. See especially the essay "The Origins of Negro Slavery," which presents a case for the thesis that slavery predated racial prejudice and discrimination in the southern colonies.

Harris, Marvin, *Patterns of Race in the Americas**. New York: Walker, 1964. ▪ A brilliant economic interpretation of the differing racial patterns in North and South America.

Higginson, Thomas Wentworth, *Army Life in a Black Regiment**, ed. John Hope Franklin. Boston: Beacon Press, 1962. Originally published in 1870. ▪ A highly readable book by a white abolitionist who shared in the Port Royal experience and became the commanding officer of the first regiment of soldiers recruited among the liberated blacks.

Jordan, Winthrop D., *White Over Black: American Attitudes Toward the Negro, 1550–1812**. Chapel Hill: University of North Carolina Press, 1968. ▪ A monumental study of the white community's changing attitudes, with heavy emphasis on psychological factors.

Litwack, Leon F., *North of Slavery: The Negro in the Free States, 1790–1860**. Chicago: University of Chicago Press, 1961. ▪ An excellent description of race relations in the ante-bellum North which reveals much about the depth and the extent of anti-Negro sentiment.

Logan, Rayford W., *The Betrayal of the Negro: From Rutherford B. Hayes to Woodrow Wilson**. New York: Collier Books, 1965. ▪ A thorough and detailed account of the triumph of extreme racist ideas and policies in late nineteenth-century America.

McPherson, James, ed., *The Negro's Civil War**. New York: Pantheon, 1965. ▪ A collection of primary source material that tells the story of the black man during the Civil War.

Morner, Magnus, *Race Mixture in the History of Latin America**. Boston: Atlantic-Little, Brown, 1967. ▪ A judicious and revealing interpretation of Latin American racial attitudes.

Rose, Willie Lee, *Rehearsal for Reconstruction: The Port Royal Experiment**. Indianapolis: Bobbs-Merrill, 1964. ▪ A sensitive and disciplined book describing Southern blacks as they moved from slavery to freedom. The author takes a close look at the black people on the Sea Islands of South Carolina, most of whom were liberated in the first year of the Civil War, and at the liberators who attempted to make them over in the Northern image.

Van Den Berghe, Pierre L., *Race and Racism: A Comparative Perspective**. New York: John Wiley, 1967. ▪ An imaginative sociological analysis of differing patterns of race relations in Mexico, Brazil, the United States, and South Africa.

Williamson, Joel R., *After Slavery: The Negro in South Carolina During Reconstruction, 1861–1877**. Chapel Hill: University of North Carolina Press, 1965. ▪ One of the best studies of black people in a particular state following Emancipation—and, perhaps, an understatement about black assertiveness in Reconstruction.

————, ed., *The Origins of Segregation**. Lexington, Mass.: D. C. Heath, 1968. ▪ An interesting collection that bears on the history of racial prejudice in the United States.

Woodward, C. Vann, *The Strange Career of Jim Crow**. New York: Oxford University Press, 1951. ▪ An influential and provocative study of the development of segregation in the American South.